Demand Better!
Revive Our Broken Healthcare System

by
Sanjaya Kumar, MD, MSc, MPH
and
David B. Nash, MD, MBA

SECOND RIVER
HEALTHCARE

Demand Better!
Revive Our Broken Healthcare System

Second River Healthcare
26 Shawnee Way
Suite C
Bozeman, MT 59715

Phone (406) 586-8775
FAX (406) 586-5672

Editor: Diane Dannenfeldt
Cover Design: Lan Weisberger — Design Solutions
Typesetting/Composition: Neuhaus/Tyrrell Graphic Design

Kumar, Sanjaya & Nash, David B.
Demand Better / Sanjaya Kumar, MD, MSc, MPH & David B. Nash, MD, MBA

ISBN-13: 978-1-936406-00-5 (hardcover)
ISBN-13: 978-1-936406-01-2 (softcover)
ISBN-13: 978-1-936406-02-9 (e-book)

1. Patient safety   2. Quality care   3. Health services administration

Library of Congress Control Number: 2010937923

First Printing   February 2011
Second Printing   November 2014

Innovative Healthcare Speakers, a speaker's bureau and division of Second River Healthcare, provides a wide range of authors and nationally recognized experts for speaking events. To find out more, go to www.InnovativeHealthcareSpeakers.com or call (406) 586-8775.

Second River Healthcare books are available at special quantity discounts.

Please call for information at: (406) 586-8775 or order from the websites:
www.SecondRiverHealthcare.com   or   **www.DemandBetter.com**

CONTENTS

PREFACE

As patient safety and quality advocates, we are very pleased to bring this book to fruition. We have devoted our professional lives to measuring and improving the quality and safety of medical care and addressing the ways healthcare is delivered. Although we have come to the same juncture with our careers and our dedicated mission to improve patient safety practices and the delivery of quality care, we each have traveled on different paths to arrive here.

For me (Sanjaya), this has been a journey with healthcare consumers on three continents and across three different healthcare delivery systems and various payment models. Very early on, the science of quality-of-care measurement and its impact on patient safety caught my attention. I journeyed on a path to provide robust and scalable data-management and decision-support analytics to help healthcare providers address gaps in quality, improve patient safety concerns and continually review and mitigate risk to avert harmful, preventable medical errors.

For David, his devotion to twenty-five years in academic medicine, has, in large part, been a tireless mission to create a new type of medical practitioner. After twenty years at Thomas Jefferson University and directly mentoring scores of new clinical leaders, he is beginning to see safety- and quality-conscious practitioners emerge. Via scores of peer-reviewed publications, books and public appearances, he has touched thousands more.

Through this work, we are gradually making an impact on improving quality of care by helping providers to identify safety gaps and put mitigating safeguards in place, thus saving lives. Every life saved from a fatal, preventable medical error is mission accomplished! We are quickly reaching the time of the empowered healthcare consumer. This type of consumer needs to know more and "demand better."

We are both confident that *Demand Better!* will help broaden our audience to include thoughtful persons across the nation who are eager to engage in the conversation about real change for healthcare. This book should give our "change agents" what they really need — insightful knowledge and context to demand better safety and quality from their doctors, hospitals and other healthcare delivery systems.

This book can serve as a one-stop shopping platform for the twenty-first-century healthcare consumer. It represents a succinct distillation of two decades of background knowledge, research and analysis focused on how to really fix our broken healthcare system. This book pulls no punches. It is provocative. It will no doubt infuriate some and encourage others.

Regardless, every reader will come away with a deeper under-standing of the core issues that underlie the journey towards improving patient safety and quality. Issues that got short shrift during the years of debate leading up to the passage of national "healthcare reform." Issues that everyone thought would get addressed but that got buried under political agendas. And many more!

All concerned citizens and consumers of healthcare are potential readers. If you've ever been a patient, we recommend that you read this book.

ACKNOWLEDGEMENTS

We are both grateful to Christopher Guadagnino who took advantage of our collective experience and turned our musings into wonderful prose. He knows how to weave a compelling and engaging story from research results that may seem dry to others, but not to us. Chris provided the much needed embellishment to the contextual framework of this book. For this, the book's success in engaging the reader will be to his credit.

We are also grateful to T.J. Tedesco for his marketing insights and relentless attention to the details of publishing a book like this one — a book with mass appeal rooted in solid research and backed by more than four decades of combined experience with national health policy and healthcare services research.

We are grateful to Beth O'Brien for helping to frame the book from the perspective of a lay healthcare consumer and for assisting in editing the draft manuscripts.

We thank our respective families for their tolerance, patience and understanding of our singular drive. Without their collective support, we would never have been able to even contemplate writing such a book.

Finally, we dedicate this book to our patients, real and virtual, individual and collective. As hard-working citizens of our great nation, they really do deserve much more from the most expensive healthcare system in the world. Americans know in their hearts that you do get what you pay for — except from our nation's healthcare system! It is time for them to rise up and "demand better!"

We sincerely believe that this book will help to fix this mess for our children and their children.

Sanjaya Kumar
David B. Nash

INTRODUCTION

Why Myths about Our Healthcare System Conceal the Real Problem

Much of the healthcare reform debate is centered on cost: the skyrocketing cost of medical care, spiraling health insurance premiums, the cost to insure the uninsured, administrative costs that eat up a sizeable chunk of every healthcare dollar and the cost of defensive medicine to avert malpractice lawsuits. All of these issues are important. But they miss the core driver of our healthcare cost problem: the quality and safety of healthcare delivery in the United States.

In 2011, we spend more than $2 trillion each year on medical care, $700 billion of which fails to improve patients' health and often harms them, in comparison to other countries that spend significantly less, according to testimony to the U.S. Senate Budget Committee in January, 2008, by Peter Orszag, then director of the Congressional Budget Office.

Tell that to people, and most of them will scratch their heads in confusion. Patient safety, maybe, but deficiencies in healthcare quality? Driving the cost crisis? More specifically, variation in healthcare quality causes deeply disturbing safety and cost problems in the form of overused, underused and misused healthcare services. The status quo is broken! To appreciate the gravity of the situation we are required to examine several tightly held beliefs about American healthcare.

We collaborate in a collective mythology about American healthcare. We "know," for example, that modern medicine is largely backed by solid science. We boast that the U.S. healthcare delivery system is superior because we offer access to more services than any other country. We've focused a great deal on safety improvement over the past decade, and we trust that our healthcare will rarely harm patients. Our physicians and hospitals are paid to reliably deliver the right care in a way that is expertly coordinated. Our medical schools are the envy of the world and offer the best training of future physicians. All of this we know.

But we are wrong. Each of these assumptions is an idealized and largely unchallenged belief about our healthcare system. These beliefs are not falsehoods, per se. Each contains some truth, enough that we confidently embrace it. And that is precisely the problem.

Our confidence in these assumptions is expensive and dangerous: the scientific certainty of medicine, the trust that more healthcare means higher quality, the ever-improving safety of that care, the reliability of fee-for-service provider payment to spur the best care, the adequacy of training physicians as autonomous scientists. The reward for our confidence in these myths is continuing lapses in quality and patient safety that fuel a staggering healthcare cost problem that no one seems prepared to address (including legislators who recently passed an insurance reform bill but called it healthcare reform).

Certainly, Americans enjoy the most technologically advanced healthcare delivery in the world. And yet, physicians deliver the right care only about half of the time, as we will see later in this book. Different physicians treat the same illnesses using different treatments, often with little scientific evidence to back up their clinical decisions.

The explosion of medical research over the past several decades gives a physician a "best practice" indicator for only about 20 percent of all medical care delivered. Where do physicians turn in making decisions about the remaining 80 percent of their care delivery? They fall back on their training ("That's the way we always did it at the medical college"), their habits ("That's how we do it in our group practice") and their limited anecdotal experience ("What I've seen in cases like this..."), often with very little feedback on whether their treatment decisions are the best, or even appropriate. The result is tremendous variation, waste and danger of preventable medical errors due to a lack of compliance with quality-of-care practices based on scientific evidence.

That is the core dilemma for physicians: despite a large "gray zone" in medical evidence and the lack of a performance feedback loop to drive improvement, they confidently recommend specific treatments for specific conditions, as they are trained to do, but those recommendations vary wildly. As mentioned earlier, most of the time science doesn't provide clear answers as to which treatment is best. As we will see, experts tell us that one-third of all healthcare delivered to patients is unnecessary — ranging from simple treatments and prescriptions to invasive procedures and surgeries. That is shocking and sometimes deadly.

Even when science does support a given drug or treatment, and we're finding that science is not as strong as we thought, research trials typically strive to demonstrate that a new drug, treatment or procedure is literally better than nothing by testing it against a placebo. Does the science always demonstrate that the drug or treatment in question is superior to competing drugs, treatments or procedures? Definitely not. Often there is no way to know.

If somebody were to ask, "Can you explain, in three words or less, what's wrong with our healthcare system?" the answer would be easy: *unexplained clinical variation*. Different doctors practice different ways to treat the same illnesses with little scientific backing. Care patterns vary by ZIP code, even in an individual city. This central problem leads to a cascade of corollary problems: waste, overuse of dangerous procedures and preventable medical errors.

Why do doctors diagnose and prescribe treatments for the same illness differently? We will see that most doctors, especially in the primary-care setting, practice in a completely data-free environment, devoid of feedback on the correctness of their practice. That staggering truth is incredibly scary for doctors, let alone patients. When no countervailing data exists to say that someone ought to change what he or she is doing, the natural human reaction, even among physicians and other highly trained professionals, is to continue what they are used to doing.

Politically, this is the third rail of medical practice. A politician can't say publicly, "Half of what doctors do is wrong," or "Most of what doctors do doesn't have solid research to support it." Or, "When doctors do the right thing, system and process failures can still occur to harm patients." Or, "Doctors who deliver more services to their patients may actually be harming them by exposing them to the unnecessary risk of complications and errors." Or, "Over the past decade of heightened patient-safety awareness, we've not made any measurable progress in reducing the rates of preventable medical errors." But all of those statements represent the status quo of twenty-first-century medicine.

Cost is a toxic by-product of unexplained clinical variation. The U.S. healthcare delivery system spends more than $700 billion each year on medical care — representing one-third of the procedures that doctors perform — and fails to improve a patient's health, and may even produce unwanted harm.[1] This can't be explained in 15 seconds on *Meet the Press*, which is why national health reform doesn't tackle this issue.

Our current healthcare payment system rewards reactive care, rather than proactive or preventive care, or both, and financially encourages doctors to treat acute episodes of illness and disease, rather than managing those illnesses or diseases to avert future crises. Most doctors are still paid to do piecework; they are paid more for the higher volume and greater intensity of the acute care they provide. They are underpaid, or not paid, to coordinate effective preventive healthcare to keep their patients out of hospitals. Doctors are in the disease business, not the wellness business, driven principally by the toxic payment system that undermines fiscal incentives for promoting wellness.

The same can be said for hospitals. The mission statement of most hospitals goes something like this: "Our mission is to improve the health of our community." That can't be true, because that's not how hospitals are paid. If they really were to reduce admissions for diabetes, smoking, asthma and coronary disease, they'd all be out of the hospital business! Hospitals are in the business of treating the episodes that are the end results of preventable diseases. That's the hospital business of the twenty-first century, driven principally by the current payment system.

If you tell a hospital president that the hospital's mission statement is an absolute lie, he or she will give you a shocked and perplexed look. But you can explain your comment: "How can it be true? If you were to really improve the health of the population, you would put yourself out of business." Hospitals look forward to the flu season. Every preventable hospital admission for asthma represents a failure to coordinate care. And yet, every asthma admission is critical to the bottom line of an acute-care community hospital. Where is the economic incentive to coordinate care? Answer: There is none.

There is no easy fix to these problems, of course. But there is a best place to look. Focus on quality-of-care compliance checks.

This is a book about debunking healthcare myths for the healthcare consumer through the lens of quality: what quality is and is not, why it is lacking in so much of our present system and how to reclaim it. Poor healthcare quality derives from uncertainty in clinical decision-making, which comes from persistent unexplained variation in physician practice patterns, from (still) inadequate accountability for patient safety, from payment for piecework and from a medical-training curriculum that is decades behind the curve regarding quality and safety. Reclaiming quality by addressing each of these deficiencies can transform the economics of our healthcare system. Greater safety, effectiveness and efficiency are possible.

This is not a utopian critique. It is based on a quality revolution that is already under way and is gradually transforming the way medical care is delivered in the United States. This effort didn't need mandates from politicians to get started, although it will need their support to achieve fruition.

This is a pivotal moment in American healthcare delivery, marked by tremendous innovation and accelerating improvements in quality and safety. Much of that innovation is focused directly on "busting" our counterproductive myths so that we can make the changes that will improve healthcare: improving physician decision-making; building a better research base to compare the effectiveness of different treatments for the same medical condition; devising accountability mechanisms that work for healthcare providers; piloting second-generation pay-for-performance models; paying greater attention to quality improvement and patient-centered care in medical-training curricula; and expanding access to quality care in non-traditional venues.

Physicians have various tools to help them make better decisions. Hospital and physician report cards are multiplying, although they need to be redesigned if they are expected to drive quality improvement through transparency. Research on the comparative effectiveness of various treatments is in its infancy in the United States, but it has been jump-started by recent government stimulus funding and agenda-setting. Pay-for-performance initiatives continue to evolve, but they need to be supplemented with some form of bundled payment among physicians, hospitals and other caregivers to reverse the perverse incentives of fee-for-service, to minimize error and waste, and to foster superior outcomes.

Today's physicians need new forms of medical training to teach them how to close the quality feedback loop and practice collaborative, patient-centered care. Ancillary primary-care providers, like nurses in retail health clinics, are poised to bring evidence-based care to more patients more frequently.

Several pioneering innovators have already debunked myths

about healthcare delivery in their own organizations. They've recognized that the bulk of medical practice is not based on solid science; physicians and hospitals need solid performance feedback and guidance systems to help them deliver the right care reliably; prevailing healthcare practices are error-prone and often dangerous; and new payment approaches hold the keys to reliable, safe and less wasteful care.

How can all of those goals be achieved? A good place to start is by recognizing the healthcare myths that prevent us from attacking the root of the issue, which we will identify in Part I of this book. In Part II, we will examine boots-on-the-ground innovations that bust those myths and point the way to better, safer *and* cheaper healthcare.

Notes

1. Peter Orszag continues to publicize this alarming figure, as he did in a White House press briefing in early 2009, available online at: http://www.whitehouse.gov/the_press_office/Press-Briefing-by-OMB-Director-Peter-Orszag-and-CEA-Chair-Christina-Romer/

PART 1

Healthcare Myths That Prevent Effective, Safe and Efficient Healthcare Delivery

MYTH 1:

There is a High Degree of Scientific Certainty in Modern Medicine

"In America, there is no guarantee that any individual will receive high-quality care for any particular health problem. The healthcare industry is plagued with overutilization of services, underutilization of services and errors in healthcare practice."

– Elizabeth A. McGlynn, PhD,
Rand Corporation researcher,
and colleagues.

[Elizabeth A. McGlynn, PhD; Steven M. Asch, MD, MPH; et al. "The Quality of Healthcare Delivered to Adults in the United States," *New England Journal of Medicine* 2003;348:2635-2645.]

Most of us are confident that the quality of our healthcare is the finest, the most technologically sophisticated and the most scientifically advanced in the world. And for good reason — thousands of clinical research studies are published every year that indicate such findings. Hospitals advertise the latest, most dazzling techniques to peer into the human body and perform amazing lifesaving surgeries with the aid of high-tech devices. There is no question that modern medical practices are remarkable, often effective and occasionally miraculous.

But there is a wrinkle in our confidence. We believe that the vast majority of what physicians do is backed by solid science. Their diagnostic and treatment decisions must reflect the latest and best research. Their clinical judgment must certainly be well beyond any reasonable doubt. To seriously question these assumptions would seem jaundiced and cynical.

But we must question them because these beliefs are based more on faith than on facts for at least three reasons, each of which we will explore in detail in this section. Only a fraction of what physicians do is based on solid evidence from Grade-A randomized, controlled trials; the rest is based instead on weak or no evidence and on subjective judgment. When scientific consensus exists on which clinical practices work effectively, physicians only sporadically follow that evidence correctly.

Medical decision-making itself is fraught with inherent subjectivity, some of it necessary and beneficial to patients, and some of it flawed and potentially dangerous. For these reasons, millions of Americans receive medications and treatments that have no proven clinical benefit, and millions fail to get care that is proven to be effective. Quality and safety suffer, and waste flourishes.

We know, for example, that when a patient goes to his primary-care physician with a very common problem like lower back pain, the physician will deliver the right treatment with real clinical benefit about half of the time. Patients with the same health problem who go to different physicians will get wildly different treatments. Those physicians can't all be right.

Having limited clinical evidence for their decision-making is not the only gap in physicians' scientific certainty. Physician judgment — the "art" of medicine — inevitably comes into play, for better or for worse. Even physicians with the most advanced technical skills sometimes fail to achieve the highest quality outcomes for their patients. That's when resourcefulness — trying different and potentially better interventions — can bend the quality curve even further.

And, even the most experienced physicians make errors in diagnosing patients because of cognitive biases inherent to human thinking processes. These subjective, "nonscientific" features of physician judgment work in parallel with the relative scarcity of strong scientific backing when physicians make decisions about how to care for their patients.

We could accurately say, "Half of what physicians do is wrong," or "Less than 20 percent of what physicians do has solid research to support it." Although these claims sound absurd, they are solidly supported by research that is largely agreed upon by experts. Yet these claims are rarely discussed publicly. It would be political suicide for our public leaders to admit these truths and risk being branded as reactionary or radical. Most Americans wouldn't believe them anyway. Dozens of stakeholders are continuously jockeying to promote their vested interests, making it difficult for anyone to summarize a complex and nuanced body of research in a way that cuts through the partisan fog and satisfies everyone's agendas. That, too, is part of the problem.

Questioning the Unquestionable

The problem is that physicians don't know what they're doing. That is how David Eddy, MD, PhD, a healthcare economist and senior advisor for health policy and management for Kaiser Permanente, put the problem in a *Business Week* cover story about how much of healthcare delivery is not based on science.[1] Plenty of proof backs up Eddy's glib-sounding remark.

The plain fact is that many clinical decisions made by physicians appear to be arbitrary, uncertain and variable. Reams of research point to the same finding: physicians looking at the same thing will disagree with each other, or even with themselves, from 10 percent to 50 percent of the time during virtually every aspect of the medical-care process — from taking a medical history to doing a physical examination, reading a laboratory test, performing a pathological diagnosis and recommending a treatment.[2] Physician judgment is highly variable.

Here is what Eddy has found in his research.[3] Give a group of cardiologists high-quality coronary angiograms (a type of radiograph or x-ray) of typical patients and they will disagree about the diagnosis for about half of the patients. They will disagree with themselves on two successive readings of the same angiograms up to one-third of the time. Ask a group of experts to estimate the effect of colon-cancer screening on colon-cancer mortality and answers will range from five percent to 95 percent.

Ask fifty cardiovascular surgeons to estimate the probabilities of various risks associated with xenografts (animal-tissue transplant) versus mechanical heart valves and you'll get answers to the same question ranging from zero percent to about 50 percent. (Ask about the 10-year probability of valve failure with xenografts and you'll get a range of three percent to 95 percent.)

Give surgeons a written description of a surgical problem, and half of the group will recommend surgery, while the other half will not. Survey them again two years later and as many as 40 percent of the same surgeons will disagree with their previous opinions and change their recommendations. Research studies back up all of these findings, according to Eddy.[4]

Because physician judgment varies so widely, so do treatment decisions; the same patient can go to different physicians, be told different things and receive different care. When so many physicians have such different beliefs and are doing such different things, it is impossible for every physician to be correct.

Why are so many physicians making inaccurate decisions in their medical practices? It is not because physicians lack competence, sincerity or diligence, but because they must make decisions about tremendously complex problems with very little solid evidence available to back them up. (That situation is gradually changing with the explosion in medical literature. Recent surveys by the Healthcare Information and Management Systems Society (HIMSS) reveal that an increasing number of hospitals and healthcare organizations are adopting technologies to keep up with the flow of research, such as robust, computerized physician-order-entry (CPOE) systems to ensure appropriate drug prescribing.)[5]

Most physicians practice in a virtually data-free environment, devoid of feedback on the correctness of their practice. They know very little about the quality and outcomes of their diagnosis and treatment decisions. And without data indicating that they should change what they're doing, physicians continue doing what they've been doing all along.

Physicians rely heavily on the "art" of medicine, practicing not according to solid research evidence, but rather by how they were trained, by the culture of their own practice environment and by their own experiences with their patients.

For example, consider deep-vein-thrombosis (DVT) prophylaxis, that means therapy to prevent dangerous blood clots in vessels before and after operations in the hospital. Research offers solid, Grade-A evidence about how to prevent DVT in the hospital. But only half of America's hospitals follow these practices. That begs an important question: Why? We have the science for that particular sliver of care. How come we still can't get it right?

The core problem we would like to examine here is that a disturbingly large chunk of medical practice is still "craft" rather than science. As we've noted, relatively little actionable science is available to guide physicians and physicians often ignore proven evidence-based guidelines when they do exist. A guild-like approach to medicine — where every physician does it his or her way — can create inherent complexity, waste, proneness to error and danger for patients.

A great example comes from Peter Pronovost, MD, PhD, a patient-safety expert and a professor of anesthesiology, critical-care medicine and surgery at the Johns Hopkins University School of Medicine. He is co-author of *Safe Patients, Smart Hospitals: How One Doctor's Checklist Can Help Us Change Health Care from Inside Out.*[6] In a televised interview about his book, Pronovost said that we (that is, physicians) knew that we were killing people with preventable central-line bloodstream infections in hospitals and we accepted it as a routine part, albeit a toxic side-effect, of practice. We were killing more people that way, probably, than those who died of breast cancer. We tolerated it because our practices didn't use available scientific evidence that showed us how to prevent such infections. We ignored the science and patients paid the price with their lives.

Cost is another toxic by-product of care delivery practices that are not based on solid science and the tremendous clinical variation that results from them.

Doing the Right Thing Only Half of the Time

When we look at how well physicians are really doing, it's scary to see how off the mark they are. Anyone who feels self-assured about receiving the best medical care that science can offer is in for a shock, considering some eye-opening research that shows how misplaced that confidence is. Let's start with how well physicians do when they have available evidence to guide their practices.

The best answer comes from seminal research by the Rand Corporation, a respected research organization known for authoritative and unbiased analyses of complex topics. On average, Americans only receive about half of recommended medical care for common illnesses, according to research led by Elizabeth McGlynn, PhD, director of Rand's Center for Research on Quality in Health Care. That means the average American receives care that fails to meet professional evidence-based standards about half of the time.[7]

McGlynn and her colleagues examined thousands of patient medical records from around the country for physician performance on 439 indicators of quality of care for thirty acute and chronic conditions as well as preventive care, making the Rand study one of the largest of its kind ever undertaken. The researchers examined medical conditions representing the leading causes of illness, death and healthcare service use across all age groups and types of patients. They reviewed national evidence-based practice guidelines that offer physicians specific and proven care processes for screening, diagnosis, treatment and follow-up care. Those guidelines were vetted by several multispecialty expert panels as scientifically grounded and clinically proven to improve patient care.

For example, when a patient walks into the doctor's office, the physician is supposed to ensure that when the patient shows up for hip surgery, he or she will receive drugs to prevent blood clots and then a preventive dose of antibiotics.

Even though clinical guidelines exist for practices like these, McGlynn and her colleagues found something shocking: physicians get it right about 55 percent of the time across all medical conditions. In other words, patients receive recommended care only about 55 percent of the time, on average. It doesn't matter whether that care is acute (to treat current illnesses), chronic (to treat and manage conditions that cause recurring illnesses, like diabetes and asthma) or preventive (to avert acute episodes like heart attack and stroke).

How well physicians did for any particular condition varied substantially, ranging from about 79 percent of recommended care delivered for early-stage cataracts to about 11 percent of recommended care for alcohol dependence. Physicians prescribe the recommended medication about 69 percent of the time, follow appropriate lab-testing recommendations about 62 percent of the time and follow appropriate surgical guidelines 57 percent of the time. Physicians adhere to recommended care guidelines 23 percent of the time for hip fracture, 25 percent of the time for atrial fibrillation, 39 percent for community-acquired pneumonia, 41 percent for urinary-tract infection and 45 percent for diabetes mellitus.[8]

Underuse of recommended services was actually more common than overuse: about 46 percent of patients did not receive recommended care, while about 11 percent of participants received care that was not recommended and was potentially harmful.

Here is disturbing proof that physicians often fail to follow solid scientific evidence of what "quality care" is in providing common care that any of us might need:[9]

- Only one-quarter of diabetes patients received essential blood-sugar tests.
- Patients with hypertension failed to receive one-third the recommended care.
- Coronary-artery-disease patients received only about two-thirds of the recommended care.
- Just under two-thirds of eligible heart-attack patients received aspirin, which is proven to reduce the risk of death and stroke.
- Only about two-thirds of elderly patients had received or been offered a pneumococcal vaccine (to help prevent them from developing pneumonia).
- Scarcely more than one-third of eligible patients had been screened for colorectal cancer.

These findings have shaped the conversation among experts on American healthcare quality by establishing a national baseline for the status quo. That baseline is jarring and disturbing. The gap between what is proven to work and what physicians actually do poses a serious threat to the health and well-being of all of us. That gap persists despite public- and private-sector initiatives to improve care. Physicians need either better access to existing information for clinical decision-making or stronger incentives to use that information.

Inappropriate use of medical services (both underuse and overuse) by physicians is rampant, affecting millions of patients. We know that because some of the nation's leading healthcare quality and safety experts reviewed several large-scale national studies and presented their findings to the President's Advisory Commission on Consumer Protection and Quality in the Health Care Industry, which was formed during President Bill Clinton's administration.

The commission released a report in March, 1998, that stated: "Exhaustive research documents the fact that today, in America, there is no guarantee that any individual will receive high-quality care for any particular health problem. The healthcare industry is plagued with overutilization of services, underutilization of services and errors in healthcare practice." The central problem, as the Rand study had revealed, is clinicians' failure to follow evidence-based best practice guidelines that exist and have been proven to enhance the quality of healthcare delivery.[10]

The commission's report acknowledged that physicians may have difficulty keeping up with an explosive growth in medical research, noting that the number of published randomized, controlled trials had increased from an average of 509 annually between 1975 and 1980 to 8,636 annually from 1993 through 1997.[11] That's just for randomized, controlled trials. Several other types of studies considerably increase the number of annual research articles that physicians must keep up with to be current on scientific research findings. Plus, that was more than ten years ago; the numbers grow more rapidly each year.

From these data, the report concluded that a troubling gap exists between best practices and actual practices and that the likelihood that any particular patient will get the best care possible varies considerably. Translation: physicians aren't following the evidence.

Hospitals are on the hook as well and show wide gaps in their delivery of recommended care. The Leapfrog Group is a consortium of large employers that reports and compares hospital quality-performance data to help companies make healthcare purchasing decisions. (Full disclosure: Sanjaya Kumar is president and CEO of Quantros, the company that hosts the Leapfrog Group's Hospital Safety Survey.) The group tracks more than 1,200 U.S. hospitals that voluntarily report how well they adhere to a variety of evidence-based quality measures that are endorsed by the National Quality Forum (NQF) or are consistent with those of The Joint Commission and the Federal Centers for Medicare & Medicaid Services.

Results from the Leapfrog Group's 2009 hospital survey show that just over half of hospitals meet Leapfrog's quality standard for heart-bypass surgery; under half meet its standard for heart angioplasty; and under half of hospitals meet Leapfrog's quality standards for six common procedures, including high-risk surgery, heart-valve replacement and high-risk deliveries, even though nationally accepted scientific guidelines for these procedures exist and have been proven to save lives.[12]

It's disturbingly clear from these studies that too many physicians and hospitals are not applying known, evidence-based and available guidelines for quality practice. Physicians are either ignoring or unaware of much better ways to treat their patients.

Knowing the Right Thing Only One-Fifth of the Time

Failing to follow existing guidelines is only part of what makes so much of medical practice "unscientific." Another key reason is that there are so few solid, actionable scientific guidelines to begin with, and those that are available cover a relatively small slice of clinical care.

Part of the problem is that science, technology and culture are all moving targets. Today's dogma is tomorrow's folly, and vice versa. Many examples show that what physicians once accepted as truth has been totally debunked. Twenty years ago, for instance, physicians believed that lytic therapy for post-myocardial infarction would prolong a heart attack. The therapy involves clot-busting medication given to heart-attack patients. Today it is standard practice. Angioplasty and intracoronary lysis of clots are other examples. Years ago, surgery for benign prostatic hypertrophy (enlarged prostate) was one of the top DRGs (illnesses billed by hospitals) under Medicare. Today, we do far fewer of these procedures because of new drugs.

The public has little idea that physicians are playing a sophisticated guessing game every single day. That is a scary thought. We hope that one day we'll look back, for example, on cancer chemotherapy the same way we look back at the use of leeches, cupping and bloodletting.

Another part of the problem is that clinical knowledge generated by randomized, controlled trials takes far longer to reach the front lines of medical care than most people realize. Turning basic scientific discoveries into innovative therapies — from "laboratory bench to bedside" — takes up to 17 years.[13] Existing scientific literature is being added to and undergoing overhaul every two years, which adds to the knowledge gap at the bedside.

Time lag notwithstanding, thousands of research articles are published every year, which presents a different challenge to delivering care based on the strongest evidence. Physicians can't always keep up with the volume of knowledge to be reviewed and put into practice, and those who don't provide poorer quality care. Medical advances occur frequently, and detailed knowledge quickly goes out of date.

Here's a counterintuitive consequence: the more years of practice experience a physician has, the more out-of-date his or her practice patterns may be. Research has documented this phenomenon of decreasing quality of clinical performance with increasing years in practice.[14] Although we generally assume that the knowledge and skills that physicians accumulate during years of practice lead to superior clinical abilities, those physicians may paradoxically be less likely to provide what the latest scientific evidence says is appropriate care! It's all about the evidence and keeping up with it.

But just how comprehensive is the available scientific evidence for effective clinical practices? It is slimmer than most people think. Slice a pie into five pieces, and remove one piece. That slice represents the roughly 20 percent of clinical-care practices for which solid randomized, controlled trial evidence exists.[15] The remaining four-fifths represent medical care delivered based upon a combination of less reliable studies, unsystematic observation, informed guesswork and conformity to prevailing treatments and procedures used by most other clinicians in a local community.

To illustrate how little scientific evidence often exists to justify well-established medical treatments, David Eddy researched the scientific evidence underlying a standard and widely used glaucoma treatment designed to lower pressure in the eyeball. He searched published medical reports back to 1906 and could not find one random-ized, controlled trial of the treatment. That was despite decade after decade of confident statements about it in textbooks and medical journals, statements which Eddy found had simply been handed down from generation to generation.[16] The kicker was that the treatment was harmful to patients, actually causing more cases of blindness rather than fewer.

Similar evidence deficits exist for other common medical prac-tices, including colorectal screening with regular fecal-occult-blood tests and sigmoidoscopy; annual chest x-rays; surgery for enlarged prostates; bone-marrow transplants for breast cancer; and common approaches to pain control, depression, immunizations, cancer screen-ing, alcohol and drug abuse, smoking and functional disabilities.[17] The problem is rampant across medicine; a huge amount of what physi-cians do lacks a solid base of scientific evidence.

In the past, many standard and accepted practices for clinical problems were simpler and more straightforward than those that today's clinicians face — and these practices seem to have worked, despite the paucity of good research evidence. Physicians simply made subjective, intuitive decisions about what worked based on what they observed. The problem today is that the growing complexity of med-icine bombards clinicians with a chaotic array of clinical choices, ambiguities and uncertainties that exceeds the inherent limitations of the unaided human mind. As a result, many of today's standard clini-cal practices bear no relation to any evidence of effectiveness.[18]

Instead, physicians frequently base their decisions on shortcuts, such as the actions of the average practitioner ("if everyone is doing it, the intervention must be appropriate"); the commonness of the disease ("if the disease is common, we have no choice but to use whatever treatment is available"); the seriousness of the outcome ("if the outcome without treatment is very bad, we have to assume the treatment will work"); the need to do something ("this intervention is all we have"); and the novelty or technical appeal of the intervention ("if the machine takes a pretty picture, it must have some use").[19]

Drug prescribing is another blatant example of medical practice that is often evidence-free. Drugs that are known to be effective may work well for only 60 percent of people who take them. But about 21 percent of drug prescriptions in the United States are for "off-label" use, that is, to treat conditions for which they have not been approved by the U.S. Food and Drug Administration.[20] That's more than 150 million prescriptions per year. Off-label use is most common among cardiac medications (46 percent) and anticonvulsants (46 percent). Here's the real punch line: in 73 percent of the cases where drugs are used in unapproved ways, there is little or no evidence that they work. Physicians prescribe drugs well over a million times a year with little or no scientific support.

These are fighting words, saying that such a big chunk of medical practice is not based on science. To illustrate just how provocative this topic is, look at what happened in the 1990s when the Federal Agency for Health Care Policy and Research (now the Agency for Healthcare Research and Quality) released findings from a five-year investigation of the effectiveness of various treatments for low back pain — one of the leading reasons that Americans see physicians.

Between 1989 and 1994, an interdisciplinary Back Pain Patient Outcomes Assessment Team (BOAT) at the University of Washington Medical School in Seattle set out to determine what treatment strategies work best and for whom. Led by back expert Richard A. Deyo, MD, MPH, the team included orthopedic surgeons, primary-care physicians, physical therapists, epidemiologists and economists. Together, they examined the relative value of various diagnostic tests and surgical procedures.[21]

They conducted a comprehensive review of clinical literature on back pain. They exhaustively examined variations in the rates at which different procedures were being used to diagnose and treat back pain. Their chief finding was deeply disturbing: what physicians thought worked well for treating low back pain doesn't. The implication was that a great many standard interventions for low back pain may not be justified. And that was immensely threatening to physicians, especially surgeons who perform back operations for a living.

Among the researchers' specific findings: no evidence shows that spinal-fusion surgery is superior to other surgical procedures for common spine problems, and such surgery leads to more complications, longer hospital stays and higher hospital charges than other types of back surgery.[22]

Disgruntled orthopedic surgeons and neurosurgeons reacted vigorously to the researchers' conclusion that not enough scientific evidence exists to support commonly performed back operations. The surgeons joined with Congressional critics of the Clinton health plan to attack federal funding for such research and for the agency that sponsored it. Consequently, the Agency for Healthcare Policy and Research had its budget for evaluative research slashed drastically.[23]

The back panel's guidelines were published in 1994. Since then, even though there are still no rigorous, independently funded clinical trials showing that back surgery is superior to less invasive treatments, surgeons continue to perform a great many spinal fusions. The number increased from about100,000 in 1997 to 303,000 in 2006.[24]

What are physicians to do? They need a great deal more reliable information than they have, especially when offering patients life-changing treatment options. Before recommending surgery or radiation treatment for prostate cancer, for example, physicians and their patients must compare the benefits, harms and costs of the two treatments and decide which is the more desirable.

One treatment might deliver a higher probability of survival but also have bad side effects and high costs, while the alternative treatment might deliver a lower probability of survival but have no side effects and lower costs. Without valid scientific evidence about those factors, the patient may receive unnecessary and ineffective care, or fail to receive effective care, because neither he nor his physician can reliably weigh the benefits, potential harm and costs of the decision.

Recognizing that the quality and reliability of clinical-research information vary greatly, entities like the U.S. Preventive Services Task Force (USPSTF) have devised rating systems to rank the strength of available evidence for certain treatments. The strongest evidence is the scarcest and comes from systematic review of studies (randomized, controlled trials) that are rigorously designed to factor out biases and extraneous influences on results. Weaker evidence comes from less rigorously designed studies that may let bias creep into the results (for example, trials without randomization or cohort or case-control analytic studies). The weakest evidence comes from anecdotal case reports or expert opinion that is not grounded in careful testing.

Raymond Gibbons, MD, a professor of medicine at the Mayo Clinic and past president of the American Heart Association, puts it well: "In simple terms, Class I recommendations are the 'do's'; Class III recommendations are the 'don'ts'; and Class II recommendations are the 'maybes.'"[25] The point is this: even physicians who follow guidelines must deal with scientific uncertainty. There are a lot more "maybes" than "do's."

Even the "do's" require value judgments, and it is important to be clear about what evidence-based practice guidelines can and cannot do, regardless of the strength of their scientific evidence. Guidelines are not rigid mandates or "cookie-cutter" recommendations that tell physicians what to do. They are intended to be flexible tools to help physicians and their patients make informed decisions about their care.

Even guidelines that are rooted in randomized, controlled trial research do not make clinical decisions for physicians; rather, they must be applied to individual patients and clinical situations based on value judgments, both by physicians and their patients. Clinical decision-making must entail value judgments about the costs and benefits of available treatments. What strong guidelines do is to change the anchor point for the decision from beliefs about what works to evidence of what works.[26] Actual value-based treatment decisions are a necessary second step.

For example, should a physician recommend an implantable cardioverter-defibrillator (ICD) to his or her patient when a randomized-control trial shows that it works? The device is a small, battery-powered electrical-impulse generator implanted in patients at risk of sudden cardiac death due to ventricular fibrillation (uncoordinated contraction of heart chamber muscle) and ventricular tachycardia (fast heart rhythm). A published randomized trial compared ICDs to management with drugs for heart-attack patients and found that ICDs reduced patients' probability of death at 20 months by about one-third.[27]

Armed with such a guideline, the physician and patient must still make a value judgment: whether the estimated decrease in chance of death is worth the uncertainty, risk and cost of the procedure. The ultimate decision is not in the guideline, but it is better informed than a decision made without the evidence to help guide it. The guideline has lessened uncertainty but not removed it.

The lesson here is that there are huge gaps in the scientific evidence guiding physician decision-making, and it wasn't until healthcare-quality gadflies like David Eddy began to demand to see the evidence that we learned about those gaps. This revelation has had at least two beneficial effects: it informs us about the lack of evidence so that we can be more realistic in our expectations and more aware of the uncertainty in medical decision-making, and it exhorts the medical community to search for better evidence.

"Nothing should be affirmatively promoted unless there is good evidence of at least some benefit," writes Eddy.[28] It is simply amazing that applying such a statement to modern medicine represents such a ground-breaking development. But it has literally changed the face of medicine.

Physicians are People, Too

Having good clinical evidence for decision-making is not the whole story. Clinical decisions inevitably rely heavily upon physician judgment — the "art" of medicine — irrespective of the evidentiary basis. Nonscientific, human dimensions of physician decision-making greatly affect the quality of medical care, sometimes for better, sometimes for worse. Let's look at both. Aggressive ingenuity can transcend practice guidelines and yield superior patient care, while biases inherent to human thinking can lead to diagnostic error.

We are used to thinking that a physician's ability depends mainly on science and skill. It would seem serendipitous to bring ingenuity into the picture. But even physicians with the greatest knowledge and technical skills can have mediocre results, and the subtleties of medical care can depend extensively on more nebulous factors such as how active and resourceful a physician is in trying different and potentially better interventions, argues Harvard surgeon Atul Gawande, MD, in his book, *Better: A Surgeon's Notes on Performance.* [29]

Gawande contradicts the widespread belief that scientifically based medical practice allows nearly all physicians to do their job as well as it can be done. He does so by explaining how all human activities, including physician performance, can be described by a bell curve. When outcomes can be measured reliably for any given medical specialty, a bell curve of performance is revealed: some physicians or hospital programs will achieve mediocre outcomes; most will achieve undistinguished outcomes; and some will achieve remarkably good outcomes. The insight is distressing and important.

For hernia operations, Gawande notes that the chances of recurrence are one in 10 for surgeons at the poor-performing end of the spectrum, one in 20 for average performers, and under one in 500 for a handful of superior performers. If someone has treatable colon cancer, his or her survival rate after surgery can range from 20 percent to a little above 60 percent, depending on the surgeon. Even when practice guidelines are available, these differences persist. Why?

Gawande explains that science is not always sufficient to produce superior results. He illustrates the point by comparing the cystic fibrosis (CF) programs at two hospitals. Cincinnati Children's Hospital is among the most respected pediatric hospitals in the country. One of the hospital's pediatricians wrote the chapter on CF in the most respected textbook in the field, the *Nelson Textbook of Pediatrics*. And yet, in the late 1990s, Cincinnati Children's was well below average, according to some measures, for treating children with CF. For example, lung function (the best predictor of life expectancy) for the hospital's CF patients under the age of twelve was in the bottom 25 percent of the country's CF patients.

That Cincinnati Children's results were not better is truly puzzling. Its system for CF care is sophisticated and highly specialized. The program undergoes a rigorous certification process. Its pediatricians have a great deal of experience caring for patients with CF, and they all participate in research trials to search for new and better treatments. They follow detailed national guidelines for CF, which two of the hospitals physicians had helped write.

Enter the role of human ingenuity in medical decision-making. Gawande describes the remarkable performance of Warren Warwick, MD, a pediatrician at the Minnesota Cystic Fibrosis Center at Fairview-University Children's Hospital in Minneapolis, one of the top-five performing centers in the country. Warwick believed that national practice guidelines were not enough, and that constant, ad-hoc experimenting was necessary to find new ways to keep CF patients' lungs as open as possible. Warwick has achieved better outcomes than anyone else.

Patients at Warwick's center received the same evidence-based treatments as patients in other centers: nebulized treatments to unclog passageways, antibiotics and chest thumping to loosen secretions. However, Warwick was almost contemptuous of settling for care based on national clinical guidelines, which he believed to be inherently out of date and in need of supplementation with ongoing experimentation at the bedside. His innovations helped to propel Fairview's CF care performance to the top of the national charts.

Warwick established a weekly meeting among his clinic's physicians to review each other's care and to uniformly adopt the care plans that work best. The center's physicians are not content when their patients' lung function is 80 percent or 90 percent of normal. They aim for 100 percent. Several children at the center have had tubes surgically inserted into their stomachs, even though no published research says it is necessary, because Warwick believed they were not gaining enough weight. Not a single child or teenager at the center has died in years, and its oldest CF patient is now 64 — all tremendous accomplishments.

The lesson from Gawande's bell curve is that average performance is a disturbing fact of medical practice, and more than the help of science may be required to rise above it. The physicians in Cincinnati and in Minneapolis are equally capable and well versed in the data on CF. The subtleties of medical decision-making must be identified, learned and passed on. The ingenuity of physicians themselves — their intense drive and constant experimenting — is a core ingredient in superior medical decision-making. As Gawande's illustration demonstrates, such ingenuity can transcend and improve upon the formal channels of scientific evidence.

As we've seen, physicians' treatment decisions are fraught with inexactitudes: insufficient scientific backing, lack of adherence to existing scientific backing and perhaps even the need to transcend existing science with human ingenuity.

Another realm of physician decision-making that is rife with nonscientific influence is diagnosis. There's a whole body of research on flaws in the diagnostic decision-making process, from which we know that as many as 15 percent of all diagnoses are inaccurate. Decisions that physicians make when diagnosing patients are susceptible to distortion and error. Because they are human, physicians make mistakes in their thinking. Those mistakes stem not from inadequate technical knowledge but from influences on the cognitive process itself.

When reviewing symptoms to diagnose illnesses, physicians rely heavily on their intuition and experience with thousands of patients, trying to sort through that knowledge to retrieve information that might be relevant to the patient in front of them. But as Harvard Medical School Chair of Medicine Jerome Groopman, MD, points out in his book *How Doctors Think*, the mind does not always weigh knowledge appropriately during decision-making.[30] The "informed intuition" approach to diagnosis is prone to various kinds of thinking pitfalls and traps that lead to errors. Different doctors may come up with different diagnoses for the same patient. Why?

Research on misdiagnoses is like "a window into the medical mind," writes Groopman, revealing that doctors sometimes fail to question their assumptions and that they focus on the wrong observations. The overwhelming majority of misdiagnoses are not caused by technical mistakes or inadequate medical knowledge, but by cognitive errors, Groopman argues.

Physicians may seize upon an initial symptom and make a snap judgment (anchoring error). They might discount clinical findings that don't fit that judgment and cherry-pick information that confirms their suspicions (confirmation bias). They might stereotype a patient, for example as "a complainer" and attribute an observed symptom to that trait (attribution error). They might inappropriately compare the present case to other cases they've seen most recently and that, therefore, are highly memorable (availability error).

The process of pattern recognition is a core element of clinical diagnosis. Within seconds of attending to key cues of a patient's problem, including medical history, physical exam, x-rays or lab test, a physician will identify a pattern that translates into a specific disease or condition. That pattern draws most heavily on the physician's visual appraisal of the patient. Most physicians, writes Groopman, quickly come up with two or three possible diagnoses within moments of meeting a patient, developing their hypotheses from a very incomplete set of information.

Groopman describes the case of a forest ranger near Halifax, Nova

Scotia, who had come into the emergency room complaining that it hurt each time he took a breath and that he had had growing discomfort in his chest over the past few days. The ER physician noted that the man was muscular, not sweating or lightheaded; didn't have pain in his arms, neck or back; had reportedly never smoked or been overweight; and had no family history of heart attack, stroke or diabetes. The man's blood pressure and pulse were normal. His lungs and heart sounded normal, and his cardiac enzymes (which can reveal heart damage) tested normal after an electrocardiogram, a chest x-ray and blood tests. The physician told the man he might have overexerted himself and strained a muscle, and sent the man home.

The man suffered a heart attack the very next day (which he survived). The physician from the day earlier had missed the diagnosis of unstable angina (in which the heart doesn't get enough blood flow and oxygen), but not because of negligence. The unstable angina didn't show on the EKG because 50 per cent of such cases don't. It didn't show up on the cardiac-enzymes test because no damage to the patient's heart muscle had occurred yet. And, it didn't show up on the chest x-ray because the heart had not yet begun to fail and no fluid had backed up in the lungs.

The mistake the physician made was failing to consider possibilities that contradicted his mental templates of heart disease — in other words, allowing his thinking to be overly influenced by what is typically true, thus attributing symptoms to the wrong cause. The physician could have considered the atypical clinical possibilities and kept the patient under observation, perhaps doing a second cardiac-enzyme test or having him take a cardiac stress test to explore the source of his chest pain. But instead, the physician's judgment was overly influenced by the man's absence of heart-disease risk factors and by how healthy he looked, leading the physician to reassure himself and his patient too quickly that the chest pain was not related to a heart problem.

Physicians can also color their decisions based on their feelings for a patient, what Groopman describes as "affective error." Research in cognitive psychology backs this up: when people are confronted with uncertainty (which means every doctor attempting to diagnose a patient), they are susceptible to unconscious emotions and personal biases. How doctors think can affect the quality of their care as much as how much they know or how much experience they have.

Modern marvels of high-tech medicine notwithstanding, the belief that there is a high degree of scientific certainty in medical practice needs to be challenged. The insights of McGlynn, Eddy, Gawande and Groopman sum up the problem. The gap between what the medical community knows to work and what physicians actually do is still huge. Physicians often don't have strong evidence to back up what they are doing. Physicians who think beyond the evidence sometimes achieve superior results. Clinical decisions are influenced by flawed and biased thinking processes. We will examine what to do about this problem in the first section of Part II, the "myth buster" section of this book, when we examine physician decision-making.

We will now examine in some detail the most troubling manifestation of physician uncertainty: the widespread, unwarranted and unexplained variation in physicians' clinical practice patterns. Embedded in that variation is the unjustified belief that more healthcare automatically means better quality.

Reflection

In our travels around the country, we get the greatest pushback from physicians over this part of the story. "How could it be?" they ask us. "Say it ain't so, Joe. It can't be as bad as you're making it out to be." And that's only when we cite the evidence.

Doctors believe that *they* practice based on the evidence, and the problem lies elsewhere. They blame it on medical liability: doctors reorder treatments and tests because they're worried about getting sued for malpractice. But there's really good evidence that the liability issue accounts for only eight percent or nine percent of the total cost to the healthcare system. Doctors find this problem of medical uncertainty hard to internalize, and they express a lot of incredulity surrounding both the size and scope of the dilemma.   – *S.K. and D.B.N.*

Notes

1. John Carey. "Medical Guesswork: From Heart Surgery to Prostate Cancer, the Health Industry Knows Little about Which Common Treatments Really Work," *Business Week*, May 29, 2006.

2. David M. Eddy, MD, PhD. "The Challenge," *Journal of the American Medical Association* 1990; 263(2):287-290.

3. Ibid.

4. Ibid.

5. HIMSS News, "Healthcare IT Continues to Grow, Despite Economy." Available online at: http://www.himss.org/ASP/ContentRedirector.asp?ContentId=69099&type=HIMSSNewsItem.

6. Peter Pronovost, MD, PhD, and Eric Vohr. *Safe Patients, Smart Hospitals: How One Doctor's Checklist Can Help Us Change Health Care from Inside Out* (New York: Hudson Street Press, 2010).

7. Elizabeth A. McGlynn, PhD; Steven M. Asch, MD, MPH, et al. "The Quality of Healthcare Delivered to Adults in the United States," *New England Journal of Medicine* 2003; 348:2635-2645.

8. Ibid.

9. Ibid.

10. Ibid.

11. The President's Advisory Commission on Consumer Protection and Quality in the Healthcare Industry. Available online at: www.hcqualitycommission.gov.

12. Leapfrog Group, From "The 2009 Leapfrog Hospital Survey: Quality Not Adequate & Waste A Major Problem," April 13, 2010. Available online at: http://www.leapfroggroup.org/news/leapfrog_news/4775498.

13. Committee on Quality of Health Care in America, Institute of Medicine. *Crossing the Quality Chasm: A New Health System for the 21st Century* (Washington DC: National Academy Press, 2001).

14. Niteesh K. Choudhry, MD; Robert H. Fletcher, MD, MSc; Stephen B. Soumerai, ScD. "Systematic Review: The Relationship between Clinical Experience and Quality of Health Care," *Annals of Internal Medicine* 2005; 142:260-273.

15. David Eddy bases that figure on estimates by the Congressional Office of Technology Assessment that only 10 percent to 20 percent of practices are supported by randomized, controlled trials. Institute of Medicine, *Assessing Medical Technologies* (Washington, DC.: National Academy Press, 1985).

16. Richard Smith. "Where is the wisdom?" *British Medical Journal* 1991; 303:798-799.

17. Issues in Permanente Medicine. Focus: Evidence-Based Medicine. July, 1999. Available online at http://www.kpcmi.org/pdf/ebm.pdf.

18. Ibid.

19. David M. Eddy, MD, PhD. "Anatomy of a Decision." *Journal of the American Medical Association,* 1990; 263(3):441-443.

20. David C. Radley, MPH; Stan N. Finkelstein, MD; Randall S. Stafford, MD, PhD. "Off-Label Prescribing among Office-Based Physicians," *Archives of Internal Medicine* 2006; 166:1021-1026.

21. Agency for Healthcare Research and Quality. Back Pain Patient Outcomes Assessment Team (BOAT). Available online at: http://www.ahrq.gov/clinic/medtep/backpain.htm.

22. Ibid.

23. Ezekiel J. Emanuel; Victor R. Fuchs; Alan M. Garber. "Essential Elements of a Technology and Outcomes Assessment Initiative," *Journal of the American Medical Association,* 2007; 298(11):1323-1325.

24. Shannon Brownlee. *Overtreated: Why Too Much Medicine Is Making Us Sicker and Poorer* (New York: Bloomsbury USA, 2007).

25. Ibid.

26. Sean R. Tunis. "Reflections on Science, Judgment, and Value in Evidence-Based Decision-Making: A Conversation with David Eddy." *Health Affairs.* 2007; doi: 10.1377/hlthaff.26.4.w500 (Published online June 19, 2007: http://content.healthaffairs.org/cgi/content/abstract/hlthaff.26.4.w500v1.)

27. Ibid.

28. Ibid.

29. Atul Gawande, MD. *Better: A Surgeon's Notes on Performance.* (New York: Metropolitan Books, 2007).

30. Jerome Groopman, MD. *How Doctors Think* (New York: Houghton Mifflin, 2007).

MYTH 2:

More Healthcare Means Better Healthcare

"We all know that our arsenal of clot-busters, MRI scanners, gene therapies and columns of specialists maim and kill the patients we aim to heal with shocking regularity, but our profession has reacted to this knowledge mostly with a collective shrug of its shoulders."

– Robert M. Wachter, MD, and Kaveh G. Shojania, MD, patient safety experts.

[Robert M. Wachter, MD, and Kaveh G. Shojania, MD. *Internal Bleeding: The Truth behind America's Terrifying Epidemic of Medical Mistakes* (New York: Rugged Land, 2004)]

When we're sick, we see a doctor. When we're really sick, we go to the hospital. The more doctors we see and the more services they provide us, the better we will get and the faster we will return to health. Well, not exactly. Healthcare doesn't quite work out that way.

In fact, patients who receive less intense treatment for their illness, or fewer tests and procedures, often have outcomes that are as good, on average — a bit better, in fact — than patients receiving the more numerous or intense services, as we will see in this section. In medicine, less is truly more. This proposition sounds less absurd when we look more closely at what "more" really means.

For most activities, you get better at something the more you do it. If you're following the right procedure the first time, your technical proficiency will improve with practice. Clear evidence supports this "proficiency volume" principle for various medical procedures, such as heart surgery. Patient mortality and hospital readmission rates tend to be lowest for surgeons who perform hundreds of surgeries a year and highest for those who perform only a few. That isn't surprising. Who wouldn't want the most experienced surgeon?

But experience is not the whole picture. The very decision of whether or not to operate must be sound. It often is. But sometimes it is not. When physicians make clinical decisions based on sound evidence, patients get the care they need, and they don't get services they don't need. The trouble, as we saw in the previous section, is that there are huge gaps in the scientific evidence, and physicians often don't follow the evidence that does exist. Instead, they practice according to how they were trained ("this is how my mentors did it"), follow local practice customs ("this is how we do it here"), or rely on their own experience ("this is how to do it based on what I've seen in cases like this").

Physicians often practice in a data-poor environment, devoid of feedback on the correctness of their practice and knowing little about the quality and outcomes of their diagnosis and treatment decisions. As a result, we witness one of the most troubling phenomena in medicine: physicians tend to do things their way; and their way differs from the way of other physicians.

When different physicians recommend different treatment for similar patients with the same illness and the same health status, it is impossible to claim that these physicians all are doing the right thing. The variation cannot be justified scientifically.

Unexplained clinical variation sums up, in three words, the core problem of American healthcare. It produces the toxic by-products of waste and uneven quality; it exposes patients to considerable unnecessary risk and causes considerable unnecessary harm. It means that some physicians underuse effective, evidence-based care. Other physicians overuse ineffective care for which there is no clinical benefit. Some will recommend conservative treatment as the best option, while others will recommend surgery. The magnitude of the problem of unexplained clinical variation is enormous.

Because of it, our healthcare delivery system spends more than $700 *billion* of its $2.3 trillion in annual health spending on medical care that does nothing to improve a patient's health and even produces harm, according to testimony that Peter Orszag, then Congressional Budget Office director, gave to the Senate Budget Committee in January 2008. That's *annual* spending. Seven hundred billion dollars every year. And, most alarmingly, all of that ineffective and harmful care represents *one-third* of the tests, treatments and procedures that physicians perform. These findings are absolutely staggering, and they are backed up by decades of research on the problem.

ZIP code by ZIP code, inexplicable differences exist in the types and amounts of healthcare delivered, and these differences are not related to illness, medical evidence or patient preference. When researchers analyze these differences, they can level the playing field by factoring out all of the differences among patients. When researchers statistically remove the influence of age, health status, type of illness and several other variables that might explain treatment differences — when everybody's heart attack is statistically the same — there are still huge differences in healthcare utilization and spending.

You may be two or three times as likely to have a heart operation than someone in an adjacent city, just because physicians in your city tend to prefer surgery to medical management of your chest pains. Physician preference, not science, makes the difference. If more people knew this, we believe, there would be widespread and justifiable outrage.

The point that is hardest to believe about all of this is that these differences are not driven by the patients' protoplasm. They are driven by unexplained variation in physicians' practice patterns. One-third of medical spending and service utilization leads to care that does not make patients better and may even make them worse. Why?

Partly because of physician culture, partly due to lack of an evidentiary basis for their decisions, partly due to failure to follow existing evidence and partly due to lack of countervailing data to say that physicians ought to change what they're doing.

The evidence exposing unexplained clinical variation slaps us in the face. It could make your hair stand on end. The other arm of the problem, remember, is risk and medical error. The more physicians do, the more error-prone they become and the more they expose patients to the dangerous environment of hospitals. That leads to more testing, procedures, risk of complications and exposure to potential error. The decision to get those tests and procedures is often not based on science. That is how, in healthcare, more is not always better — and is often much worse.

Unexplained Variation is Rampant

"Geography is destiny" when it comes to healthcare delivery. That's the conclusion reached by the Christopher Columbus of unexplained clinical variation, John "Jack" Wennberg, MD, MPH, founder of the Center for the Evaluative Clinical Sciences, now the Dartmouth Institute for Health Policy and Clinical Practice. Decades of research by Wennberg and his Dartmouth colleagues reveal that the amount of medical care a patient receives for a specific illness is determined by where he or she lives.

A patient may get twice as many tests and procedures as a comparable patient with the same illness who lives in a different part of the country, or sometimes just in a different ZIP code. That's because most of the clinical decisions that physicians make are driven by local medical opinion and the local supply of medical resources, rather than by sound science or the preferences of their patients.[1]

Early in his work, Wennberg discovered marked variation in medical practice everywhere. He once lived in Vermont, between Stowe and Waterbury. In Waterbury, 20 percent of kids had had their tonsils removed by the time they were fifteen years old. In Waterbury, 70 percent had![2] Wennberg found a similar phenomenon with prostate surgeries in Maine. In some parts of the state, 20 percent of men with noncancerous enlargement of the prostate had their prostates removed by age eighty, while in other parts of the state the rate was 60 percent. Hysterectomies for women by age 70 followed a similar pattern: in some parts of Maine 20 percent of women had the operation, while in other parts 70 percent did.[3]

Why the variation? When scientific evidence on the value of specific medical treatments is ambiguous or incomplete, physicians' practice-style factor — the subjective reasoning that guides their clinical decision-making — is a major influence on practice variation. That practice-style factor affects whether patients with menopausal symptoms, enlarged tonsils or prostate, mild angina or other ailments receive conservative treatments or undergo a surgical operation.[4] It affects whether patients with relatively minor medical conditions, such as bronchitis or gastroenteritis, or who need minor surgical procedures, such as cystoscopy (bladder scope) or breast biopsy, receive their care in a hospital or in a physician's office.

In fact, the most important driver of per-capita cost variation for the treatment of specific diseases within a region is not differences in the health of the region's residents or the incidence of their illness. It is the different opinions of doctors about the need to hospitalize their patients.

Reflect, for a moment, on the implications of that "second opinion." It could mean the difference between going to the hospital or not, getting an operation or not, and possibly getting harmed by invasive and perhaps unnecessary tests and procedures. It could mean catching a preventable infection because you wound up in a hospital when more conservative outpatient treatment might have sufficed. That's not merely frightening. It is outrageous.

Absence of clear information makes a huge difference. Wennberg took what he discovered about Vermont's large variations in tonsillectomy rates to the Vermont Medical Society, which in turn circulated the information to Vermont hospitals. Physicians in the area with a high tonsillectomy rate then reviewed the most recent medical literature and convinced their colleagues that hospital policy on the use of tonsillectomy should be changed, and that the procedure should be used only after a second opinion was obtained. Astonishingly, the rate for tonsillectomy in that area eventually dropped to less than 10 percent of its initially measured rate. Physicians had replaced their data vacuum and subjective practice styles with evidence-based guidance, virtually eliminating unwarranted practice variation, at least for boys and girls getting tonsillectomies.

For decades, Wennberg and his Dartmouth colleagues — including Elliott Fisher, MD, MPH; Jonathan Skinner, PhD; and others — have documented that practice variation in healthcare delivery is rampant across the United States. They are perhaps best known for the *Dartmouth Atlas of Health Care* (www.dartmouthatlas.org), a series of reports that closely examine millions of Medicare claims for regional variations in healthcare usage and spending. The *Atlas* divides the U.S. into more than 300 hospital referral regions designating where clusters of patients tend to seek care. The findings are startling:

- Higher-spending regions in the country provide significantly more care to comparable Medicare patients than lower-spending regions do. Patients in higher-spending regions are more likely to be admitted to the hospital, spend more time in the hospital, receive more tests, see more medical specialists and have many more different physicians involved in their care.
- That extra care does not produce better outcomes overall or result in better quality of care, whether one looks at measures of technical quality (such as providing appropriate medication to heart-attack patients), or survival following such serious conditions as a heart attack or hip fracture.
- Up to 30 percent of medical care and spending does not improve patients' health outcomes and might even hurt them.

That last finding means the United States could save up to $700 billion a year in health spending just by attacking unwarranted clinical variation. If physicians in the highest-spending regions, like Miami or Los Angeles, adopted the practice patterns of physicians in the lowest-spending regions, like Minneapolis, health outcomes would be just as good or better.

Examining the costs of healthcare across the country — say, for hip fracture, colorectal cancer and acute myocardial infarction — shows huge variation in per-capita Medicare spending across geographic regions. That doesn't sound too surprising; after all, patients in Miami are much older and sicker, on average, than patients in Seattle. But remove all of the potentially confounding variables — such as patients' age, race, sex, income, education, health status and regional Medicare reimbursement differences — and surprisingly, per-capita Medicare spending still varies widely across geographic regions.

That is precisely what landmark *Dartmouth Atlas* research found.[5] Keep in mind that the researchers leveled the playing field and statistically factored out the differences among patients in their analysis. Yet spending and healthcare utilization to treat heart attacks, hip fractures and colorectal cancers still vary considerably. And, no good medical reason explains that variation.

Patients in higher-spending regions receive approximately 60 percent more care: more frequent physician visits, especially in the hospital; more frequent tests and minor procedures; more frequent consultations with medical specialists; and greater use of the hospital and intensive care unit. Pulmonary-function tests, for example, are performed nearly three times more often in the highest-spending regions than in the lowest-spending ones.

Some of the most dramatic differences are in rates of services provided to severely ill patients. For example, patients in their last six months of life spend more than two extra days in intensive care units in the highest-spending regions than in the lowest-spending regions and have tubes inserted into their bodies (heart tubes, feeding tubes, emergency tubes) more than twice as frequently.

The amount that Medicare spends on hospital care varies more than two-and-a-half times across regions (again, after leveling the playing field by factoring out differences in the prices Medicare pays for similar services in different regions, differences in patients' illness and other variables).[6] Patients who live in higher-spending areas are neither sicker, nor do they prefer more care. That means differences in spending are almost entirely driven by unexplained differences in the volume and intensity of healthcare services that comparable patients receive. Geography is destiny.

The Dartmouth research repeatedly demonstrates that underlying illness rates do not account for the spending differences among regions. One of the healthiest regions in the country, around Provo, Utah, draws seven percent more than the national average in Medicare spending; while the Richmond, Virginia region, whose residents tend to be sicker than the national average, draws 21 percent less in Medicare spending than the national average.

Why does volume of services vary so much? The spending and volume differences are not based on differences in patients or their medical needs. They are the product of physician choices of tests, treatments, and procedures. Physician practice-style factor is what varies. That is what is meant by unexplained clinical variation.

Why does practice-style factor vary so much? Higher-spending regions have a greater per-capita supply of providers or medical resources, or both. That greater supply of physicians and resources never sits idly; it gets used. Researchers call the phenomenon "supply-sensitive care," because the higher-spending regions have more hospital beds (especially in intensive care units), more CT scanners per capita, more physicians overall and more specialists per capita. Physicians adapt their hospital admission decisions to the presence of resources, meaning that patients in these regions — even those who may be less ill — get hospitalized more frequently, stay in the hospital longer, receive more CT scans, spend more time in the ICU, see physicians more frequently and get more diagnostic tests than identical patients in lower-spending regions.

The region's capacity to provide services strongly influences physicians' treatment decisions, rather than medical evidence or severity of illness justifying that service. In the absence of evidence, the prevailing cultural assumption that "more medical care is better" takes hold, leading physicians unconsciously to use available resources until they are exhausted. This assumption is amplified in a fee-for-service environment that pays providers more for doing more."[7]

More Care, But Not More Benefit

It's bad enough that there is widespread, unexplained variation in the quantity of healthcare delivered across the United States. But, are patients any better off when they get all that extra care? Shockingly, the answer is no. Dartmouth researchers measured quality in several ways: survival rate, whether patients got appropriate medication, whether their health deteriorated any more slowly and whether they were satisfied with their care. Extra care fails to deliver on all counts, they found.

The increased use of specialists, diagnostic tests and hospital-based care in higher-spending regions does not bring additional clinical benefit. Residents of high-spending regions do not show improved survival, slower decline in functional status or improved satisfaction with care. Quality of care in higher-spending regions is no better on most measures and is worse for several measures of preventive care. Access to care in higher-spending regions is no better or worse; neither is patient satisfaction. In regions where Medicare spends less, patients get less care and yet they fare just as well or better than their peers in the higher-spending regions.

What, then, is the relationship between healthcare quantity and quality? The answer is clear, based on years of research with remarkably consistent results: higher spending does not result in better quality of care, whether quality is measured as adherence to evidence-based guidelines, or survival following such serious conditions as a heart attack or hip fracture, or patient perceptions of the accessibility or quality of their care.

Here's the multibillion-dollar question: Why doesn't higher spending and more intense use of medical services — at both the regional and hospital levels — lead to higher-quality care? Answer: Because of clinical uncertainty, a poor base of scientific evidence to guide best practices and the resulting unexplained practice variation.

Hospitals are where many of the most costly and least studied clinical decisions are made — whether to readmit patients with congestive heart failure, whether to care for them in the ICU, or how many specialist referrals should be made. The research literature is largely silent, for example, on the appropriate interval between repeat visits or the value of additional diagnostic tests, hospitalizations and stays in the ICU for patients with specific chronic conditions. And, where care guidelines exist, adherence among physicians and hospital staff is spotty. The result in both cases is unexplained variation in clinical practices.

Unexplained clinical variation means that many unproven or ineffective practices get used anyway, including treatments that entail risk to the patient. Variation in treatment intensity is primarily a problem of overuse and waste, not underuse or healthcare rationing.

Healthcare experts have been aware of these findings for years.

But the message that more healthcare is not necessarily better healthcare made headline news in June, 2009, when *The New Yorker* magazine published a provocative article, "The Cost Conundrum: What a Texas Town Can Teach Us about Health Care," written by Harvard surgeon Atul Gawande, MD. The article made it all the way to the White House. President Obama made it required reading in the Oval Office, citing it while meeting with a group of Democratic senators as "what we've got to fix."

In his article, Gawande vividly illustrates the astonishing fact that physicians can *double* the amount of healthcare they deliver, yet achieve no better health outcomes for their patients. Gawande compares two towns in Texas to showcase how wildly physician treatment decisions vary and how more is not better. Healthcare costs arise because of the decisions physicians make about which services and treatments to write an order for. "The most expensive piece of medical equipment," Gawande writes, "is a doctor's pen."

Gawande visited McAllen, Texas, the border-town setting for the television miniseries *Lonesome Dove*. Situated in Hidalgo County, McAllen has the lowest household income in the United States, and yet it is one of the most expensive healthcare markets in the country (second only to Miami). The average cost per Medicare patient in 2006 was $15,000, nearly twice the national average.

Gawande calls McAllen "the most expensive town in the most expensive country for healthcare in the world." He also visited El Paso County, which he says has essentially the same ethnic, economic and public health demographics as Hidalgo County. But El Paso spent about $7,500 per Medicare patient in 2006 — half as much as in McAllen.

Why are McAllen's healthcare costs so high? Hidalgo County's public-health statistics revealed that an unhealthy population isn't the reason. Is McAllen providing unusually good healthcare? No evidence indicates that the treatments and technologies available there are better than those found elsewhere in the country. Both McAllen and El Paso offer comparable technologies — PET scans, neonatal intensive care units, advanced cardiac services and the like. Physician supply is no different; Hidalgo County actually has fewer specialists than the national average. Public health statistics are similar, so the variation isn't explained by differences in patient needs.

And yet, McAllen costs Medicare $7,000 a year more per person than the national average without delivering better healthcare. The primary cause of McAllen's extreme costs is across-the-board overuse of medicine.

Gawande provides a couple of examples of that overtreatment. What should a physician do when he sees a patient with uncomplicated, first-time gallstone pain? In such a case, the pain usually goes away on its own or with pain medication. Most patients have no further trouble if they eat lower-fat foods. Some do have recurrent episodes and need to have their gallbladder surgically removed. But McAllen surgeons are quicker to operate.

What about a 40-year-old woman with no family history of heart disease who comes in with chest pain after a fight with her husband, has a normal EKG, and then says the chest pain has gone away? She might get a stress test to confirm that there's no issue and then be sent home. In McAllen, she would likely get a stress test, an echocardiogram, a mobile Holter monitor and perhaps even a cardiac catheterization.

To examine whether McAllen's physicians really were overusing medical services, Gawande turned to Dartmouth's Medicare data, to commercial insurance data from D2Hawkeye, an independent company and to Ingenix, UnitedHealthcare's data-analysis company. There was no mistake: Gawande found that McAllen's patients got more testing, hospital treatment and surgery than El Paso's patients or patients nationwide.

That amounts to a lot more healthcare — twice as much — without additional benefit to the population. Gawande's examples of two Texas towns mirror the Dartmouth team's national findings. We must reject the conventional assumption that more healthcare services and higher spending will automatically improve health benefits across the population.

More Care and More Harm

The reality is even starker: more healthcare may in fact be worse. Mortality is slightly higher in regions where the intensity of care is higher. That seems like a bizarre finding. How can it possibly be true?

Can more healthcare provide *less* benefit? The research suggests yes. States with the highest per-capita Medicare spending — Louisiana, Texas, California and Florida — score poorly on quality-of-care measures.[8] Researchers also found better-quality care in states with lower Medicare spending, for example, a higher rate of beta-blocker prescribing for heart-attack patients, better adherence to breast-cancer screening for women and blood sugar and eye exams in diabetics.

Once again, remember that the comparisons were made after factoring out patient differences and comparing apples to apples — these were statistically comparable patients. Cutting spending is not the answer to improving quality. What is? Reducing unexplained clinical variation through better physician adherence to national practice benchmarks for basic quality measures and encouraging greater access to primary-care services that can pre-empt expensive acute-care episodes.

The question still stands: how can more healthcare be worse for patients? Just as failure to provide needed services such as bypass surgery in high-risk patients may cause harm in some settings, seemingly low-risk interventions like a hospitalization or ordering a diagnostic test can also cause harm.

Hospitals are dangerous places. Hospitalized patients face the risk of medical error, adverse events and complications and hospital-acquired infections. The more physicians involved in a patient's care, the greater the potential for miscommunication and medical error. The more diagnostic tests performed, the greater the risk of finding and then operating on other abnormalities — like a benign lump that would never have caused symptoms or other health problems — exposing patients to more risk.

The strange irony is that for patients with chronic illnesses, more aggressive interventions result in shorter life expectancy, probably because of the risks associated with hospitalization. Many of these interventions bring marginal clinical value along with greater risk of harm. We are certainly not suggesting that physicians withhold aggressive and potentially lifesaving care to extend the life of people with chronic illness, but rather that they focus on more conservative, less risky and potentially more effective interventions, like better control of blood pressure for people with diabetes, rather than on heroic end-of-life care. That is how less can be more.

Each year Americans receive millions of MRIs, CT scans and blood tests that do little to help physicians diagnose a suspected disease but instead lead them to discover other potentially benign conditions for which they perform invasive procedures. The dangers of excessive scanning and intervention are not minor. This point has been driven home vividly by Shannon Brownlee,[9] former *U.S. News & World Report* medical writer, current science writer for the *Atlantic Monthly* and senior fellow at the New America Foundation in Washington, D.C., a not-for-profit, nonpartisan public policy institute. She describes a study of nearly 1,200 whole-body CT scans. Eighty-seven percent of those scans found something abnormal. Forty percent of those required follow-up tests and fewer than one percent of questionable images on the scans turned out to be tumors.[10]

Physicians looking to "cover all the bases" often ignore data showing that many of the tests they order do not help patients. Some lead to unnecessary surgeries. For example, even though the American College of Radiology recommends against imaging studies for patients with simple low back pain (not caused by cancer or a major accident), the National Committee for Quality Assurance found that physicians still gave nearly a quarter of managed-care patients with low back pain an unnecessary imaging test. Spending on lumbar fusion surgery rose 500 percent between 1993 and 2003, in the absence of sound evidence that this risky surgery is effective, Brownlee writes.

Then there's the radiation from imaging. A whole-body CT scan delivers a radiation dose equivalent to about one-tenth of the lifetime exposure we get from natural sources and the average head CT delivers as much radiation as 200 chest x-rays.[11] An angioplasty procedure delivers the equivalent of more than 1,000 chest x-rays. How much impact will the radiation from all of these tests have on cancer rates in the coming years? That remains an open question.

We are seeing a rapid increase in CT usage that represents a potentially serious public-health problem, particularly among children, who are more sensitive than adults to radiation exposure. Japanese atomic-bomb survivors who were approximately two miles away from the explosions received radiation doses similar to the dose from a CT scan.[12] Study of these survivors for sixty years has provided direct evidence of an increased cancer risk, though small, for individuals who have experienced this same dose of radiation from CT scans. In a few decades, about 1.5 to two percent of all cancers in the United States may be due to the radiation from CT scans being done now.

The National Cancer Institute is concerned about the dangers of too much scanning. The institute projects 29,000 excess cancers from the 72 million CT scans that Americans got in 2007 alone, nearly 15,000 of which could be fatal.[13] Perhaps even more alarming is the *thirteen-fold difference* in radiation dose for the *same* CT scan across hospitals. In other words, a CT scan at one hospital may expose a patient to thirteen times the radiation dose that he would have experienced during the same CT scan test at another hospital. Needless to say, if all institutions were to use the lowest-dose technique for their CT scans, patients would be a lot better off.

Hospitalizations are also dangerous. Patients contract lethal infections while in the hospital for elective procedures and suffer complications when they undergo surgeries. Carotid endarterectomy (a surgery performed on about 150,000 patients a year to prevent stroke by removing plaque from the lining of the carotid artery) actually poses a *greater* risk of triggering a stroke in two-thirds of patients.[14]

Just by sheer volume of exposure, unnecessary care makes medical errors more likely — like receiving the wrong drug or the wrong dose or a drug that interacts badly with another drug.

A lack of clear clinical evidence often leads to unwarranted clinical variation, which in turn leads to harmful overtreatment. Over the years, more than 40,000 women with advanced breast cancer have received high-dose chemotherapy with a bone-marrow transplant. The treatment wound up killing 9,000 patients before ultimately being shown in clinical trials to be no better than standard treatment.[15]

Thousands of Americans have back surgery each year, even with little evidence that the surgery works better than more conservative treatments. Some patients improve. Others end up in far worse shape. Dartmouth researchers found that patients with back pain in Boise, Idaho, were getting surgery three times as frequently as comparable patients in Manhattan. Miami residents suffering from arthritis were five times more likely to receive arthroscopic knee surgery than comparable patients in Iowa City, even though the surgery was eventually proven ineffective as a treatment for arthritic knee pain.[16]

Overutilization of medical care, particularly spending far more time than warranted in the risky environment of a hospital, kills 30,000 elderly Americans a year, writes Brownlee. Death from unnecessary care is about as clear cut a case of "less is more" as you can get. If overtreatment were a disease, Brownlee adds, patient advocacy groups would be clamoring for a cure.

Are patients getting risky treatments that they don't want? Yes, because if they knew more about the risks and trade-offs of their elective treatment options, many would choose more conservative treatment. Poor communication between physicians and their patients is a big problem because patients often don't fully understand or appreciate the risk-benefit trade-offs and physicians are often poor judges of how much their patients' values and preferences may (or should) affect treatment decisions.

Some patients might be willing to risk a treatment even if its benefits are uncertain. But many would not. Some men, having tested positive for prostate cancer, would rather live with a relatively harmless and slow-growing cancer than risk incontinence or impotence from prostate surgery. Women with early breast cancer can choose either mastectomy or lumpectomy with radiation. If they are very concerned about losing a breast, they'll be more likely to choose lumpectomy.

Doing a better job of making patients aware of the risks and trade-offs of their treatment choices can effectively reduce overutilization of potentially harmful elective procedures. Most clinical trials show that using decision aids — such as short videos, brochures and interactive computer programs that provide detailed, balanced, evidence-based information about treatment options — results in patients being more knowledgeable about their options and medical decisions that are more in line with patient preferences. Properly integrating the preferences of fully informed patients leads to a *decline* in demand for surgery by about 25 percent — a reduction that would result in savings of about $4 billion a year for Medicare's eleven most common surgical procedures.[17]

The bottom line is that we wrongly embrace a cultural belief that more medicine is better, that scientifically backed reasoning drives most physician decision-making and that the treatments that physicians recommend are reliably effective. A mountain of evidence exposes these beliefs as myths — grounded in some fact, but danger-ously misleading when looked at carefully. Most physicians probably do not even know that a good chunk of the care they provide may in fact be unnecessary, harmful or even fatal to their patients.

Scientific uncertainty is integral to a great deal of modern medi-cine. When evidence is incomplete about the effectiveness of so many treatments, subjective "practice-style factor" kicks in, and we see huge clinical variation across physician practices. Where you live can determine how much medicine you get. Too little necessary medicine or too much unnecessary medicine is dangerous. We now know that more aggressive treatment styles, when combined with clinical uncertainty, do not always benefit patients and sometimes harm or even kill them. The problem only grows worse as new, more numer-ous and more invasive technologies become available. Most of us will probably benefit, but others will not, and still others may suffer.

Reflection

A brand-new book has been written on the topic covered in this section — *The Treatment Trap: How the Overuse of Medical Care Is Wrecking Your Health and What You Can Do to Prevent It*, by Rosemary Gibson and Janardan Prasad Singh (Ivan R. Dee, pub-lisher, 2010). It explains, in far more detail than we could do here, the size and scope of this challenge. The punch line remains the same, though: there's so much variation that it's too great to claim that every doctor is doing a good job. Variation leads to error, waste and worse — mistakes and com-plications.

When confronted with good data about the size and scope of clinical variation, it is amazing how fast doctors will change behavior. There's very good evidence that when you give doc-tors good information, they do work hard to improve.

– S.K. and D.B.N.

Notes

1. John E. Wennberg, MD, MPH; Shannon Brownlee; et al. "An Agenda for Change: Improving Quality and Curbing Healthcare Spending-Opportunities for the Congress and the Obama Administration," *Dartmouth Atlas White Paper*, December, 2008. Available online at: http://www.dartmouthatlas.org/downloads/reports/agenda_for_change.pdf.

2. Fitzhugh Mullan. "Wrestling with Variation: An Interview with Jack Wennberg," *Health Affairs Web Exclusive*, October 7, 2004, 73-80. Available online at: http://content.healthaffairs.org/cgi/reprint/hlthaff.var.73v1.

3. John E. Wennberg, MD, MPH. "Dealing with Medical Practice Variations: A Proposal for Action," *Health Affairs*, 1984; 3(2): 6-32.

4. Ibid.

5. There are two landmark articles on the subject: Elliott S. Fisher, MD, MPH; David E. Wennberg, MD, MPH; et al. "The Implications of Regional Variations in Medicare Spending. Part 1: The Content, Quality, and Accessibility of Care," *Annals of Internal Medicine*, 2003; 138:273-287. And Elliott S. Fisher, MD, MPH; David E. Wennberg, MD, MPH; et al. "The Implications of Regional Variations in Medicare Spending. Part 2: Health Outcomes and Satisfaction with Care," *Annals of Internal Medicine*, 2003; 138:288-298.

6. Elliott Fisher, MD, MPH; David Goodman, MD, MS; et al. "Healthcare Spending, Quality, and Outcomes: More isn't always better," *Dartmouth Atlas Project Topic Brief*, February 27, 2009. Available online at: http://www.dartmouthatlas.org/downloads/reports/Spending_Brief_022709.pdf.

7. Ibid.

8. Katherine Baicker, PhD, and Amitabh Chandra, PhD. "Medicare Spending, the Physician Workforce, and Beneficiaries' Quality of Care, *Health Affairs Web Exclusive*, April 7, 2004, 184-197. Available online at: http://content.healthaffairs.org/cgi/reprint/hlthaff.w4.184v1.

9. Shannon Brownlee, *Overtreated: Why Too Much Medicine Is Making Us Sicker and Poorer*. (New York: Bloomsbury USA, 2007).

10. Claudia D. Furtado, et al. "Whole-Body Screening: Spectrum of Findings and Recommendations in 1192 Patients," *Radiology*, 2005; 237:385-394.

11. Brownlee, *Overtreated*.

12. David J. Brenner, PhD, DSc, and Eric J. Hall, DPhil, DSc. "Computed Tomography-An Increasing Source of Radiation Exposure," *New England Journal of Medicine*, 2007; 357(22):2277-2284.

13. Rita F. Redberg, MD, MSc. "Editorial: Cancer Risks and Radiation Exposure from Computed Tomographic Scans," *Archives of Internal Medicine*, 2009; 169(22):2049-2050.

14. Shannon Brownlee. "Information, Please," *The Atlantic Monthly*, January-February, 2004.

15. Ibid.

16. Ibid.

17. Ibid.

MYTH 3:

Our Healthcare is Safe

"Must we wait another decade to be safe in our health system?"

> – *1999 report by the U.S. Institute of Medicine,* To Err is Human.

"Despite a decade of work, we have no reliable evidence that we are any better off today. More than 100,000 patients still needlessly die every year in U.S. hospitals and healthcare settings — infected because of sloppy compliance with basic cleanliness policies, injured by failure to follow simple checklists for safety — the equivalent of a national disaster every week of every year."

> – *2009 report by Consumers Union,*
> To Err is Human — To Delay is Deadly:
> Ten Years Later, a Million Lives Lost,
> Billions of Dollars Wasted.

[Linda T. Kohn, Janet M. Corrigan, and Molla S. Donaldson, Editors. *To Err Is Human: Building a Safer Health System Committee on Quality of Healthcare in America* (Washington, DC: Institute of Medicine National Academy Press, 1999).]

[Kevin Jewell and Lisa McGiffert. *To Err is Human — To Delay Is Deadly: Ten Years Later, a Million Lives Lost, Billions of Dollars Wasted* (Austin, TX: Consumers Union, May 2009).]

Most readers of this book are aware of the dangers of medical errors. More than ten years have passed since the federal Institute of Medicine (IOM) released its watershed report, *To Err is Human: Building a Safer Health System*, which planted the issue into the consciousness of the public.[1] The report's message lingers in our minds to this day: as many as 98,000 people die each year from medical errors in hospitals — the equivalent of one fully loaded jumbo jet crashing every day (or six to eleven preventable deaths every hour of the day), and more deaths than from car accidents, breast cancer or AIDS. Medical error is the nation's fourth leading cause of death.

The release of the IOM report in late 1999 put the patient-safety issue on the map in a way that no study ever had. The subject is no longer confined to journal articles and theoretical assumptions. The report catalyzed a national focus on reducing medical errors and improving quality of care. It jump-started transparency and quality-improvement initiatives by stakeholders across the board, involving hospitals, health systems, legislators, regulators, insurers, purchasers and even patients.

Medicare and commercial health insurers have begun to collect hospital and physician quality metrics and experiment with payment policies that use this data, even withholding payments to hospitals for some preventable errors. Hospital quality and safety data are now public, and physician data soon will be. No one can deny the ripple effect that 1999 IOM report has had.

But is all of this activity making patients safer? The fact is that we don't know for sure. We've certainly made progress since that IOM report, but we have no national entity comprehensively tracking patient safety that can tell if we are any better off than we were a decade ago.

We do know that significant dangers remain in our healthcare delivery. Underuse, overuse and misuse of healthcare services are still widespread. The hospital is still a very dangerous place. Unexplained clinical variation and failures in care processes are still rampant, as best as we can tell. Patients continue to be harmed and killed by healthcare.

Medical errors don't only happen in the hospital. In fact, new research reveals that errors are even more common in physician offices and other outpatient-care settings. Our healthcare delivery system has become so complex that errors are inevitable. The system leaves too many gaps that invite danger to patients, ranging from lost or fumbled patient information when multiple physicians are involved to sound-alike drugs with look-alike labels begging to be mixed up. Even patient names get mixed up, with calamitous results.

As long as human beings deliver healthcare in complex systems, that care will never be error-free. The status quo is still dangerous to patients. Physicians and hospitals have a way to go to reduce the potential harm of the healthcare they provide.

Epidemic of Medical Error and Harm

Our healthcare system is a breeding ground for medical errors, which the IOM's, *To Err is Human,* report defines simply as "the failure of a planned action to be completed as intended or the use of a wrong plan to achieve an aim." Examples abound: adverse drug events causing patient harm of some kind, improper transfusions, surgical injuries and wrong-site surgery, restraint-related injuries or death, falls, burns, pressure ulcers and mistaken patient identities. The highest error rates with serious consequences are most likely to occur in intensive care units, operating rooms and emergency departments. Besides harming and killing patients, the IOM report claims, preventable medical errors cost between $17 billion and $29 billion per year in hospitals nationwide and erode trust in our healthcare system.

Sanjaya Kumar's book, *Fatal Care: Survive in the U.S. Health System*, documents in detail a number of recent fatal and serious medical errors and adverse events. All of them were preventable. Many such events go unrecognized, with only a few getting the attention they deserve.[2]

There are diagnostic errors, like wrong or delayed diagnosis, failure to order necessary tests, use of outmoded tests or failure to act on results of tests. There are treatment errors during operations, procedures or tests; or in the dose or method of using a drug. There are avoidable delays in treatment or in responding to an abnormal test. There are failures to provide prophylactic treatment (for example, to prevent infection during a procedure). There is inadequate monitoring or follow-up of treatment. There is failure of communication among caregivers. There are all kinds of system errors. Hospitalized patients see multiple providers in different settings; none of those providers has access to complete information and it is easy for things to go wrong.

Medication errors are the deadliest kind of error, accounting for one out of 131 outpatient deaths and one out of 854 inpatient deaths. Their contribution to avoidable morbidity and mortality can only grow as new medications are introduced for a wider range of illnesses, as the, *To Err is Human,* report notes. Another IOM report, *Preventing Medication Errors*, concluded that at least 1.5 million patients are harmed in U.S. hospitals each year by preventable medication errors, at a cost of $3.5 billion.[3]

New drugs and treatments for heart attacks, which have cut mortality rates by nearly two-thirds since a generation ago, have paradoxically also increased the number and intensity of harmful complications waiting to happen. Medical journalist Shannon Brownlee illustrates this point vividly in her book, *Overtreated: Why Too Much Medicine Is Making Us Sicker and Poorer.*[4] An injection of the blood thinner heparin can cause hemorrhaging if a physician doesn't first perform a rectal exam to make sure the patient isn't bleeding in his gut. Catastrophic bleeding in the brain can be triggered by thrombolytic drugs that break up clots in coronary arteries. Cardiac arrest can result from beta-blockers that cause a patient's blood pressure to drop rapidly. A patient can die from an allergic reaction to the dye that is injected into the bloodstream for a CT scan to detect an aortic aneurysm. An artery can be perforated during cardiac catheterization. Higher-intensity treatment brings more risk.

In their book, *Internal Bleeding: The Truth behind America's Terrifying Epidemic of Medical Mistakes*, Robert Wachter, MD, and Kaveh Shojania, MD, offer a glimpse of the kinds of safety breaches that patients face:[5]

- About 12,000 heart-attack patients are mistakenly discharged from hospital emergency departments each year because a physician failed to diagnose them as having had a heart attack or restricted blood supply.
- Twenty percent of hand surgeons operate on the wrong hand or finger at least once in their career.

- An estimated one out of 10,000 surgery patients end up with a surgical instrument or sponge left in them.
- Physician fatigue degrades performance. Staying awake for 24 hours is like being legally drunk with a blood alcohol level of 0.1 percent. And yet, extended-duration work shifts remain common for physicians doing their medical residencies.

Not all medical harm stems from errors, though. The broader category of "medical harm" means that patients suffer unintended physical injury stemming from medical care that requires additional monitoring, treatment or hospitalization, or that kills the patient.[6] Medical harm also includes failing to provide indicated medical treatment, which winds up harming the patient.

This broader index of patient safety applies whether or not the medical harm is considered preventable, whether or not it results from a medical error and whether or not it occurs within a hospital. Medical harm is not the same as medical error: some errors cause medical harm but many do not, while many incidents of medical harm (for example, infections and complications) are not necessarily the result of errors. Although this notion of physical injury stemming from medical care is broader than medical error, it somehow seems an even more broadly compelling measurement of the dangers of healthcare.

How often does healthcare harm patients? The Institute for Healthcare Improvement (IHI) has an alarming answer: about *40,000 times per day*. The IHI reviewed patient records against a list of known triggers of adverse event and estimates that 40 to 50 incidents of medical harm happen to patients for every 100 hospital admissions. Assuming 40 incidents of harm per 100 admissions and roughly 37 million hospital admissions per year in the United States (according to the American Hospital Association), that translates to approximately *15 million* incidents of medical harm per year in the United States.[7] That is nothing short of appalling.

Consider hospital-acquired infections (HAIs), or those that patients didn't have when they were admitted to the hospital, which may be resistant to antibiotics and potentially life-threatening, especially for frail and elderly hospital patients. Every year, an estimated 1.7 million Americans are victims of HAIs, more than 4,600 per day, according to the Centers for Disease Control and Prevention (CDC).[8]

Many of those HAIs are believed to be preventable. The CDC estimates that 99,000 deaths per year in the United States are associated with HAIs, including pneumonia, bloodstream infections, urinary tract infections and surgical site infections, among others.

Another form of medical harm is the underuse of interventions that have been proven effective — like undetected and untreated hypertension or depression, failure to immunize children and prenatal care begun too late in pregnancy. Underuse leads to potentially major foregone opportunities to avert illness and improve health and function, notes Mark Chassin, MD, now President of The Joint Commission in Chicago, Illinois, and his colleagues from the National Roundtable on Health Care Quality.[9]

Failure to use effective treatments such as beta-blockers and aspirin for heart-attack patients, for example, may mean that as many as 18,000 of these patients die each year in the United States. These are deaths that could have been prevented. Millions more are not reached by proven effective interventions that can save lives and prevent disability. Perhaps an equal number suffer needlessly because they are exposed to the harms of unnecessary health services, and large numbers are injured because of preventable complications of medical treatment. That is the deadly triad of healthcare delivery: underuse, overuse and misuse.

Are Patients Safe Outside the Hospital?

The patient-safety world has focused primarily on hospital care. What's not often talked about is that the physician's office is more dangerous than the hospital, in terms of number of errors. On a statistical basis, four times as many errors occur in the ambulatory, or outpatient, setting as in the hospital. Think about it: doctors' offices and ambulatory surgery centers are subject to far less rigorous accreditation and regulatory oversight than hospitals. Without checks and balances or a safety and performance feedback loop, the physician office is a guild or craftsman-like setting.

Research on patient safety in the outpatient setting is beginning to reveal the troubling news that patients cared for outside of the hospital are at serious risk.[10] Although safety lapses tend not to be as severe as those occurring in hospitals (not surprising, since hospitalized patients are the sickest and frailest, and the treatments are often complex and invasive), the frequency of those errors is far greater because of the sheer volume of patients involved and the multiple junctures for error to occur. Diagnoses can be missed or delayed; physicians can fail to order the appropriate diagnostic or laboratory tests; tests can be incorrectly interpreted; and follow-up can be inappropriate or inadequate.

The more we learn about patient-safety lapses in physician offices, the more we realize that the office setting is a whole different world from the hospital. There are several key differences between hospital practice and office practice.[11] Whereas the hospital patient safety movement has emphasized the prevention of errors related to treatment (for example, medication errors, surgical errors, handoff and communication errors and hospital infections), missed diagnoses (especially of cancer) are potentially much more consequential in the physician office setting.

Because patients are not passive or captive in the office, their understanding of and agreement with physicians' treatment recommendations are far more important than in the hospital, and patients get hurt when they don't adhere to those recommendations. Compared to hospitals, small physician practices have scant resources to invest in electronic medical records and an error analysis infrastructure. In addition, physician office practices receive far less regulatory scrutiny than hospitals and, therefore, have less of an incentive (other than sheer professionalism) to launch safety-improvement efforts.

As the veil is slowly being removed, here is what we are learning about patient safety in the outpatient setting. Surgical procedures performed in physician offices bring ten times the risk of adverse incidents and death over those performed in an ambulatory surgery center.[12] Patients are harmed when their after-hours calls to their physicians' offices are not forwarded to the on-call physician. Some experience discomfort from that delay, while others end up requiring emergency transport.

Patients are also vulnerable after discharge from the hospital. One study found that 19 percent had problems after leaving the hospital, including injuries from adverse drug events attributable to poor medical management. One-third of these problems were preventable. Three percent resulted in permanent disabilities.[13]

The processes of making referrals and reporting test results are two particularly vulnerable aspects of ambulatory care. Both processes are fragmented and leave plenty of communication gaps and opportunities for potentially dangerous loss of information.

In surveys, most primary-care physicians report that they are dissatisfied with the current referral process, primarily because of the lack of timeliness of the information they receive and the inadequate content of referral letters (containing patient information from another physician). Most specialists report receiving no information from the primary-care physician before specific referral visits, and many primary-care physicians report not having received any information from specialists by four weeks after specific referral visits.[14]

When patients are discharged from the hospital, the records that summarize their care, medication and treatment plans are often missing or incomplete. Two-thirds of the time, a patient's primary physician doesn't have the discharge summary in time for the patient's first visit out of the hospital. When discharge summaries are available, they often lack information such as diagnostic test results (missing up to two-thirds of the time) and test results pending at discharge (missing two-thirds of the time).[15]

Many physician practices do a poor job of notifying patients of test results and ensuring follow-up visits. Up to one-third of attending physicians and residents at family medicine and internal medicine practices have no reliable method to ensure that the results of all ordered tests are received, while one-third do not always notify patients of abnormal results (usually because the patient is scheduled for follow-up) and only one-quarter have a reliable method for identifying patients overdue for a follow-up visit.[16]

There is no question that we need to pay a lot more attention to patient safety gaps in physician offices.

Broken Systems

Why do errors happen? One of the IOM, *To Err is Human,* report's main conclusions is that medical error is not a "bad apple" problem and that most medical errors do not result from recklessness or malfeasance by individual clinicians. Errors are more commonly caused by broken systems and flawed processes that trip up even the most competent physicians.

This notion of systems error may not be intuitive for most people. But it is absolutely pivotal to understanding the root cause of most medical errors and "near miss" patient-safety events. It does not absolve individual clinicians of the need to be vigilant and accountable. But blaming an individual when an error occurs does little to make the system safer or prevent someone else from committing the same error.

The decentralized and fragmented nature of the delivery system, with its rigidly defined areas of specialization and multiple providers in different settings, creates fertile opportunities for error. The problem is largely structural and endemic to the way in which our complex healthcare systems are organized. That is why improvement will be slow.

And that's not counting when the patient is handed off across various caregivers and care-delivery settings, a notoriously dangerous time for patients, when information "voltage drop" — lost or delayed clinical information about the patient — can harm or kill.

That lesson is powerfully communicated by the heartbreaking death of 18-month-old Josie King, who died in 2001 from severe dehydration and inappropriate use of narcotics at one of the finest hospitals in the nation.[17] Josie had been admitted to the Johns Hopkins Hospital after suffering first- and second-degree burns from climbing into a hot bath. She spent ten days in the pediatric intensive care unit (PICU), healed well and was sent to the intermediate care floor with the expectation of being sent home in a few days.

Josie's central-line catheter had been taken out, and she suffered an infection from it that caused vomiting, diarrhea and dehydration. Josie's mother, Sorrel, was told by the nurses not to give Josie anything to drink by mouth, as they were monitoring her fluid intake and did not want her to drink anything that went unrecorded.

Upon returning to the hospital early the next morning, Sorrel frantically summoned help when she looked at Josie. The little girl's medical team arrived and administered two shots of Narcan (which is used to counteract depression of the central nervous system and respiratory system caused by narcotics), believing that over-sedation with methadone, a painkiller she had been receiving during the healing process of her skin-graft surgeries, had caused Josie's lethargy. Josie was finally offered something to drink and gulped down nearly a liter of juice. Josie's attending physician ordered that she not be given any more pain medication until he was consulted.

Josie started perking up, was more alert, and had kept all liquids down. Around noon, a pediatric anesthesiologist from the pain team was concerned that Josie would suffer withdrawal symptoms without another shot of methadone and paged Josie's attending physician for permission to resume the shots. But Josie's attending physician was still in surgery. After consulting with another pediatric surgical team member, the anesthesiologist ordered a lower dose of methadone.

In the early afternoon a nurse entered Josie's room with another syringe of methadone. Sorrel was alarmed and told the nurse that Josie's doctor had agreed to cancel the methadone, but the nurse said the orders had been changed and administered the drug. Josie went into cardiac arrest within minutes. Sorrel stood helpless as a crowd of physicians and nurses came running into her daughter's room. Josie was rushed back up to the PICU, but she couldn't be resuscitated.

Josie, now brain dead, was taken off life support after two days. A little girl who was to be sent home in a couple of days died because of oversights and miscommunication among different members of her care team. They had failed to connect crucial clinical pieces: diarrhea and vomiting, dehydration, intense thirst, weight loss and lethargy. A simple, small dose of narcotic had killed a severely weakened and dehydrated toddler in one of the most prestigious medical centers in the world.

Josie's death led Sorrel to form the Josie King Foundation. With its mission to prevent others from dying or being harmed by medical errors, the foundation provides pilot funding for patient-safety programs throughout the country.

It is a myth that everything that happens to a patient in the hospital happens because somebody thought it through carefully, that it was planned. Multiple clinicians are involved in the care of a single patient. Specialists have myopic perspectives that may not overlap with other specialists — like a pain-management physician concerned that a patient may suffer narcotic withdrawal symptoms. They often "communicate" with each other by scribbling notes in the patient's chart. Who integrates those notes and sees the big picture, particularly when the patient's attending physician is momentarily unreachable?

Potentially life-threatening consequences can occur from even mundane failures in the system, such as a fax machine that fails to transmit a stat order (meaning "immediately") to the pharmacy, or a hospital that is short staffed with no runner to transport the pill.

As many as fifty steps stand between a physician's decision to order a medication for a hospitalized patient and the patient actually receiving the medication, write Wachter and Shojania. Even if each of those steps goes right 99 percent of the time, there is still a 39 percent chance that one error will occur in that fifty-step process.

As ridiculous as it seems in twenty-first century medicine, patients are still harmed and killed by illegible handwritten prescriptions, mix-ups of very different drugs with near-identical packaging and mix-ups of sound-alike drug names. There are Zyprexa and Zyrtec (an antidepressant and an antihistamine), Cerebyx and Celebrex (anticonvulsant and anti-inflammatory), Lamictal and Lamisil (mood stabilizer and antifungal), Clomiphene and Clomipramine (fertility stimulator and antidepressant).

Patients have inadvertently been injected with fatal doses of insulin because its bottle and label were nearly identical to heparin, a blood thinner routinely injected in small doses through intravenous lines to prevent clogs from clots. We need to identify broken parts of the system like this and learn how to fix them.

But the problem is more than a couple of broken parts. The "chassis" is broken on our current delivery system because it was not built to support the best and safest approach to medical care, declares David M. Lawrence, MD, former chairman and CEO of Kaiser Permanente, the largest not-for-profit healthcare system in the world, and a member of the committee that worked on the, *To Err is Human,* report.

"Imagine arriving at the airport and being invited to board an airplane that is little more than a horse and buggy with jet engines attached. Yet that is what we ask our patients to do every day — put their lives in the hands of a healthcare delivery system built in the nineteenth century for the solo-practice doctor with a black bag and trust it to support teams of doctors and other professionals using twenty-first-century technology," writes Lawrence. [18]

The root cause of our system's high variations in quality and high levels of error rates is that the system itself is too fragmented to function effectively, safely and efficiently. It is largely composed of loose networks of physicians and hospitals that give only the illusion of integration. The best and safest approach to medical care requires a comprehensive team of professionals to correctly manage patients and information as they are handed off from one part of the healthcare system to another.

Lawrence's observations are echoed by others, including Brownlee. Organizationally speaking, American medicine is still practiced much as it was fifty years ago. Often, one physician doesn't know that another physician has already ordered certain tests for a patient, or that the two physicians have prescribed two different drugs that do the same thing, or that the other physician has recommended a conflicting drug or treatment.

Counting on individual competence and good intentions to prevent errors is destined to fail, because medical practice takes place within broken systems. Wachter and Shojania describe the case of Joan Morris, a woman recovering from repair of a brain aneurysm (a ballooning in a cerebral blood vessel), who was scheduled to be released from the hospital the following morning. Ms. Morris instead found herself the next morning in a cardiac electrophysiology study (EPS) lab with a catheter inserted through an incision in her groin, snaked through a major blood vessel, and into the cavity of her heart, which had been stopped and started several times by physicians who were puzzled why they could not localize the abnormal electrical activity they expected to find. It turns out that Joan Morris had been mixed up with Jane Morrison, another patient who was suffering from arrhythmia (erratic heartbeat) and who had been scheduled for the EPS procedure.

The fundamental lesson here is that healthcare delivery is embedded within complex systems with many moving parts, each prone to error. After a major accident, people typically blame the "sharp end of the chisel," the action that occurred at the moment of error, like the surgeon who performs a procedure on the wrong patient. But often the blunt end of that chisel — deeper and more fundamental causes, like not having reliable patient ID systems in hospitals and ensuring that people use them — enables the errors in the first place.[19]

That is what is meant by the buzz-phrase "system failure" in healthcare. Individual competence and good intentions are not enough to prevent errors if the operational "blunt end" of the hospital remains broken (for example, if there are flawed processes for checking patient IDs or institutional pressure to hustle patients to procedures the moment a slot opens up in a lucrative service line like a catheterization lab).

Culture of Silence

When patients suffer injury or death, our healthcare system is often very poorly equipped to handle the aftermath. The way in which our system treats family members whose loved ones have been harmed or killed by medical errors can be deplorable, marked by a culture of fear, blame and cover-up. Healthcare safety researchers Rosemary Gibson and Janardan Singh offer a glimpse of these dynamics in their book, *Wall of Silence*.[20]

Hospitals and physicians, they write, say they can't disclose medical errors because their attorneys fear such disclosures will make them vulnerable to medical malpractice liability. What patients and their families want most of all is to be told the truth about what went wrong and to be reassured that steps are being taken to prevent something similar from happening to other patients. Some patients express appreciation when they are told the truth.

Our system isn't set up to provide support to the grieving family of patients in the aftermath of a medical mistake that the system won't admit. In one instance recounted by Gibson and Singh, a mother whose little boy just died from a medical mistake cleared his belongings out of his hospital room with his body still lying on the bed and then was driven back to her motel room in a police car by two security guards who were talking to each other about paint. That was the extent of the hospital's "support services." The only call she got from the hospital was asking if she would be willing to donate her son's eyes.

In another case, Gibson and Singh describe a retired store manager whose colon was punctured during a colonoscopy and who suffered a raging infection that nearly killed him. Months afterward, while he was still recovering, the man received several bills from the physician who performed the colonoscopy, along with a form letter asking, "How are we doing?" and "Would you recommend us?"

In a third case, a woman whose mother had died from a medical mistake tried to make an appointment with the CEO of the hospital where it happened. It took months to get the appointment, and she traveled several hours to meet the CEO in his office. The meeting took place in a corporate conference room where the mother was greeted by an entourage of lawyers and administrators. The woman asked about the circumstances that allowed her mother to die and what had been done to prevent events like that from happening again.

The CEO had a rote answer — "I don't know. I'll have to check into that and get back to you" — to each of her questions. "After a short while," Gibson and Singh recount the woman as saying, "he looked at his watch and said he only had a few minutes because he had to take his daughter to the beach." The woman never heard from the CEO again.

Healthcare organizations still need to make the transformation from denial and secrecy to honesty and openness when preventable errors harm patients.

Impossibility of Being Error-Free

Compounding system complexity and failure are additional factors of culture and human fallibility, which can't be re-engineered with simple fixes. When information is exchanged in a faulty or incomplete way so frequently, as it was in the Joan Morris case, miscommunication can become the norm among caregivers, who grow to tolerate it when patients are handed off from one physician to another.

Human fallibility manifests itself in how positive workers feel about their jobs and how well they work together, how freely information is shared across departments (which resemble "fiefdoms" in many institutions) and how comfortable staff feel about questioning the actions of superiors — like a nurse questioning a physician about to operate on a patient who has not been affirmatively identified.

The airline industry has done perhaps more than any other complex industry to engineer system improvements and safety protocols to avert error. Yet, there are documented cases in which fatal crashes have occurred because a copilot or navigator didn't feel comfortable questioning an apparent slip-up of a senior pilot.

John J. Nance, J.D., a best-selling author, pilot, licensed attorney, and *ABC News* and *Good Morning America* aviation correspondent, describes the problem in compelling detail in his book, *Why Hospitals Should Fly: The Ultimate Flight Plan to Patient Safety and Quality Care.*[21] Nance also explains how flight crews are now trained to expect errors and taught ways to handle them when they occur to assure safety. The medical community would do well to adopt one lesson from crew resource-management training: anyone who fears a possible safety lapse is expected to express that concern immediately to anyone else involved, ignoring status hierarchies.

A culture of low expectations is unacceptable. As Wachter and Shojania put it, "Most organizational errors are made by well-intentioned human beings — most highly educated, well trained and experienced — who have become accustomed to small glitches, routine foul-ups and a culture that suppresses doing much about them in the name of an overriding goal. The saga of human error is not a story about people who aren't good enough, but merely one about people."[22] That is why we can never prevent error, unless we figure out a way to redesign the human condition.

Since error is inevitable, and we must do the best we can to minimize harm to patients from error, where should we focus our efforts? Repetitive tasks pose the most frequent danger to patients because clinicians are most likely to switch to "automatic pilot" while doing these tasks, write Wachter and Shojania. Well-trained and experienced physicians and nurses are most likely to slip up doing things they've done automatically hundreds or thousands of times and, therefore, do without paying close attention. Some examples: remembering to verify a patient's identity before beginning a procedure, verifying a patient's blood type before a surgical operation, asking if a patient has any allergies to medication before writing a prescription or loading a syringe with heparin (not insulin) to flush an IV line.

Even though proven protocols exist to minimize harm to patients from activities like these, many hospitals still do not follow the protocols. Why not? Safety improvement is not simply a matter of removing hazards and instituting well-intentioned safety rules, like forbidding the storage of concentrated potassium (which is commonly added to patients' IV bags) on medical wards to prevent fatal patient overdoses. Caregivers have routinely violated authoritative top-down rules, for example, by hoarding concentrated potassium solution and hiding it in refrigerators next to their lunch so they will not be hassled when they need it.

Doctors, nurses and other hospital staff members won't buy in to safety protocols simply because someone higher up in the organization orders them to do so. It takes tremendous determination and leadership to create a "culture of safety" and to transform the way in which physicians and nurses think about their work and carry out safety improvement. That leadership is often lacking. Congress underfunds research on patient-safety improvement. Hospitals focus their attention and dollars on high-tech, profitable services. Medical and nursing schools focus on science and give short shrift to safety.

Wachter and Shojania explain, "We all know that our arsenal of clot-busters, MRI scanners, gene therapies and columns of specialists maim and kill the patients we aim to heal with shocking regularity, but our profession has reacted to this knowledge mostly with a collective shrug of its shoulders... It's as if we spent the last thirty years building a really souped-up sports car, but barely a dime or a moment making sure it has bumpers, seat belts and air bags."[23]

Status Quo Still Dangerous

The IOM's, *To Err is Human,* report declared that it would be irresponsible to expect anything less than a 50 percent reduction in errors over five years. Ten years after *To Err is Human*, we have no national entity comprehensively tracking patient safety, and we are unable to tell if we are any better off than we were a decade ago. That conclusion is corroborated by several researchers and entities.

Patient safety has actually been getting worse instead of better. That's the finding of the Federal Agency for Healthcare Research and Quality (AHRQ), which uses twenty individual measures to quantify progress on patient safety in its Congressionally mandated annual National Healthcare Quality Report (NHQR). The 2008 NHQR[24] notes that preventable medical injuries are actually increasing each year: one in seven hospitalized Medicare patients suffers from one or more adverse events; more patients develop avoidable bloodstream infections from catheters each year (thousands from central line-associated bloodstream infections); and a growing number of people suffer accidental cuts and tears to their organs during surgery each year.

How are we doing overall on patient safety? We still don't know. That is not for lack of safety metrics to study; in fact, there may be too many. Trying to track and understand dozens of patient-safety indicators simultaneously is analytically difficult, according to AHRQ's director Carolyn Clancy, MD.[25] The industry may instead be moving toward using a single measure — hospital-acquired infections (HAIs) — as the "canary in the coal mine" proxy for all others.

Like the canary's sentinel ability to alert miners to toxic gases, severity-adjusted HAI rates function as an early warning system to identify overall patient-safety problems. HAIs turn out to be reliable proxies for other safety variables and are probably the best generalized indicators of patient safety in a hospital. A hospital that has a higher severity-adjusted HAI rate (the rate is adjusted for patient demographics and level of illness) than its peer institutions probably performs more poorly on other patient safety indicators, as well.

Using the HAI rate as a measure, the canary appears to be in trouble. Each year, nearly two million patients suffer from HAIs, resulting in 99,000 deaths and incurring an estimated $28 billion to $33 billion in excessive healthcare costs. For example, AHRQ has found that hospital-acquired cases of *Clostridium difficile* infection, or *"C. diff,"* more than doubled between 2001 and 2005. *C. diff* is an antibiotic-resistant bacterium that causes diarrhea and serious intestinal conditions such as colitis.

AHRQ's Clancy says she is frustrated with the tepid rate of progress in preventing and reducing medical errors. A fragmented, paper-based healthcare system has predominated over the past ten years. Patient-safety improvement has largely been left to individual hospitals and provider organizations to undertake, or not.[26] Improvement is episodic, haphazard and voluntary.

Although the groundwork for improving safety has been laid over the past ten years, building a culture of safety is a formidable task and the deck seems to be stacked against substantial or rapid improvement. As Clancy states, "Addressing medical errors involves each organization changing its culture and systems for care delivery. It involves improving communication and teamwork — one organization or unit at a time *and* organization-wide — in a healthcare system that still rewards volume and highly compensated procedures over preventive care and improving patient outcomes." Some hospitals have stepped up to the plate and implemented meaningful improvements, but we still don't even know which organizational strategies and tools are most effective, and how soon we can expect tangible results.

Some stakeholders are fed up with the wait for meaningful progress in patient safety. In a May, 2009, report titled, *To Err is Human — To Delay is Deadly: Ten Years Later, a Million Lives Lost, Billions of Dollars Wasted*, the Consumers Union (the not-for-profit publisher of *Consumer Reports*) gives the country a failing grade on progress to rid our healthcare system of preventable medical harm.[27]

The IOM asked in 1999, "Must we wait another decade to be safe in our health system?" Ten years later, we find ourselves asking the same question.

We have reason to be frustrated about our apparent lack of progress. According to the most recent estimates, using the best patient-chart review methodologies, one of ten patients admitted to hospitals still experiences some type of adverse medical event, about half of which are preventable. About one-third of adverse medical events cause patients harm, ranging from minor harm like protracted hospitalization to permanent disability or death. That translates to more than a *half-million* people in the United States being harmed by *preventable* medical errors each year.[28]

According to Wachter, the average hospitalized medical patient experiences one medication error per day. Patients who are on multiple medications are more likely to be harmed, as are elderly patients and patients on risky medications like anticoagulants, opiates, insulin and sedatives. The average patient in an intensive care unit experiences 1.7 errors in his or her care per day in the ICU.[29]

Drug confusion errors persist, and regulatory oversight doesn't seem to prevent them. The Consumers Union recounts the high-profile case in 2007 of near-fatal overdoses when the blood thinner heparin was accidentally given to the infant twins of actor Dennis Quaid at Cedars-Sinai Medical Center. Quaid sued Baxter Healthcare Corp., saying that heparin and a lower-dose version called Hep-Lock are both packaged in similar blue vials with small print on the labels.[30]

In his book, *Fatal Care: Survive in the U.S. Health System*, Sanjaya Kumar, MD, notes that a year before the Quaid incident, a similar mix-up occurred when six infants in a newborn ICU at an Indianapolis hospital were given overdoses of heparin, killing three of them. Two infants at that same Indianapolis hospital had received a similar overdose in 2001. Although the drug manufacturer issued a letter after the Indianapolis deaths warning hospitals of the potential for confusion, the packaging was not changed for at least 12 months, and the same packaging was still being used at Cedars-Sinai during the Quaid incident. Regulators fined Cedars-Sinai for failure to follow its own safety policies.

Technologies like computerized physician order-entry (CPOE) and bar-code medication administration systems are estimated to cut medication errors in half or more by warning of medication allergies or interactions, taking illegible handwriting out of the picture, checking that the right patients get the right medication and electronically linking to pharmacies to directly transmit prescriptions. But according to a 2008 survey of American Hospital Association members, only 17 percent of hospitals have an operational CPOE system in all of their units, the Consumers Union notes.

New federal legislation may improve that picture by offering bonus Medicare payments to physicians who use e-prescribing and penalizing those who don't. The 2009 economic stimulus bill provided $19.2 billion to encourage the adoption of health information technology, and we'll have to wait to see the impact of this incentive.

For now, patient-safety improvement is still a work in progress. An epidemic of medical error and patient harm appears to continue unabated. Complex healthcare delivery systems remain broken. The ways in which physicians, hospitals and other providers handle the aftermath of errors is deplorable. Care delivery outside the hospital turns out to be fraught with its own dangers. Healthcare can never be error-free. Can it be made harm-free? If so, we're not there yet.

Reflection

Consumers Union has recently given America's healthcare system a failing grade for safety. Wouldn't it be wonderful if Consumers Union President Jim Guest were to write a column exonerating our healthcare system and giving us all a passing grade, at last? We're hoping that the day is not far away when his organization publishes a report explaining the great progress we have made, in leaps and bounds, and that, on average, we've beaten this problem and our hospitals and doctor offices are far safer than they ever were.

– S.K. and D.B.N.

Notes

1. Institute of Medicine. *To Err is Human: Building a Safer Health System*. (Washington, DC: National Academies, 1999).

2. Sanjaya Kumar, MD. *Fatal Care: Survive in the U.S. Health System*. (Minneapolis: IGI Press, 2008).

3. Philip Aspden, Julie Wolcott, J. Lyle Bootman, Linda R. Cronenwett, Editors. Committee on Identifying and Preventing Medication Errors, Institute of Medicine: *Preventing Medication Errors: Quality Chasm Series*. (Washington, National Academy Press, 2006).

4. Shannon Brownlee, *Overtreated: Why Too Much Medicine Is Making Us Sicker And Poorer*. (New York: Bloomsbury USA, 2007).

5. Robert M. Wachter, MD, and Kaveh G. Shojania, MD. *Internal Bleeding: The Truth behind America's Terrifying Epidemic of Medical Mistakes*. (New York: Rugged Land, 2004).

6. Institute for Health Improvement. "Frequently Asked Questions about the 5 Million Lives Campaign." Available online at: http://ihi.org/IHI/Programs/Campaign/Campaign.htm?TabId=6.

7. Ibid.

8. R. Monina Klevens, DDS, MPH; Jonathan R. Edwards, MS; et al. "Estimating Healthcare-Associated Infections and Deaths in U.S. Hospitals, 2002," *Public Health Reports*, March-April, 2007; 122(2):160-166.

9. Mark R. Chassin, MD, MPP, MPH; Robert W. Galvin; and the National Roundtable on Health Care Quality. "Consensus Statement: The Urgent Need to Improve Healthcare Quality," *Journal of the American Medical Association*, 1998; 280(11):1000-1005.

10. Eric J. Moskowitz and David B. Nash. The Quality and Safety of Ambulatory Medical Care: Current and Future Prospects, *American Journal of Medical Quality*, 2007; 22:274.

11. Robert M. Wachter, MD. "Is Ambulatory Patient Safety Just Like Hospital Safety, Only without the 'Stat'?" *Annals of Internal Medicine*, 2006; 145(7):547-549.

12. H. Vila, R. Soto, et al. "Comparative Outcomes Analysis of Procedures Performed in Physician Offices and Ambulatory Surgery Centers," *Archives of Surgery*, 2003; 138(9):991-995.

13. A.J. Forster, H.J. Murff, et al. "The Incidence and Severity of Adverse Events Affecting Patients after Discharge from the Hospital," *Annals of Internal Medicine*, 2003; 138(3):161-167.

14. T.K. Gandhi, D.F. Sittig, et al. "Communication Breakdown in the Outpatient Referral Process," *Journal of General Internal Medicine*, 2000; 15(9):626-631.

15. S. Kripalani, F. LeFevre, et al. "Deficits in Communication and Information Transfer between Hospital-Based and Primary-Care Physicians," *Journal of the American Medical Association*, 2007; 297(8):831-841.

16. E.A. Boohaker, R.E. Ward, et al. "Patient Notification and Follow-Up of Abnormal Test Results: A Physician Survey," *Archives of Internal Medicine*, 1996; 156(3):327-331.

17. As detailed on the Josie King Foundation website: www.josieking.org. Additional details provided by Shannon Brownlee in her book, *Overtreated: Why Too Much Medicine Is Making Us Sicker and Poorer*. (New York: Bloomsbury USA, 2007).

18. David M. Lawrence, "Improving Patient Safety: Building Teams, Trust, and Technology-Confronting the 'Chassis Gap' in American Health Care," *New Visions for Health Care*. (Picker Institute). August, 2000. Available online at: http://www.pickerinstitute.org/documents/Pt%20safety-%20building%20trust.pdf.

19. Wachter and Shojania borrow this terminology from James Reason, a British psychologist and professor.

20. Rosemary Gibson and Janardan Prasad Singh, *Wall of Silence: The Untold Story of the Medical Mistakes That Kill and Injure Millions of Americans*, (Washington, DC: LifeLine Press, 2003).

21. John J. Nance, J.D. *Why Hospitals Should Fly: The Ultimate Flight Plan to Patient Safety and Quality Care*. (Bozeman, MT: Second River Healthcare Press, 2008).

22. Wachter and Shojania, *Internal Bleeding*, pp. 52-53.

23. Ibid, p. 26.

24. Agency for Healthcare Research and Quality. "2008 National Healthcare Quality Report." Rockville, MD: U.S. Department of Health and Human Services, Agency for Healthcare Research and Quality; May, 2009. AHRQ Pub. No. 09-0001, pp. 8-9, 101.

25. Carolyn Clancy, MD "Editorial: The Canary's Warning — Why Infections Matter," *American Journal of Medical Quality*, 2009; 24(6):462-464.

26. Carolyn Clancy, MD "Commentary: Ten Years After To Err Is Human," *American Journal of Medical Quality*, 2009; 24(6): 525-528.

27. Kevin Jewell and Lisa McGiffert, *To Err is Human — To Delay is Deadly: Ten Years Later, a Million Lives Lost, Billions of Dollars Wasted*. (Austin (TX): Consumers Union, 2009). Available online at: http://www.safepatientproject.org/safepatientproject/pdf/safepatientproject.org-ToDelayIsDeadly.pdf.

28. Robert M. Wachter. *Understanding Patient Safety*. (New York: McGraw-Hill, 2008).

29. Ibid.

30. "Dennis Quaid Sues Again over Twins' Drug Overdose," *Reuters*, May 25, 2010. Available online at http://www.reuters.com/article/idUSTRE64O6R220100526.

MYTH 4:

Our Healthcare Payment System Works

"Healthcare costs ultimately arise from the accumulation of individual decisions doctors make about which services and treatments to write an order for. The most expensive piece of medical equipment, as the saying goes, is a doctor's pen."

– Atul Gawande, MD, author and Harvard surgeon

[Atul Gawande, MD. "The Cost Conundrum: What a Texas Town Can Teach Us about Healthcare." *The New Yorker*, June, 2009.]

We pay physicians and hospitals to provide more services to more people across all age groups at a greater intensity than any other country. That would be a good thing in most industries: more goods and services mean a more vibrant industry. But healthcare is different. "More" does not mean better when our payment system rewards unexplained clinical variation in medical care that does not improve health and sometimes threatens safety and lives. "More" means a spiraling cost-and-quality crisis.

Our healthcare payment system is based on the principle of piecework, which essentially means that providers get paid more for providing more healthcare services, often irrespective (or in the absence) of evidence to justify them. That is gradually changing with the evolution of pay-for-performance and other new payment programs, as we'll see in Part II of this book.

Managed care's utilization control apparatus did put the brakes on costs in the 1980s and 1990s, but spending has bounced right back, partly because physicians reacted by increasing the volume of their services, and partly because a massive consumer and media backlash against restrictions on choice has driven the industry to loosen most of those policies.

We are left with a provider compensation status quo that is largely one of piecework fee-for-service, paying physicians per procedure or test. The Medicare physician fee schedule, for example, lists the value of more than 10,000 physician services using a complex formula.[1] Commercial insurers base their physician fee schedules on Medicare reimbursement amounts.

The key point is this: fees paid to physicians reward the volume and intensity of the care they provide, rather than the value and health outcomes of patients. Medicare and other payors pay hospitals by diagnosis-related groups (DRGs), each a lump sum for a group of specific illnesses or patient diagnoses. This form of payment gives hospitals the incentive to shorten a patient's hospital stay, but they still get paid more for higher-intensity services and, of course, for more hospital visits.

Certainly, other factors are driving our spiraling cost crisis. Direct-to-consumer pharmaceutical drug advertising is a multibillion-dollar business and surely drives a lot of physicians to prescribe expensive drugs. Many of these advertised drugs are just marginally better than much cheaper alternatives. Many of them (like Cialis for erectile dysfunction) are more lifestyle enhancing than life saving or health promoting. Fear of medical malpractice lawsuits surely drives physicians to practice defensive medicine, ordering tests and procedures that may not be necessary out of fear of being sued for "not doing all they could to save the life of my client."

But these are not the main drivers of our healthcare cost crisis. Pharmaceutical marketing fuels about eight percent of the growth in medical care costs. Defensive medicine accounts for seven percent or eight percent, depending on which researchers you read. Both are certainly part of the problem, but well under 20 percent of it.

The main driver of our nation's spiraling healthcare cost crisis is unexplained variation in physician decision-making at the bedside, driven by pernicious financial incentives. The problem is simultaneously about quality and cost. If we could reduce that unexplained variation, we could eliminate an estimated 30 percent of healthcare costs spent on wasted and sometimes dangerous care that is of no benefit to patients.

The key problems are these. We spend the most on healthcare among industrialized nations, but we achieve very poor quality results for our money. Our payment system trumps market forces that drive quality and efficiency in most other industries. It perpetuates the misuse of medical care. It nourishes unexplained clinical variation by rewarding physicians for using unproven therapies and technologies that don't improve health. It punishes physicians for providing services proven to improve health, particularly preventive health and chronic-disease management services.

Let's put it another way. Why is Anthem Blue Cross and Blue Shield raising its healthcare insurance premium rates by 39 percent in 2010 and incurring the wrath of Kathleen Sebelius, secretary of the U.S. Department of Health and Human Services, and the President? Rising costs. And what's the cause of rising costs? Utilization. And what's the ultimate cause of rising utilization? Physician decision-making. The insurance industry, then, is the canary in the coal mine, telling us that utilization is out of control. We, as physicians, say, "We have seen the enemy, and he is us."

More Spending, Fewer Positive Results

We spend the most on healthcare among industrialized nations but achieve comparatively poor quality results for our money. The United States has the most expensive health system in the world per capita, spending two to four times per capita what other developed nations spend, but it lags behind many developed countries on vital health statistics.

Medical journalist Shannon Brownlee illustrates the problem well.[2] For life expectancy at birth, the United States ranks near the bottom of countries in the Organization for Economic Cooperation and Development (OECD), just ahead of Cuba but far behind Japan, France, Italy, Sweden and Canada. Our infant mortality rate of 6.8 per 1,000 births is more than twice as high as in Japan, Norway and Sweden and worse than in Poland and Hungary. We spend more per capita on healthcare than the Chinese spend, per capita, on everything.[3]

Our healthcare spending continues to outpace inflation and national income growth. The Centers for Medicare & Medicaid Services (CMS) say health costs took up 17.3 percent of our gross domestic product in 2009, representing the largest single-year increase in the annual growth rate in fifty years. Commercial health-plan premiums have more than doubled in a decade. The CMS predicts that our annual healthcare costs will eat up more than 20 percent of our national economy by 2016.

Healthcare spending is by far the single most important factor in determining our nation's long-term fiscal health, and if it continues to grow as projected, future budget deficits will rise to levels that will seriously jeopardize the long-term economic growth of our country, Peter Orszag, then director of the Congressional Budget Office, told the Senate Budget Committee in January, 2008.

Enough waste could be removed from the healthcare system to trim between $1.5 trillion and $3 trillion from national health expenditures over ten years, while simultaneously *improving* access, quality and healthcare outcomes, according to a recent Commonwealth Fund report.[4] How can both goals be achieved? By fixing our pernicious payment system: aligning financial incentives with quality and efficiency, correcting price distortions in healthcare markets, producing better information for healthcare decision-making, incorporating that information into how we pay physicians and hospitals and promoting health and enhancing disease prevention. All of that is a tall order, to be sure.

But it is amply clear, the Commonwealth Fund report says, that we need to change the way our health system is organized and financed. Plenty of evidence from Dartmouth and Rand Corporation researchers and elsewhere shows that many of the factors that drive up spending do not improve quality or value. We are paying to perpetuate and aggravate the problem.

Unless checked, our current healthcare growth rate will continue to outpace wages and incomes, the report notes. It will force government and employers to make difficult budget choices, putting economic pressure on businesses and placing future generations of retirees at risk as health costs erode pensions and retirement savings. No grand policy panacea is going to save us, but we can begin by examining how sick our reimbursement system really is and addressing glaring defects.

What distinguishes the U.S. healthcare system from those of other countries is the volume of services we consume, especially the most expensive kinds of care, notes Brownlee. We get three times the number of MRI scans as the OECD average, and compared with other countries, we have many more specialists, who often recommend expensive procedures or surgeries.[5]

Surely many medical innovations have proven to be worth it. Clot-busting drugs, angioplasty and stents to open coronary arteries as well as drugs that can prevent damage to the heart muscle, have dramatically lowered the mortality rates of heart-attack patients, Brownlee notes. But many expensive medical innovations have been overused and have not led to better health outcomes or have proven to be more harmful than beneficial.

The cost differences among those testing modalities are staggering. A $20 blood-pressure test turns out to be superior to a $32,973 electroencephalography test, a $24,881 CT scan and a $22,397 cardiac enzymes test.[6] But our fee-for-service reimbursement system pays for the latest technologies, as long as they have regulatory approval. We often don't know how many of the new technologies and treatments that physicians use actually help patients and how many represent unnecessary waste, Brownlee notes, because we devote the equivalent of one-tenth of one percent of our healthcare spending to research that tries to find out.

But we do know that there has been an explosive rise in the use of these expensive tests: about 40 million CT scans were performed on American patients in 2000 and 72 million in 2007.

Hospitals don't discourage physicians from ordering excessive scans because they make, on average, a $1,000 profit per scan, according to Brownlee.[7] Our payment system pits the interests of profit against patient health in some pernicious ways. (Recall that many of these new scanning technologies increase cancer risks in patients.)

When it comes down to a fight against reducing image-test overutilization and keeping a hospital solvent with a highly profitable service, the hospital will win, says Brownlee. Technology brings top-name specialists, who bring profitable business to the hospital. They attract research grants. A hospital will spend millions of dollars to acquire the latest scanning technology and advertise it widely in the community. The hospital surely won't let that expensive equipment sit idle.

Physicians also profit from the medical-technology arms race. While Medicare and Medicaid payments for physician services rose 31 percent between 1999 and 2004, payments for imaging services rose twice as fast because physicians ordered more (and more expensive) images per patient, writes Brownlee. CT payments went up 112 percent over that time interval. Brownlee cites research performed for the Medicare Payment Advisory Commission finding that more imaging tests did *not* improve patient care for heart attacks, hip fractures or colon cancer.

If we spend the most on healthcare per capita of all developed countries, why do we have a quality deficit? We can answer that in three words: *unexplained clinical variation*. That is the core problem in American medicine, and it stems from large gaps in scientific backing for much of what physicians do. More tests ordered do not always reduce uncertainty about a patient's condition (and occasionally lead to more risky, invasive care). More procedures performed do not always improve a patient's health. Combine that with an irrational payment system that rewards the excess services, and you get toxic results.

As physicians fall back on subjective practice styles to guide their clinical decision-making, patients end up with a huge amount of inappropriate care: underutilization of necessary services like preventive care to keep chronically ill patients out of the hospital and overutilization of unnecessary services that don't work or cause more harm than good. Our reimbursement system pays for it all, for the most part. As medical economist J.D. Kleinke puts it in his book, *Bleeding Edge: The Business of Health Care in the New Century*, our fee-for-service payment system gives a blank check to patients that physicians and hospitals are only too willing to cash.[8] Physicians' decisions directly affect between 70 percent and 90 percent of all healthcare spending in the United States, including whether to hospitalize patients, recommend surgery, prescribe drugs and order diagnostic tests, he adds.

Market Perversity

Our healthcare system doesn't obey the same economic principles as other industries. Kleinke explains why the economic behaviors that drive our healthcare system are irrational, perverse and counterproductive. A normal marketplace contains rational consumers who demand better products at better prices and producers who are rewarded by supplying both. That's not what happens in our healthcare marketplace. Third-party reimbursement does not reward rational behavior by either consumers or producers — and, in many cases, actually penalizes it.

Try to think of an industry in which the *producer* of a product determines the need for that product, is paid more for producing more of it and has no incentive to reduce its cost. That is the perverse situation in fee-for-service medicine, Kleinke notes. It rewards physicians and hospitals financially for heroic treatment, redundant treatment or any treatment at all, regardless of its economic or scientific merit.

Harvard surgeon Atul Gawande, MD, offers a vivid glimpse into how piecework payment works. In his book, *Better: A Surgeon's Notes on Performance*, he recounts asking his physician group's billing office for a copy of its master fee schedule listing what various insurers paid staff doctors for the care they provided. The list had 24 columns across the top, one for each insurance plan, and a row for every service for which a doctor can bill. Medicare's physician reimbursements, which Gawande says were in the middle range, paid $77.29 for a simple patient office visit, $151.92 for a more complex office visit, $621.31 for removing an appendix, and so on.

Physicians, as the "producers," are the major cost-drivers in healthcare because their clinical decisions determine what services get dispensed. For the patients he sees in the office in a single day, Gawande says he prescribes somewhere around $30,000 worth of medical care, including specialist consultations, surgical procedures, hospital stays, x-ray imaging and medicines. He confesses that how well these services are reimbursed affects how lavish he can be in dispensing them. Since insured patients are insulated from most of the costs, they are typically receptive to the services that their physician recommends, even those services with marginal or uncertain benefits — what economists call a moral hazard. Healthcare is far from a rationally functioning market.

The fee-for-service system makes cultural sense and reflects our national character, Kleinke notes. We believe in the miracles of science in our heroic battle against disease. We jealously defend our right to access all the resources our healthcare system can offer us. But from a quality, safety and economic standpoint, our healthcare payment system is an absolute mess.

Complicating the situation further is what Kleinke describes as "clinical apartheid," in which most physicians are separate economic entities from the hospitals in which they practice, and yet these physicians' treatment decisions have the greatest impact on hospitals' costs, profits, quality and reputation. The result is tremendous waste and inefficiency when different surgeons treat comparable patients with different methods, using different brands of medical equipment and with different outcomes. They have little or no economic incentive to change practice patterns to save resources or to reduce clinical variation.

Managed care (often in the form of health maintenance organizations, or HMOs) tried but ultimately failed to fix the problem of unwarranted clinical variation and the waste it generates. Managed-care companies scrutinized physicians and hospitals that used far more medical resources than their peers and required permission (preauthorization) before agreeing to pay for expensive scans, treatments and procedures. Denials for "medically unnecessary" care were common.

These utilization-review tactics did indeed "bend the cost curve," putting the brakes on the growth of medical spending. But managed-care companies were confrontational with physicians and patients, and they were administratively expensive to the insurers themselves. Preauthorization's return on investment was less than expected, and the companies' heavy-handed tactics were self-defeating, spawning resentment and a (victorious) market backlash among the media, providers and patients.

Kleinke explains why managed care's "near-lethal dose of chemo-therapy for a sick healthcare market" ultimately failed. Aggressive intervention by an emboldened third-party payor wasn't perceived as a goodwill effort to eliminate unwarranted practice variation and thereby improve the quality and safety of patient care. To physicians and patients, it was a "ham-fisted cost-control hammer," second-guessing clinicians' professional judgment in a search-and-destroy mission to identify "bad" doctors and hospitals, writes Kleinke.

Utilization review targeted overuse of services but not underuse of needed services, like preventive care, which further tarred managed-care companies as cost-control cops more concerned with their bottom line than with patients' health. Managed care's "heavy-hand-ed and cumbersome command-and-control systems" managed cost, not care, writes Kleinke. Marketing claims about quality were only window dressing. The public sided with physicians, whose professional ethic was to do what's best for patients, rather than with managed-care companies, who were sworn to their shareholders to do what was cheapest. Chastened by the great public backlash against cost-control tools like utilization review and preauthorization, managed-care companies have scaled back those tools to weak echoes of what they once were.

Managed care's zealous cost-control practices paradoxically drove costs up, Brownlee observes. When insurers ratcheted down the amount they paid for each individual physician service, physicians responded like "pieceworkers in a shirt factory" by increasing the volume of their work. They saw more patients, ordered more tests, and performed more ancillary and discretionary procedures. Between 2000 and 2005, notes Brownlee, there was a 40 percent rise in colonoscopies per-formed on Medicare patients, a 34 percent rise in angioplasties and a 45 percent rise in cardiovascular stress tests.

In 1990, the average visit with a family physician lasted 20 min-utes. That plunged to seven to 10 minutes in 2000, notes Brownlee, as physicians pumped up their patient volume to recoup lost income. Of course, with less than half as much time as before to spend with a patient, primary-care physicians had less time to diagnose and explain treatments to patients. To cope with the time crunch, they shunted more of their patients to specialists and dispensed a lot more of the latest, most expensive brand-name prescription drugs. Healthcare costs began rising by double-digit rates.

Managed care ended up doing serious damage to primary care by driving existing physicians into early retirement and medical students into the more lucrative specialties. Even fee-for-service plans grossly underpay for primary-care services relative to specialty services. The research demonstrating that America faces a dire shortage of primary-care physicians would fill a room. Chalk up another pyrrhic victory for our pernicious payment system.

Rewarding Uncertainty

Here's another way to look at the problem with reimbursing physicians and hospitals based on the volume and intensity of the services they deliver. Much of medicine, particularly when solid evidence is scant, amounts to a reflex behavior by physicians that is determined by the sheer presence of resources. When a greater supply of healthcare resources is available, physicians tend to order more services.

We don't know, for example, the optimum number of physician office visits that a patient with mild congestive heart failure should have, but we do know that the actual number of visits a patient gets is determined by the number of available time slots in a given market, and that a greater number of visits brings no improvement in health condition.[9] Dartmouth researcher Jack Wennberg calls this phenomenon "supplier-induced demand," and the Dartmouth research backs it up persuasively.

The Dartmouth research shows that populations living in regions with high Medicare spending do not live longer or have an improved quality of life, even though the healthcare they receive is twice (or more) as expensive as in low-spending regions. Where more physician and hospital services are available, spending is greater, and more tests and procedures, like hip replacements and back surgeries, are performed.

That increased spending is not due to heavier demand or a greater need for services. Remember that the Dartmouth researchers statistically leveled the data playing field to factor out all of the possible influences they could think of, including population demographics and patients' disease severity. The supply of medical services in higher-spending regions is driving the increased utilization.

Wennberg explains the problem this way. The amount that Medicare and commercial health insurers reimburse physicians and hospitals in a given market (healthcare prices) is typically stable and doesn't fluctuate much over time. Having an oversupply of a certain kind of service in a market, like cardiac surgery centers or high-tech scanning equipment, doesn't reduce the price, as it would in most other industries with oversupply and competition. In healthcare, perversely, an oversupply means that service will be provided more frequently. Reimbursement per service is unchanged, volume of services increases and outcomes are the same or worse. There is another term for that: *waste*.

That is why we see a high volume of back surgery, for example, in markets with many orthopedic surgeons. We see more diagnostic tests and physician office visits in markets with a high number of internists. The variations in utilization can't be explained on the basis of illness, patient preference, or the dictates of scientific medicine.[10] It is overutilization, driven by supply.

Our healthcare reimbursement system fuels the problem. Physicians are the "purchasing agents" for their patients, as Wennberg puts it: their decision-making determines what kind of care is provided, how much care is provided and where it is provided (for example, in or out of a hospital). Throw in large amounts of clinical uncertainty and practice variation, and you get a huge amount of waste, error and potential harm to patients — about 30 percent worth, according to Dartmouth estimates. And fee-for-service reimbursement pays for it, just the same. Why?

Brownlee puts her finger on the central problem. Because of all of this clinical uncertainty, nobody — not patients or employers or insurers — can reliably choose the best care at the most reasonable price. This lack of reliable information prevents even physicians and hospitals from learning what constitutes the best or most efficient care.

Insurers don't have enough reliable data to judge the effectiveness of most of the hospitalizations, tests, office visits and procedures they are paying for. They rely on physician judgment and they (for the most part) pay for it all.[11] Hospitals are therefore encouraged to invest in expensive technologies and services, perpetuating a technological arms race.

The *Dartmouth Atlas* amply demonstrates that our current health-care payment system is grossly inefficient at seeing that the right kind of care gets delivered to the right patients. Instead of trying to control costs, we should instead concentrate on improving the *quality* of medicine, which requires generating better research evidence to reduce medical uncertainty about what works best for whom. We need to reduce uncertainty, and reward physicians who use evidence-based medicine, to reduce unwarranted variation in medical practice and the toxic waste it produces. That will mean some patients get more treatments that are currently underused, while others will get fewer overused or unnecessary treatments.

Few have argued that physicians purposefully waste resources to enrich themselves under the current reimbursement system. But that system and our cultural values serve up a ready answer to physician uncertainty as to what tests and treatments to order for their patients: more is better. When evidence is incomplete or conflicting about when to use a particular procedure, surgery or diagnostic test, Brownlee notes, some physicians will treat more aggressively, especially if piecework reimbursement rewards that.

Brownlee quotes Wennberg as saying that, under a piecework payment system, a medical license is like a hunting license. Specialists — like orthopedic surgeons who earn more for each knee replacement, hip repair or back surgery they perform — hunt for opportunities to do those procedures, perhaps unconsciously deciding that patients will be helped by the procedures even when those patients won't be.

Economics journalist David Leonhardt illustrates the "blank check" nature of our healthcare payment system in a July 7, 2009 *New York Times article*, "In Health Reform, a Cancer Offers an Acid Test" with the example of slow-growing, early-stage prostate cancer, the most common form. Physicians and their patients can choose from several different courses of treatment, all with roughly similar benefits but very different prices, ranging from a few thousand dollars for watchful waiting to $50,000 for intensity modulated radiation therapy (IMRT), and $100,000 for proton radiation therapy.

No therapy has been shown superior to another, according to Rand Corporation analysis, as well as several cancer experts. "Which treatments are becoming more popular?" Leonhardt asks rhetorically. The use of IMRT rose tenfold from 2002 to 2006, and proton treatment centers have been opening at hospitals around the country. The result? Our healthcare system is paying at least several billion more dollars for prostate treatment than it should, writes Leonhardt. Drug and device makers have no reason to fund research to see which works best because insurers already pay for expensive treatments even if they aren't more effective.

Failure to Reward Preventive Care

There are some situations in which more healthcare really is better: preventive care and care to manage chronic illness. Our reimbursement system often penalizes appropriate care by underpaying for essential preventive care services. Providers get paid much more for treating more serious and expensive medical problems than they do for effective preventive medicine, which requires considerable time and effort to provide.

This problem is the other end of unexplained clinical variation: underutilization of effective medical services, such as immunizations, high-risk pregnancy screenings, diagnosis of previously undiagnosed patients with hypertension and depression and the dispensing of cholesterol-lowering medication.

The burden of chronic illness, such as diabetes and cardiovascular disease, is a pivotal problem that has risen dramatically in the United States. These chronic conditions are correlated with obesity, smoking and diet. They are very expensive to treat over long periods of time and account for a whopping 75 percent of all healthcare spending in the United States, according to estimates by the Centers for Disease Control and Prevention.[12] The costliest 15 percent of Medicare patients, the CDC notes, account for 75 percent of total spending because they need a lot of complex treatments.

The problem is ubiquitous. In 2005, 133 million Americans — almost one of every two adults — had at least one chronic illness, and about seven of ten deaths among Americans each year are from chronic diseases, according to the CDC. Addressing chronic illness with better preventive care is clearly a top priority.

The galling fact is that we already know where to focus much of our preventive care effort. The CDC notes that four behaviors within our control greatly exacerbate the morbidity and mortality related to chronic disease: lack of physical activity, poor nutrition, tobacco use and excessive alcohol consumption.[13] The message here is simple, but its implications are maddeningly complex. Healthy behavior and lifestyle change is a tremendously valuable medical investment. Behavior and lifestyle choices drive a large chunk of our healthcare spending. A great deal of chronic illness is preventable or ameliorable. But those goals prove to be elusive. Our current payment system structure seems designed to keep things that way.

Most of the money spent on healthcare for chronic illness is spent on hospitalization for preventable complications, writes Brownlee. But keeping chronically ill patients out of the hospital requires constant monitoring of diet, exercise and blood sugar levels. Under our current system, physicians are paid very little for the intense amount of preventive care that established guidelines say is required for the chronically ill. Physicians frequently lose money by administering the necessary but labor-intensive routine testing and care coordination. Many insurers don't pay providers to teach diabetics how to modify their diet or how to inspect their own feet to avert a blood-circulation crisis.

There is a one in four chance that a diabetic's physician will actually perform the necessary hemoglobin test on a routine basis or spend the time to teach the patient to check his or her own blood sugar regularly.[14] Brownlee cites a Rand Corporation study estimating that 2,600 diabetics go blind every year and 29,000 suffer kidney failure because they didn't get their blood sugar checked in time. Physicians fail to do it in part because the payment system punishes them financially when they do, Brownlee adds.

Then there is the impact on hospitals and specialists. You don't need to be an economist to figure out what happens financially when hospitals lose a large chunk of their admissions or when fewer services are required by cardiologists and surgeons. Under our pernicious payment system, they lose money when patients stay healthy.

Brownlee offers an example. The Robert Wood Johnson Foundation has developed a program called Pursuing Perfection, which is aimed at improving the care of patients with chronic diseases like diabetes, emphysema, hypertension, high cholesterol, ischemic heart disease, asthma, arthritis, depression and anxiety disorders and others. The program is being piloted around the country, and it involves multidisciplinary care teams including nutritionists and nurses, patient counseling on diet and exercise and information technology to facilitate effective care coordination among providers.

The program has all of the right ingredients. It has successfully reduced blood-sugar levels of diabetics and cut deaths from diabetes in half. It prevents heart failure crises. It saves Medicare and private insurers thousands of dollars per patient.

But the Pursuing Perfection program is killing the local hospital at the Bellingham, Washington, site, Brownlee writes, costing it $7.7 million in lost revenue because patients are staying out of the hospital. Specialty physicians in the county stand to lose $1.6 million because patients require far fewer procedures and office visits. Primary-care physicians participating in the program coughed up $500 a month for four years for an electronic medical-record system. Many of the program's activities — like group office visits, e-mail exchanges with patients and follow-up calls by nurses to check on patients' medication regimens — are poorly compensated, if at all. One sixty-physician group that helped plan the local initiative withdrew from it because participating would cost them too much.

Piecework payment is set up to reward more office visits and more complications. It does not reward care coordination, or hiring ancillary nurses and nutritionists, or reimbursing for extra time spent with patients. Instead of encouraging physicians and hospitals to become cooperative and coordinated care teams, our payment system works against the health of patients.

The Medicare program does a particularly poor job of chronic care prevention. It spends nearly one billion dollars a day on healthcare, mostly on hospitalizations for acute events, but not for activities that might reduce the need for hospitalization, many of which are correlated with chronic conditions.[15]

Hence, the Medicare paradox.

The Medicare program is, in reality, a program serving people with chronic conditions, typically multiple chronic conditions, whose health status presents a tremendous cost and quality challenge. According to the Congressional Budget Office, nearly half of Medicare patients suffer from three or more chronic conditions. The problem is that the traditional Medicare program remains a "passive payer," precluded from using even basic tools to try to make care more coordinated, efficient and effective at pre-empting hospital admissions for preventable flare-ups of chronic disease.

In addition, because program rules of Medicare must be uniformly applied across the country, exemplary performance cannot be rewarded, while poor performance is tolerated. Can you think of any other major national program costing hundreds of billions of dollars with similar rules and regulations? Only very recently has that begun to change, with several pilot projects designed to improve this situation, as we'll see in later sections.

But the primary, traditional Medicare program is a passive goose laying golden eggs, rewarding more care and higher-intensity care for a great many hospitalizations that could have been prevented in the first place. Our fee-for-service system makes preventable heart attacks profitable for physicians and hospitals. The Medicare paradox raises its sinister visage.

There's yet another vexing problem with hospital DRG reimbursement: since hospitals are paid a lump sum to treat a patient for a specific set of illness diagnoses, they have the financial incentive to discharge the patient as soon as possible. The same reimbursement system that rewards hospitals for providing more complex acute care encourages them to get patients out of the hospital quickly. Many of those patients wind up back in the hospital for conditions that could have been prevented.

Readmission costs are staggering. For every five Medicare patients who leave the hospital, one of them ends up back in the hospital within a month, costing Medicare between $12 billion and $15 billion a year, according to Institute for Healthcare Improvement consultant Stephen Jencks, MD, MPH, and colleagues.[16] By three months, the rate rises to one in three. Within a year, two out of three are rehospitalized or die.

Even younger patients are not exempt: for the population as a whole, the readmission rate is 14 to 19 percent for the first 30 days. Perhaps most alarming of all, rehospitalization within 30 days represents about 25 percent of *all* admissions for a quarter of hospitals across the country.

Rehospitalization is a frequent, costly and sometimes life-threatening event, and it stems from poor follow-up care, Jencks and colleagues conclude. Our healthcare system does a poor job of keeping patients healthy enough to stay out of the hospital, and hospitals and physicians collaborate poorly to ensure prompt and reliable follow-up care. As proof, the authors note that most of the readmissions within 30 days are unplanned, and half of the readmissions related to medical conditions (for example, heart failure, pneumonia, chronic obstructive pulmonary disease, psychoses and gastrointestinal problems) involve patients who had not seen a physician between admissions.

Conceptually, keeping people out of the hospital is not an overwhelming challenge. We have proven strategies at our disposal to reduce readmission rates. Hospitals have programs and staff devoted to discharge planning, and some of these programs are quite innovative. But the fee-for-service payment rewards repeated hospitalizations, notes Amy Boutwell, MD, a content director and policy specialist at the Institute for Healthcare Improvement.[17] Hospitals stop getting paid when a patient leaves, and they receive a new payment when the patient returns.

The patient's primary-care physician often doesn't even know the patient has been in the hospital, leaving patients on their own to figure out what medications to take and when to take them, how to recognize red-flag symptoms and when to make follow-up appointments, adds Boutwell. The ultimate cause of preventable rehospitalizations is the fragmented nature of our healthcare system and the financial incentives to continue business as usual. Boutwell knows of a hospital that actually discontinued a program that lowered readmission rates because the hospital could not afford the empty beds the program created.[18] It is hard to find better proof that our healthcare payment system is broken.

Here are the lessons. Spending more on healthcare delivery does not bring more quality. Healthcare delivery does not function as a normal market, as the suppliers (providers) determine demand. Price does not obey the law of supply and demand, except in a perversely twisted way in which more supply leads to greater utilization.

Our largely fee-for-service-based system rewards reactive acute care and penalizes effective preventive care. It is largely blind to quality and encourages higher volume and intensity of services. Its siloed nature impedes effective care coordination, paying physicians and hospitals separately with their incentives working at cross-purposes. Physicians are rewarded for keeping patients in hospitals longer; hospitals have the incentive to discharge quickly. From a financial standpoint, hospitals may welcome readmissions, as Medicare currently pays for all rehospitalizations except those within 24 hours after discharge for the same condition.

Put simply, physicians and hospitals are in the disease business, not the wellness business. The mission statement of most hospitals goes something like this: "Our mission is to improve the health of our community." That *can't* be true, because that's not how they are paid. If they really were to reduce admissions for diabetes, for smoking, for asthma and for coronary disease, they'd all be out of the hospital business. Hospitals are in the business of episodically doing the best they can to care for the end result of lots of preventable diseases.

When you tell a hospital president that their mission statement is an absolute lie, they'll give you a shocked and perplexed look. But you can explain it to them: How *can* it be true? If you really improve the health of the population, you would put yourself out of business. Hospitals look forward to the flu season. From a population health perspective, every hospital admission for asthma represents a failure of care coordination. And yet, every asthma admission is critical to the bottom line of an acute-care community hospital. Where is the economic incentive to coordinate care? Answer: there is none. That's the hospital business of the twenty-first century, driven principally by our current payment system.

Reflection

When you have a hammer, everything looks like a nail. Doctors are paid to keep using the same hammer, doing the specific things they are trained to do. They're going to set a target income, and they're never going to stop — at least until the payment system is radically altered. Possibly, under healthcare reform, they might be paid to put the hammer down for awhile.   *– S.K. and D.B.N.*

Notes

1. Each of three elements (amount of physician work required for a given service, practice expense, and malpractice insurance cost) is assigned a relative value unit (RVU) for each procedure code (Current Procedural Terminology, or CPT, code). These RVUs are then adjusted based on medical cost and wage differences in geographic areas. A conversion factor (national dollar amount that varies each year) is multiplied by the total geographically adjusted RVU to determine how much Medicare will pay for a particular physician service.

2. Shannon Brownlee. "5 Myths on Our Sick Healthcare System," *Washington Post*, November 23, 2008.

3. Shannon Brownlee, *Overtreated: Why Too Much Medicine Is Making Us Sicker and Poorer* (New York: Bloomsbury USA, 2007).

4. Cathy Schoen, Stuart Guterman, et al. "Bending the Curve: Options for Achieving Savings and Improving Value in U.S. Health Spending," The Commonwealth Fund Commission on a High Performance Health System, December, 2007.

5. Shannon Brownlee. "America, Health Thyself," *The Washington Monthly*, September-October, 2009.

6. Mallika L. Mendu, MD; Gail McAvay, PhD; et al. "Yield of Diagnostic Tests in Evaluating Syncopal Episodes in Older Patients." *Archives of Internal Medicine,* 2009; 169(14):1299-1305.

7. Brownlee, "America, Heal Thyself."

8. J.D. Kleinke, *Bleeding Edge: The Business of Health Care in the New Century* (New York: Aspen, 1998)

9. Michael T. McCue, "Clamping Down on Variation," *Managed Healthcare Executive*, February 1, 2003.

10. Fitzhugh Mullan,"Wrestling with Variation: An Interview with Jack Wennberg," *Health Affairs Web Exclusive*. October 7, 2004, 73-80. Available online at: http://content.healthaffairs.org/cgi/reprint/hlthaff.var.73v1.

11. Shannon Brownlee. "Information, Please," *The Atlantic Monthly*, January-February, 2004.

12. Centers for Disease Control and Prevention, "Chronic Disease Overview" website: http://www.cdc.gov/nccdphp/overview.htm#2.

13. Ibid.

14. Shannon Brownlee, *Overtreated*.

15. Nash, David B. "From the Editor: The Medicare Paradox," *Health Policy Newsletter,* 2003; 16(3), Article 1.

16. Stephen F. Jencks, M.D., M.P.H., Mark V. Williams, M.D., and Eric A. Coleman, M.D., M.P.H. "Rehospitalizations among Patients in the Medicare Fee-for-Service Program," *New England Journal of Medicine*, 2009; 360: 1418-1428.

17. Quoted in Lola Butcher. "How to Save a Bundle on Hospital Readmissions," *Managed Care Magazine*, July, 2009. Available online at: http://www.managedcaremag.com/archives/0907/0907.readmissions.html.

18. Ibid.

MYTH 5:

Our Medical Schools Prepare the Best Future Doctors

"We need a continuous cultural transformation to move the delivery system from being provider-centric to becoming patient-centric. We must be passionate about being customer-focused. Many strategies are required to accomplish this, including the much-discussed payment and reimbursement reform efforts. To be truly successful over the long run, however, we must focus on how we train our workforce, with a heightened emphasis on interdisciplinary education. We can never promote coordination and teamwork by educating in silos and being hostage to professional prerogative."

– Michael Dowling, CEO,
North Shore-Long Island Jewish Health System.

[Firsthand quote, received 10/18/10]

The world looks to the United States for medical education. We have what is probably the greatest medical education engine ever assembled in the world, represented at the pinnacle by 140 medical school-affiliated academic medical centers, partnerships between medical schools and hospitals that teach doctors in training. These centers assemble the most highly trained specialists and subspecialists to provide the most sophisticated patient care in the world. They offer the most advanced technology to diagnose and treat disease. They conduct breakthrough research that leads to dazzling medical advancements. They teach more than 100,000 new doctors and other health professionals each year. The world looks at this in awe.

This industry of academic medicine really represents the pinnacle of American science, drawing on billions of dollars in funding from entities like the National Institutes of Health and the Centers for Medicare & Medicaid Services. Academic medical centers are a source of national pride.

Look at Jefferson Medical College in Philadelphia as an example. The college gets 10,000 applicants annually; interviews are granted to 1,000 of those applicants; and the college offers admission to 500 to yield a class of 250. Read between the lines: in a recession, medical education is even more sought after than in booming economic times.

Getting into an American medical college is a huge achievement, confirmation of the student's grades and potential. After four years of medical school (called undergraduate medical education, or UME), graduates enter internship and residency training for three to seven years (graduate medical education, or GME) where they practice medicine under the supervision of fully licensed physicians in a hospital or clinic.

That's the good news. Here's the not-so-good news: the curricula and culture of medical education and training allows doctors to enter a lifetime of medical practice with serious competency deficiencies. Medical school graduates learn virtually nothing about quality and safety — how to evaluate it, how to improve it or even that it desperately needs improving.

Medical training curricula and culture reinforce the superhero mindset: "I made it through four tough years of medical school. I completed all those years of internship and residency training and I practiced amazing medicine under expert supervision. I'm an expert now, and I've proven my excellence. Why should I question it?"

Unexplained clinical variation in medical practice is born right there. Mentors in teaching hospitals often are faculty and senior residents who have little or no formal training or skill as educators. Rather than teach the importance of using evidence-based guidelines, they do what most doctors do: deliver treatments and procedures the way that local practice customs, or their own personal judgment and practice styles dictate.

The problem is summed up nicely by Paul Batalden, MD, a professor of the Dartmouth Institute and of pediatrics at the Dartmouth Medical School, and Frank Davidoff, MD, former editor of *Annals of Internal Medicine* and a senior fellow at the not-for-profit Institute for Healthcare Improvement. In a recent article published in the *Journal of the American Medical Association*, they wrote that doctors have two jobs to do every day: the job of doctoring and improving Job One. Doctors generally ignore Job Two. And the quality of many individual doctors' performance actually decreases with time rather than improving.[1]

Medical-school graduates themselves tell us that they lack skills that will be vital to medical practice in the coming years. The American Association of Medical Colleges (AAMC) graduating-senior questionnaire is an annual survey that every graduating medical student in every medical school fills out. Results of this survey show conclusively that students feel they get inadequate preparation in promoting quality and safety. As many as one-third or more report that they get inadequate instruction in how to interpret and use evidence-based medicine or how to improve the health of their patient populations or how to prevent disease. They also report inadequate training in teamwork and communication with other physicians and health professionals. These disastrous findings have held steady for the past several years.[2]

How can medical education fail to help new doctors build such fundamentally crucial competencies? How can it fail to impress upon them the importance of self-evaluation and improvement in the quality and safety of their care? How can it promote defensiveness against self-evaluation and improvement? The need to improve medical training is one of the foremost challenges that our healthcare system faces.

These are fighting words! But they are hardly radical. Such a critique has been levied by experts in medical education for many years.

Newly minted doctors have been telling us for years that they don't feel confident about how to use evidence-based medicine or how to help their patients stay healthy or how to communicate and coordinate effectively with other caregivers or how to improve their care. Medical education and training is burdened with several defects that militate against these crucial competencies. We'll highlight three in this section.

Quality teaching has been in decline for years at academic medical centers, as faculty are under tremendous pressure to bring in research funding and patient-care revenue to serve the corporate needs of their financially strapped institutions. Those marketplace imperatives have made excellent teaching a low priority and have crowded out time for it.

Medical training does not acculturate doctors to be open-minded to practice-improvement opportunities; it often does the opposite. Students learn that they are part of an intensely hierarchical pecking order that prizes doctor autonomy over collaboration and infallibility over openness to improvement. Mentors occasionally abuse subordinates, teaching the lessons that fallibility is shameful and that the call for improvement is threatening.

Undergraduate medical education is locked into a century-old basic educational model that focuses narrowly on biological science and almost entirely ignores practical clinical reasoning and quality and safety improvement skills. Things are a little better in graduate medical education, which is reforming its curriculum to address competencies required for safe and effective healthcare delivery. But the demand for research productivity and clinical revenue continue to crowd out time for faculty to devote to teaching the new curriculum. Instead, supervision at the GME level is often left to faculty and senior residents with little training as educators.

Teaching Takes a Backseat

Kenneth Ludmerer, a celebrated historian of medicine and medical education, writes that there was a time when the central mission of medical schools was educating medical students. But the rapid growth and funding of medical research after World War II, followed in later decades by intense marketplace pressures to bring in more clinical revenue to institutions bleeding red ink, were corrosive to effective learner-centered medical education.[3]

The post-World War II era brought economic boom times and growth in the National Institutes of Health, which currently invest more than $30.5 billion a year in medical research. In 1965 came the birth of the biggest goose that laid the golden egg: Medicare. American medical education was off to the races. By 1965, it had completely transformed itself into big science, big money, big schools and the recognition that the baby-boom generation needed a doctor boom. The number of medical schools doubled from post-World War II to the 1960s.

It's important to appreciate that the flow of dollars into American medical education is a public good. But it did not improve medical-school teaching. After World War II, when medical education expanded its activities beyond the four-year medical school into graduate-level teaching, research and patient care, those other functions rapidly outstripped teaching in importance, Ludmerer notes. Faculty were no longer rewarded and promoted for the time-consuming and labor-intensive task of good teaching, but instead based on how many dollars they could bring to their institution from research grants and other sources.

In the '80s and '90s, marketplace competition among teaching hospitals intensified. Managed-care companies ratcheted down payments and actively monitored whether the services that hospitals were billing for were medically necessary. Medicare switched from fee-for-service reimbursement for hospitals to a system known as prospective payment based on diagnosis-related groups (DRGs), which pays hospitals a fixed price for a set number of days for a patient with a particular set of medical conditions. The federal government also slashed payments it made to teaching hospitals for medical education.

Many academic medical centers bled red ink. Some still run on deficits. Corporate goals took precedence over educational missions. Medical educators were further torn from their teaching responsibilities when their institutions demanded that they see more patients to bring in more revenue from clinical care. Clinical revenue became the primary source of income for some academic medical centers and faculty were expected to see as many paying patients as quickly as possible. Medical students were (and still are) being taught by a small and shrinking percentage of medical-school faculty, many of whom have become demoralized and have less and less time to become advisors, role models and mentors, notes Ludmerer.

A prevailing paradigm in academic medicine is known as the "triple threat" — doctors who will simultaneously be superior educators, clinicians and research scientists. The triple-threat doctor sees patients, does unbelievable diagnostic work in the hospital, goes back to the lab to do NIH-funded research, writes papers about it and teaches.

Well, guess what? The triple threat never existed. It's a myth. No one can be really good at all three things. That would be way too complicated, especially with the explosion of medical knowledge each year. Becoming an excellent educator takes a lot of time and the commitment to polish one's teaching skills and update one's knowledge base. Research is extremely time consuming and its funding is very competitive. Successful researchers can devote 80 percent or more of their time to research and publishing.[4]

Medical-school faculty are held to this idealized mythology of the triple threat, while their largest incentives are to publish and to see paying patients. Teaching time and quality suffer.

Tainted Culture

Less exposure to the best and most talented teachers is only one of the impediments to fostering medical students' competencies in quality and safety improvement. The culture of medical school and residency training presents its own obstacles. That culture teaches counterproductive lessons: that vulnerability is bad, that the doctor is not to be questioned and that it is normal to heap scorn and abuse on subordinates in the care-team hierarchy.

Medical safety expert Donald Berwick, MD, (who was recently appointed by President Obama as head of the Centers for Medicare & Medicaid Services) writes that doctors who admit candidly that they made a mistake, or that they could be better at what they do, are vulnerable to ridicule, accusations of incompetence or even the threat of punishment.[5] That fear is a serious obstacle to quality and safety improvement.

But genuine learning requires vulnerability, Berwick notes. Doctors must let their guard down to admit that an opportunity for improvement exists. They must be willing to accept that they could be practicing ineffective medicine or committing medical errors. They need to evaluate their practice patterns and patient outcomes to find out. They might need to stop doing what they've been doing and start doing something else. These activities can lead to judgments about them by their patients, their colleagues and even health insurers.

Doctors-in-training learn that negative judgments can hurt and they learn to defend against them. As they learn, doctors are acculturated into an education and training environment that says they are the accountable party at the top of the care hierarchy. The doctor is the one in charge. Even though other care-team members contribute to the patient's care, or the processes used may be flawed, good and bad outcomes are attributed to the individual doctor.

This kind of cultural learning can cripple one's openness to improve. Should a medical error harm or kill a patient, the doctor becomes a "second victim" of sorts. He or she becomes demoralized in a "shame and blame" environment that does not tolerate failure. In the aftermath of a mistake or a poor quality outcome, the demoralized doctor is often psychologically disabled, unprepared to help find out what happened and to change the care process to prevent it from happening again.

"This in a nutshell is the problem at hand," according to a report from the Expert Roundtable on Reforming Medical Education, a group of medical-education leaders, students, patients and experts from related fields, which was assembled recently by the Lucian Leape Institute at the National Patient Safety Foundation, a prominent think tank.[6]

A related problem, the NPSF Roundtable notes, is rooted in the hierarchical culture of medical school and residency training, where medical students and residents are often intimidated by doctors and don't question their judgment. That "professional egocentricity" of doctors chokes off effective collaboration and team-building with other caregivers. As we've seen in previous sections of this book, the failure of care-team members to ask questions in the face of a questionable procedure can and does lead to egregious and heart-breaking medical errors.

Intimidation is part of medical training culture. Young doctors in residency training watch how their mentors treat others. These observations help form the values, behaviors and attitudes that they carry later in their medical careers. This is the so-called "hidden curriculum," and it often is based on positive experiences. But senior doctors and residents are sometimes abusive and unprofessional toward subordinates, leaving lasting lessons for impressionable young doctors.

The NPSF Roundtable regards these dehumanizing experiences as one of the more serious problems in medical school and teaching hospitals. Medical students report in surveys that they observe an increasing number of unprofessional behaviors as their training progresses. They are critical of those behaviors at first but eventually interpret them as normal. Some even begin to emulate those behaviors.

About 17 percent of respondents to the American Association of Medical Colleges' graduating senior questionnaire (out of 13,000 respondents, representing graduating students across all medical schools in the United States) reported in 2009 that they had personally been mistreated during medical school. Of those, about half said they had occasionally been publicly belittled or humiliated, and about 10 percent said that they had been threatened with physical harm or physically punished (for example, hit, slapped, or kicked).

Abusive behavior could mean making a student feel foolish for asking a question, or throwing surgical instruments in the operating room. The NPSF Roundtable documented a few examples of abuse, like this one:

"Two second-year medical students spent an afternoon observing surgery in the OR as part of a medical-school course. The chief surgical resident assigned the students to a corner of the room with instructions to be quiet and not touch anything. After the students had washed their hands and moved to their assigned place, the attending surgeon noticed them and yelled, 'Who are you? What are you doing in this OR? When you come into an OR, you introduce yourself to the surgeon. And why are you standing there? Go stand in that (pointing to a different) corner.'"[7]

Abusive and disrespectful behaviors do more than simply hurt

feelings, the NPSF Roundtable notes. In the context of medical education and training, they create a culture of fear and intimidation and
instill lessons of shame and blame that last. Abused students and residents sometimes model the behaviors and pass them on to future
learners. That's not exactly the kind of lesson that encourages doctors
to evaluate their own care for quality and safety gaps, or to seek
improvement.

Choked by Science

Most American medical schools continue to graduate doctors who
don't know how to improve their own medical care delivery. Some are
making progress, however. Jefferson Medical College, for example,
devotes a day in the third year of medical school to quality and safety.
This puts Jefferson in the top one percent of all medical schools as far
as dealing with quality and safety. We're building a Ford Pinto for a
marketplace that wants a hybrid Toyota, and not a lot has changed on
the factory floor for decades.

Or, as the NPSF Roundtable puts it, today's medical schools are
producing "square pegs for our care system's round holes," by overem-
phasizing basic science content while almost entirely neglecting pivotal
skills, behaviors and attitudes that students will need as practicing
physicians: things like human dynamics, patient safety, care delivery
improvement and even basic communication and teamwork skills.

Basic science is important. Doctors have to know about how the
human body works. But medical school perpetuates the myth that it is
training scientists and its curriculum wastes too much precious time on
course after course of bioscience, at the expense of teaching fundamental doctoring skills. Doctors are unable to fix what they don't understand. That problem begins right out of the gate, in medical school.

We're still using a century-old paradigm, known as the post-
Flexner era model, for medical education. Abraham Flexner, a research
scholar at the Carnegie Foundation for the Advancement of Teaching,
was hired by the Rockefeller Foundation to travel around the country
in the early 1900s and assess medical education. He was appalled at
the mediocre quality of many schools where students essentially paid
a fee and got a diploma.

Only a handful of schools, like Johns Hopkins, University of Pennsylvania, University of Michigan and Harvard, taught any real science. In 1910 Flexner wrote a scathing book called the *Flexner Report* that basically said that we have to completely change how we educate physicians in the United States, and that medical schools must adhere strictly to the protocols of mainstream science in their teaching and research.

Most remarkably, the nation responded, and American medical education was transformed, integrating bedside teaching (that term comes from the Flexner report) and basic science with clinical care.

But undergraduate medical education has become locked into a narrow and wasteful focus on biological science regurgitation. We've known that for decades. Dozens of reports from foundations, educational bodies and professional task forces have criticized medical school curricula for excessive use of lectures and overemphasis on rote memorization of scientific knowledge, instead of focusing on practical and professional skills like clinical reasoning and developing professional values and compassion, as pointed out by Molly Cooke, MD, an internist and medical-education advocate, and her colleagues.[8]

One such report was published by the Blue Ridge Academic Health Group, a group of academic health-center experts from around the country. The report notes that the early years of UME are devoted to lectures on the fundamentals of bioscience taught by basic science faculty, which does a poor job connecting that knowledge to clinical medicine and leaves students wondering how the knowledge is relevant to the practice of medicine.[9]

Flexner himself did not intend for value-neutral minutiae of scientific knowledge to be the sole or even predominant basis for clinical decision-making and he lamented how medical curriculum had allowed the scientific aspects of medicine to crowd out the social and cultural aspects, as Cooke and colleagues point out. But the academic culture of medical school finds it much more comfortable to teach biological science than messier real-world skills like inter-professional teamwork, self-evaluation of one's own patient care and strategies for self-improvement — topics that remain poorly represented in medical-school curricula.

Part of the problem is what we might call the "medical barge" analogy in medical education. A lot of medical educators believe, metaphorically, in a big barge of information out there in the river. The barge is weighted down with all kinds of stuff: the kidney, the heart, the human genome, biochemistry and histology. This huge barge of information is already crashing into the embankment, threatening to founder under its own weight.

Along come people who say they want to put some more stuff on that barge, like self-evaluation for quality and safety improvement, or ways to promote healthy patient populations or effective collaboration with other doctors and caregivers. The typical member of a medical-school curriculum committee replies, "Oh, no, no. We'd have to throw something off the barge to accept your new trash. What would you like us to throw off the barge? Should we omit the heart from the curriculum?"

The core group of medical educators and admission committee officers still believe that performance in organic chemistry as a nineteen-year-old is a powerful predictor of your lifetime success as a clinician. Premedical requirements are set by the AAMC, and they haven't varied much in 35 years: a year of inorganic chemistry, a year of organic chemistry, a year of calculus, at least a year of biology and a year of physics. The litmus test of the premed curriculum, though, is organic chemistry, which is a bear of a course. There's a huge volume of educational literature claiming that a student's performance in organic chemistry as an undergraduate will mirror his or her performance in the first two years of medical school. That literature is accurate. Why? Because undergrad organic chemistry and early med school are taught based on the same fundamental model: here's the information, memorize it and spit it back.

So, medical-school admissions committees use performance on organic chemistry as a barometer, the threshold performance indicator, for admission to medical school. Basically, if a student gets a C in organic chemistry, he or she is not going to medical school, end of story. The problem is that the organic chemistry grade is not predictive of anything except performance in basic science.

What we need to do is teach science better. We need to appreciate more independent learning. A great example is George Washington University School of Medicine, which no longer requires students to have microscopes or even to look in microscopes. That's an amazing sea change: giving up the microscope! They've created computer programs with digital images from histology (study of cells) and bacteriology. Why do medical students need to look with a microscope to try to find what a cancerous kidney tumor looks like when we have 500 pictures on the Web that are much better than what they'll ever see? Using new technologies like this, we can be more efficient in our teaching of bioscience.

How many lectures are enough? That's a key question. Let's pretend that you are in charge of teaching the kidney, and you're given ten one-hour slots. Of course, you're going to moan and groan that that's not nearly enough time to teach everything you need to know about the kidney. Well, of course it's not enough, but how much scientific minutiae do medical students really have to learn?

A basic understanding of renal physiology and major diseases of the renal system is certainly important. But do doctors really need cellular-level understanding and details like they are taught today? Probably not. There will always be somebody with that expertise with whom a doctor can consult and collaborate, or somebody who could look it up. Doctors of today need to be information experts and understand how best to use the knowledge databases available to keep informed and current so that they can make evidence-based decisions at the patient's bedside.

We need a total reassessment of what should be on the "barge" and what shouldn't. We can't keep loading stuff on the barge and throwing other stuff overboard. Instead, we should blow up the barge, start over, and maybe work backward by asking much more fundamental questions: What do we want a doctor to be like? What skills and competencies should he or she possess? Those are very different questions from the ones we're asking today.

Unmet Needs

Major leaders in academic medicine from Johns Hopkins University and the University of Washington in Seattle have written together in the *Journal of the American Medical Association* that when all is said and done, academic medicine has a single mission: to improve the health of the population.[10] This is a watershed event that outlines the importance of the commitment we must share to meet that goal. But we have yet to meet the goal, as a third of all graduates testify each year on the AAMC survey by saying that they don't know how to improve the population's health.

The NPSF Roundtable sums up the current challenges facing medical education this way. Healthcare has undergone a major sea change over the past two decades. The complexity and cost of healthcare have escalated; tremendous waste persists; and we've become aware of an epidemic of medical errors and patient-safety problems. Medical education and training institutions struggle to keep up with this evolving landscape and properly prepare trainees to become part of the solution.

On the GME side, you could argue that we're making some progress. In GME there's a recognition of the importance of self-improvement and awareness of health "systems-ness." The Accreditation Council for Graduate Medical Education has set a national guidepost out there called the ACGME Outcome Project. Beginning in 2006, all accredited residency programs were required to begin integrating six general competencies into their curricula: medical knowledge, patient care, professionalism, interpersonal and communication skills, systems-based practice, and practice-based learning and improvement. The latter two are particularly relevant to quality and safety improvement.

Competency in systems-based practice essentially says that by the time residents complete their training, they should understand the system that they are a part of and be able to demonstrate the ability to call effectively on other resources in the system to provide optimal healthcare. For example, they should know what a social worker does, a physical therapist and a home health aide.

Practice-based learning and improvement competency gets at Davidoff's Job Two, which basically says doctors ought to be able to pick up their own performance chart and review it against benchmarks, figure out where they fall short and then improve. They ought to be able to assimilate scientific evidence and continuously improve patient care based on constant self-evaluation and lifelong learning.

Some medical schools have begun to incorporate these competency goals into their curricula, but progress is slow going. Part of the challenge is figuring out ways to evaluate students on these competencies, since they focus less on content knowledge and more on skills, attitudes and behaviors. New curriculum needs new ways to test whether students are learning it.

Another big challenge is the teacher shortage we mentioned earlier. Not enough faculty can devote the time-intensive preparation needed to develop the new curriculum adequately. The research and patient-revenue crunch hasn't magically subsided. The triple-threat myth still lives.

There is consensus among expert panels like the Blue Ridge Group that academic medical centers must develop a core of faculty with education expertise who can develop the new curricula. The medical centers should reward that activity with heightened professional status and allocate time for teaching and for teacher development. They should "train the trainers" and fund their activities through sources like earmarked endowment funds.

Here's yet another dilemma: no comparable progress has taken place on the UME side. The Liaison Committee on Medical Education (LCME), the national accrediting authority for medical schools, has not yet established core competencies for graduating doctors. So, predictably, medical students one day turn into interns and residents with no formal understanding of pivotal issues that they're going to face going forward. They're completely ill-prepared to understand their role in the system and they're ill-prepared to understand the skill set necessary to improve Job One.

That's the current status of medical education: teachers with little time or reward to teach well and little training in the new required competencies; clinical mentors with little or no formal skill as teachers; a culture that fosters autonomy and fear of vulnerability instead of teamwork and openness to better ways of practicing; and a century-old model that fixates on biological science while giving short shrift to clinical reasoning, self-evaluation and quality-improvement skills.

It is no wonder that unexplained clinical variation persists, that healthcare quality and safety are so spotty and that a tremendous amount of waste continues to define our healthcare delivery. Once we recognize these problems and their severity, we can begin to appreciate how difficult they are to overcome. Efforts to overcome them are already in place. We'll examine several of those efforts in the second part of this book.

Reflection

One of us (David) is once again living the medical-school curriculum vicariously, through the eyes of one of his daughters, who is a freshman in medical school. Here's the good news: her generation is bringing a new level of enthusiasm and a willingness to think globally about healthcare, along with the ability to get information in an instant from every worldwide source. But regrettably, the curriculum looks all too familiar.

We're hoping that our work will stimulate medical schools to make these much-needed changes. One day, organic chemistry — which is predictive of very little, beyond how much a person can memorize — will no longer be the litmus test for the successful medical-school student. There is finally a convergence of interest in curriculum reform across all the major national stakeholders, including the Association of American Medical Colleges, the Institute for Healthcare Improvement, the American Medical Student Association, the Agency for Healthcare Research and Quality and the Lucian Leape Institute. We expect to see the fruits of that convergence very soon.   *–S.K. and D.B.N.*

Notes

1. Paul Batalden and Frank Davidoff, "Teaching Quality Improvement: The Devil Is in the Details," *Journal of the American Medical Association,* 2007; 298(9):1059-61. Available online at: http://jama.ama-assn.org/cgi/content/full/298/9/1059.

2. Association of American Medical Colleges GQ Medical School Graduation Questionnaire, 2009: All Schools Summary Report. Available online at: http://www.aamc.org/data/gq/allschoolsreports/gqfinalreport_2009.pdf.

3. Kenneth M. Ludmerer, *Time to Heal: American Medical Education from the Turn of the Century to the Era of Managed Care* (England: Oxford University Press, 1999).

4. Robert M. Centor, "Erstwhile Triple Threat," *Journal of General Internal Medicine,* 2002; 17(7):572-573.

5. Donald M. Berwick, "The Double Edge of Knowledge," *Journal of the American Medical Association,* 1991; 266(6):841-842.

6. National Patient Safety Foundation, *Unmet Needs: Teaching Physicians to Provide Safe Patient Care. Report of the Lucian Leape Institute Roundtable on Reforming Medical Education.* (Boston: National Patient Safety Foundation, 2010). Available online at: http://www.npsf.org/download/LLI-Unmet-Needs-Report.pdf.

7. Ibid. p.12.

8. Molly Cooke, David M. Irby, William Sullivan, and Kenneth M. Ludmerer, "American Medical Education 100 Years after the Flexner Report," *New England Journal of Medicine,* 2006; 355(13):1339-1344. Available online at: http://content.nejm.org/cgi/reprint/355/13/1339.pdf

9. The Blue Ridge Academic Health Group. *Reforming Medical Education: Urgent Priority for Academic Health Centers in the New Century,* (Atlanta: Robert W. Woodruff Health Sciences Center, 2003).

10. Paul G. Ramsey and Edward D. Miller, "A Single Mission for Academic Medicine: Improving Health," *Journal of the American Medical Association,* 2009; 301(14):1475-1476. Available online at: http://jama.ama-assn.org/cgi/content/full/301/14/1475.

PART 2

Myth Busters
to Transform Our
Healthcare System

MYTH BUSTER 1:

Physician Decision-Making

"We have to use data if we're going to better serve our patients and build a quality- and safety-oriented system. We can't keep doing this by best guess and best intention. It isn't going to work. Data will carry us into the 21st century of healthcare."

– Glenn Mitchell, MD,
Chief Medical Officer and Vice-President,
Clinical Safety, Sisters of Mercy Health System.

[Personal Interview, 2008]

Doubt and complexity play a large role in healthcare delivery, intruding upon its effectiveness, safety and efficiency. When making diagnostic and treatment decisions, physicians still rely heavily upon the "art" of medicine: unsystematic personal clinical experience, clinical intuition and judgments based on anecdotal evidence. After all, only about 18 percent of what doctors do is based on Grade-A randomized, controlled trial evidence; the rest is a medical gray zone about which physicians really aren't sure.

Medical gray zones contribute to wide variations in physician practice patterns which, as we've seen, often means unwarranted tests and treatments, complications and errors from medical procedures, and waste. Added to that uncertainty and practice variation is the tremendous complexity of healthcare delivery systems — especially in the often chaotic environment of hospitals, where multiple patient handoffs among providers offer plenty of opportunities for system mishaps and safety lapses.

How should we go about tackling these problems of uncertainty, variation and complexity in healthcare delivery? We need to do three things simultaneously. In the realms of healthcare for which we have solid evidence of what works, clinicians should standardize those "best practices" as best they can. For the gray zones, they need to "close the feedback loop" of their practices by testing their care approaches, measuring their outcomes and deriving their own evidence-based conclusions. Finally, dialogue between physicians and patients must be much more interactive, with patients empowered to elicit better information about the risks and benefits of their care options and to express their values and preferences more vocally. Evidence-based medicine is the foundation of each of these necessary activities.

Central Role of Evidence-Based Medicine

Evidence-based practice guidelines bring together the best scientific knowledge and expert opinion on what treatments are most effective in helping physicians to deliver the right care for the right patient at the right time, and to avoid expending scarce resources on ineffective clinical services. But what exactly do we mean by evidence-based medicine?

It's an incredibly value-laden term because it implies that most clinicians aren't practicing based on the evidence. Those are fighting words. Isn't all medicine based on evidence? Hardly. We've seen earlier in this book how little of modern medical practice is actually derived from rigorous clinical evidence: about 18 percent, according to David Eddy, MD, PhD, senior advisor for health policy and management at Kaiser Permanente.

The term "evidence-based medicine" was coined in the early 1990s by a working group of clinical epidemiologists now at McMaster University in Ontario, Canada. Professors David Sackett, OC, MD, FRSC, FRCP, and Brian Haynes, MD, MSc, PhD, introduced a set of concepts to teach clinicians how to inject more research evidence into their practices in place of primarily anecdotal experience.[1]

Sackett noticed that doctors were continuing to provide dangerous treatments without first testing them in any rigorous way. For years, physicians had prescribed anti-arrhythmic drugs for heart-attack patients, even though later research revealed that these drugs had killed more Americans than the Vietcong, writes Sackett. [2]

When physicians are not providing the right care at the right time to patients, patients often get more services that they don't need, exposing them to potential harm, according to Janet M. Corrigan, PhD, MBA, President and CEO of the National Quality Forum (NQF), a standard-setting organization.[3] Guidelines can prevent that by translating medical evidence into action steps for providers, says Corrigan.

Studies are published every month demonstrating that physicians who incorporate national guidelines into their local practices improve patient outcomes, and Corrigan cites as a prime example the American Heart Association's *Get with the Guidelines* program, which has documented quality gains in patients who have had coronary artery disease, stroke and heart failure.

Evidence-based guidelines are meant to identify proven medical practices and discourage physicians from using ineffective or unproven ones, instead blending their individual clinical expertise with the best available external evidence, say Sackett and colleagues.[4] Even excellent scientific research-based evidence may be inapplicable to an individual patient, so a physician's judgment and experience, as well as a patient's values and preferences, must still be part of the clinical decision-making process.

But some skeptics still regard evidence-based guidelines as "cookbook medicine" and as an encroachment on their professional autonomy by hospitals and insurance companies looking to save money.

Part of the problem is the culture in which physicians are trained, as we saw in the previous section. Physicians are acculturated to believe that they alone bear personal responsibility for the outcomes of treatment of their patients, and therefore they must have complete control and autonomy in the decisions about that care. Clinical autonomy is a crucial and tricky concept. Of course, physicians must be free to use their expertise, professional training and experience to make diagnoses and prescribe treatment. Of course, they must use their professional judgment effectively.

But physicians must recalibrate their conception of clinical autonomy if they have any hope of achieving a better balance between the science and the art of medicine. Do evidence-based guidelines represent cookbook medicine? Guidelines are more like jazz scores than cookbooks, according to James Reinertsen, MD, senior fellow of the Institute for Healthcare Improvement. The guideline's foundation in clinical science provides the basic melody, while the physician's clinical judgment is akin to a musician's improvisation, he writes.[5]

Several entities comb the research and formulate evidence-based guidelines for physicians to use in their practices. Those entities include medical specialty societies, the federal Agency for Healthcare Research and Quality (AHRQ), the independent not-for-profit Institute for Healthcare Improvement (IHI), the international multicenter Cochrane Collaboration and many others.

These entities review and publish disease-specific practice guidelines for common medical problems like chest pain, stroke, pneumonia and heart attack. For example, the American College of Cardiology and American Heart Association guidelines on heart-failure treatment,[6] guide physicians on treatment decisions such as use of anti-clotting medications, intensive glucose control, triage and transfer of patients for angioplasty and use of stents.

Practice guidelines give physicians a baseline for quality-improvement feedback, allowing them to observe how deviation from standardized treatment affects outcomes for different patients. Guidelines don't cover all of medical practice, but they are out there and they work. Let's look at some examples of how.

Standardizing Care Processes

We know, for example, what steps should be taken in what sequence to prevent some serious and common problems in hospitals, such as blood clots in veins, infections acquired in hospitals, pressure ulcers, and errors associated with high-alert medications (for example, anticoagulants, sedatives, narcotics and insulin). In many cases, the required change is decidedly low tech. Physicians' rates of improving the diagnosis and treatment of diabetic neuropathy injury (nerve damage) would almost certainly rise if their nurses had a protocol that any diabetic's shoes and socks are automatically taken off before the physician walks into the room, and a sticky note made clearly visible that reads, "Look at My Feet." Doctors know that these problems exist, and many know that the science is behind these best practices, but they often don't standardize their processes to fix the problem.

How should we handle clinical scenarios where we have solid proof of what works, and yet clinicians don't uniformly apply that knowledge? In those scenarios, variation itself — deviation from what research has established as the essential ingredients of effective and safe care — introduces error, complications and patient harm. In those cases, physicians must strive to standardize care according to the science and monitor outcomes while they do it.

Take the example of bloodstream infections that patients can acquire at hospitals. More than 80,000 people a year contract these infections because of preventable flaws in the way that catheters are inserted into the veins near the heart before major surgery. Such infections could potentially cost up to $2.3 billion annually to treat. An estimated 28,000 people die each year from them.[7] Five simple steps can reduce those infections dramatically in the surgical intensive care unit.

That is the important message of a new book, *Safe Patients, Smart Hospitals: How One Doctor's Checklist Can Help Us Change Health Care from Inside Out*, by patient safety expert Peter Pronovost, MD, PhD. Pronovost selected five evidence-based procedures recommended by the Centers for Disease Control and Prevention as having the greatest effect on preventing catheter-related bloodstream infection, and he advocated that all clinicians follow these procedures uniformly when inserting catheters into patients.

The checklist he developed to support the use of these procedures is surprisingly simple: wash your hands; clean the patient's catheter insertion site with the antiseptic chlorhexidine; try to avoid placing catheters in the groin, where infection risk is higher; cover the patient and yourself while inserting the catheter to keep a sterile field; remove a catheter as soon as it is no longer needed.

The checklist was key, but its successful use required addressing the traditional hospital hierarchy in which nurses are afraid to challenge physicians making a mistake, notes Pronovost. He and his team worked to encourage a cooperative culture so that nurses could speak up and halt a procedure if a step was omitted, such as a physician forgetting to wash his or her hands.

By introducing this five-step standardized checklist and cultural makeover, Pronovost has gotten infection rates down to almost zero in surgical ICUs at Johns Hopkins. When used for 18 months in Michigan, the checklist saved 1,500 lives and $75 million, while lowering the rate of catheter infections by 66 percent. Pronovost travels around the country and hopes to introduce the checklist to hospitals in all fifty states.

Physicians at Utah's Intermountain Healthcare's network of hospitals have been adapting evidence-based guidelines to their practices for several years, beginning in the late 1980s with ventilator care and eventually covering fifty clinical conditions and accounting for more than half of the network's patients. As David Leonhardt, an economics writer for the New York Times, reports, Intermountain was able to boost its patients' survival rate for acute respiratory distress syndrome to four times the national average; cut adverse drug events (including overdoses and allergic reactions) in half; cut the mortality rate for coronary-bypass surgery to half of the national average; and slash hospital readmission rates for heart failure and pneumonia patients. These evidence-driven improvements have saved thousands of lives each year across the network's hospitals.[8]

Let's look at one more example of attacking unwarranted practice variation with evidence-based guidelines. In late 2004, Donald Berwick, MD, MPP, a patient-safety guru and founder and CEO of IHI, made a dramatic proposal: a "campaign to save 100,000 lives" over eighteen months and every year thereafter by introducing proven best practices across the country to participating hospitals.

The IHI's "100,000 Lives Campaign" introduced six proven best practices to more than 3,100 participating hospitals across the country. An estimated 122,300 lives (the official IHI estimate range was between 115,363 and 148,758) were saved between January, 2005, and June, 2006, by hospitals implementing some or all of these evidence-based interventions, which are known to significantly reduce harm and death when implemented reliably.[9] Interventions included actions like delivering the correct antibiotics at the proper time to prevent surgical site infections and deploying rapid-response teams to avert Code Blues.

Several of these evidence-based guidelines are promoted by other agencies including the Centers for Medicare & Medicaid Services and The Joint Commission, a hospital accrediting organization.

There is no shortage of proof that specific guidelines improve outcomes. The key is achieving more uniform implementation. Physicians need to capitalize on computerized, clinical decision-support tools that help them to keep abreast of medical knowledge and apply it uniformly. More widespread adoption of user-friendly medical decision-support systems will play a huge role in boosting guideline adoption and effectiveness, says Mary Nix, MS, MT (ASCP), health science administrator at AHRQ and project officer for AHRQ's Center for Outcomes and Evidence.

Computerized, clinical decision-support software technologies can mine clinical literature to retrieve relevant information for clinicians at the bedside. When physicians enter patient symptoms and clinical conditions, the software displays evidence-based diagnoses, treatment recommendations and clinical summaries with references to peer-reviewed research articles. Decision-support systems like these do not tell the clinician what to do. Physicians still have to use their clinical judgment to decide which of the diagnoses they are going to investigate and treat.

Measure, Test and Close the Feedback Loop

Instead of deploying existing research-based guidelines during patient care — as Pronovost and his colleagues did against central-line infections — another form of evidence-based medicine calls upon physicians to synthesize new practice guidelines from the ground up by doing local experiments in care improvement at the bedside.

In his 2007 speech to the IHI's annual National Forum on Quality Improvement in Health Care, Berwick said he hoped to see a vast learning network of thousands of physicians testing promising changes in care delivery and gathering evidence to guide broader implementation, rather than waiting for best practice guidelines to emerge from formal research channels.[10] "Improvement, properly done, *is* research and learning. And, widespread improvement is widespread research," Berwick said, adding that "local improvement can be common, continual, disciplined and informative to all."

Physicians can attack unwarranted practice variation by paying closer attention to their own patient-care activities, looking for opportunities to improve quality and testing changes in practice style to see if they improve outcomes. These can be simple steps: standardize small elements of practice, observe outcomes, modify elements, observe outcomes, formulate home-grown practice guidelines that produce best outcomes, share what's learned with other physicians. This kind of medical practice reflects true devotion to care quality and patient safety, and we need more of it.

As Reinertsen puts it, "Given the imperfections and uncertainties of the evidence base, it might even be argued that, rather than waiting for perfect evidence, we should make good judgments using what evidence we have, implement those choices together, monitor the results and thereby use our practices to extend our knowledge base of what works and what doesn't."[11]

That approach was championed by cardiologist Richard Shannon, MD, now chairman of the Department of Medicine at the University of Pennsylvania School of Medicine in Philadelphia, who has been featured in *The Wall Street Journal*, on ABC's *20/20*, and in other high-profile media for pioneering work of this sort. A few years ago, when he oversaw the medical ICU and coronary-care ICU at Pittsburgh's Allegheny General Hospital, he attracted the national spotlight by declaring war on preventable infections that patients developed while on a central venous catheter, which is placed into a large vein in the neck, chest or groin to administer medication and fluids. These central-line catheters were causing infections that killed patients.

Shannon was determined to prove that these infections could be prevented. He spearheaded a campaign that eventually resulted in the elimination from his two ICUs of hospital-acquired bloodstream infections that are transmitted from central-line catheters. Here's how he did it.[12]

Shannon noticed that the medical and coronary ICUs had a rate of central-line infections that was higher than the regional average: 47 total infections occurred in 37 patients, 19 of whom died. He and his fellow clinicians reviewed records of all patients who had suffered a central-line infection over one year (between July, 2002, and June, 2003,) and spent weeks carefully watching how central lines were being inserted into patients.

The source of the problem eventually became apparent, he says: there were more than fifty differences in how physicians inserted central lines, and some of that variation could have been killing patients. The differences included whether or not physicians wore masks, caps, and gowns; what kind of catheter was used; and whether and what type of disinfectant was used before inserting the catheter.

Faced with what he saw to be dangerous variation in the central-line insertion process, Shannon challenged his care teams to improve the technique. By explicitly stating the steps in the care process, Shannon says, a team of care providers can detect a problem immediately when it occurs, isolate which step was missed, and fix the problem when it occurs.

His care teams took three months to agree to do several things the same way all the time, thereby eliminating chaotic and individualized variation, says Shannon. Here are the steps: Physicians should wear gowns, caps and masks; they should use one kind of disinfectant; they should drape the patient to create a sterile field around the catheter's insertion point; they should use one specific kind of catheter; and they and their nurses should adhere to a specified sequence of respective duties during the procedure.[13]

Those interventions drastically reduced the number of central-line infections, from 49 during the year before the improvements, to six in the year after, between 2004 and 2005. The following year there were 11 central-line infections, and the year after that there were two. In February 2007, Allegheny General Hospital announced that its coronary care ICU had gone a whole year without a single central-line infection, and it is now extending its variation-busting approach to eradicate infections hospital-wide.

Another excellent example of how physicians can successfully improve the quality and safety of their care by formulating practice-improvement experiments and measuring real-time changes in outcomes is the VA Pittsburgh Healthcare System's main hospital, which was able to slash its rate of hospital-acquired infections due to MRSA (a type of virulent bacteria) by over 85 percent within two years in its inpatient surgery unit.

The care teams identified problems at the bedside, standardized key steps and developed ways to communicate the improvements throughout the unit, according to Peter Perreiah, a former engineer at Alcoa and former managing director of the Pittsburgh Regional Healthcare Initiative.[14]

This experimental approach to developing best practices directly confronts clinicians' habitual and often unexamined practice patterns. If physicians and care teams took the time to observe what they did every day, closing the feedback loop, they would discover care deficiencies and be able to implement remedies.

Consider the importance of accurate biopsies to diagnose cancer and the consequences of errors in the pathology lab. An estimated three percent to five percent of the billions of lab tests performed each year are defective somehow, says Stephen Raab, MD, Director of the Center for Pathology Quality and Healthcare Research at the University of Pittsburgh Medical Center (UPMC).[15] The error rate is significantly higher and more dangerous in common tests for certain cancers. A false positive may lead to an unnecessary hysterectomy. A false negative can miss a deadly skin cancer.

Beginning in 2002, pathologists at nine major academic medical centers (UPMC, UCLA Medical Center, University of Iowa, Henry Ford Health System, Drexel University, Wake Forest University, New York University, Northern California Kaiser Permanente and Loyola University) were determined to find ways to fix outdated and error-plagued systems for collecting, labeling, handling and interpreting blood and tissue samples used to diagnose cancer. The collaborative effort was partly funded by the AHRQ.

Raab, who led the collaborative, says the main problem is poor samples: a lot of blood may be mixed with a cancer sample, obscuring the cancer cells. Or the biopsy sample may have missed existing tumor cells. Other errors may be caused by wrong ancillary information provided; for example, the patient could be identified as a 60-year-old when in fact the patient is an 18-year-old, and the diagnosis may differ depending upon age. Some patients with cancer who were diagnosed correctly may not be followed up because the information was never conveyed in the appropriate fashion to the right clinician.

False negatives of a lab test, which represent 98 percent of diagnostic errors, can miss cancer. Raab says most false negatives are due to a poor sample or difficulty in interpreting a poor sample, or both. Pathologists may also falsely interpret samples with ambiguous results as positive, which can lead to repeat tests and more invasive and expensive procedures. Given the sheer number of the tests performed in the United States, the cost burden of these errors adds up to billions of dollars.

Pathologists at the collaborating hospitals tested various ways to prevent errors. For example, when two pathologists looked at every slide of a specific tumor type, the number of lung-cancer diagnosis errors dropped. Posting a pathologist at the bedside of patients undergoing a needle biopsy meant that quality of samples could be interpreted on the spot. False-negative readings on malignant tumors dropped by up to 20 percent, says Raab.

A lot of innovation is coming out of Pittsburgh. The work of the Pittsburgh Regional Healthcare Initiative (PRHI) nicely illustrates the power of collaborative experimenting to attack practice variation and improve care delivery. The PRHI is a consortium of more than forty hospitals; hundreds of physicians; and the business, labor and health-insurance communities in southwestern Pennsylvania. The PRHI facilitates interactive forums for clinicians to share war stories and ideas for improvement.

One of the PRHI's significant accomplishments is its Cardiac Care Improvement Registry initiative, in which twelve cardiac-surgery units in the Pittsburgh region tracked more than a hundred variables involved in coronary-artery bypass (CABG) surgery and developed a consensus-based repository of best practices.[16] The PRHI's cardiac collaborative tracked thousands of cases from the region, helping heart surgeons to evaluate their own patient outcomes against others in the region and enabling the feedback loop to be closed.

The initiative ultimately identified four important care-process improvements following CABG surgery:[17] use the internal mammary artery (instead of leg) as a harvest site, administer aspirin before surgery, administer beta-blockers to get the patient's pulse rate down to under 80 beats per minute before surgery and take care that the patient doesn't become anemic while connected to the bypass pump.

Encourage Patients to Become More Active in Clinical Decision-Making

We've seen examples of how using evidence-based guidelines and closing the feedback loop of physician performance can tackle the problems of uncertainty, variation and complexity in healthcare delivery. Bringing more science and systematic observation to physician practice brings better patient outcomes, reduces or eliminates preventable errors, and increases efficiency of healthcare delivery. This need not crowd out clinical autonomy and the art of medicine, but it must bring them into better balance with science.

But other aspects of clinical care also are prone to error — such as the very manner in which physicians make decisions and the inability of any one clinician to assure the safety of care in a complex system — and require interventions other than science to assure accuracy, quality and safety. Physicians are human beings who are susceptible to judgment errors that stem from cognitive thinking traps. Physicians also practice medicine in complex care environments that invite mishap because of the number of different providers and procedures involved. In both cases, an effective antidote is the patient himself or herself. Therefore, the third thing we need in our list of uncertainty-, variation-, and complexity- busters is more active communication by patients during their encounters with clinicians.

As we saw in the first section of this book, a great deal of uncertainty can be involved when physicians diagnose patients, as the mind does not always weigh knowledge appropriately. Physicians rely heavily on their intuition and personal experience, trying to retrieve information that might be relevant to an individual patient.

Jerome Groopman, MD, Harvard Medical School Chair of Medicine, writes in his book, *How Doctors Think*, that physicians fall prey to various kinds of thinking pitfalls and traps that lead to errors, like seizing upon an initial symptom and making a snap judgment (anchoring error); discounting clinical findings that don't fit that judgment or giving too much weight to information that confirms their suspicions (confirmation bias); and inappropriately comparing the present case to the cases that are freshest in their memory (availability error).[18]

Active patient involvement is the best countermeasure to prevent these kinds of diagnostic decision-making errors, Groopman notes, and patients should help their physicians examine the assumptions they make.

Groopman suggests that patients ask their physician three specific questions when they are being diagnosed: *"What else can it be?"* *"Could two things be going on to explain my problem?"* and *"Is there anything in my history or physical exam or lab tests that seems to be at odds with the working diagnosis?"* Groopman calls these questions a "broad-spectrum antibiotic" to remedy a diversity of bugs in physician diagnostic thinking, an antidote to cognitive traps.[19]

Patients must be proactive to assure that they receive safe and reliable care under healthcare conditions that are increasingly complex and often chaotic. Being a patient is dangerous. Patients have to be on guard. They have to ask questions. They have to demand accountability. For example, the frequency of medication errors in hospitals is huge: thousands occur daily in every major hospital. Vigilance on the part of patients — asking questions about their care — is crucial to prevent error: "Yesterday my pill was purple. Today it's yellow. What does that mean?" Patients must also learn how to become valuable consultants to their physicians. The questions they ask their physicians can go a long way to help improve diagnostic and treatment decisions, and prevent common judgment errors.

Sanjaya Kumar, MD, addresses the problem dramatically and succinctly in his book, *Fatal Care*:

"Medical errors can happen to anyone, and at any institution," he writes. "As a patient in a hospital, you entrust your safety to others the moment you check in, assuming there are multiple processes in place to safeguard against preventable medical errors. You may believe your hospital and physician take every precaution to create a system of checks and balances. Maybe you think serious, life-threatening mistakes could never happen to you or your loved ones. But you would be wrong, dead wrong," he warns.[20]

Kumar's book illustrates in vivid detail the tragedy of preventable medical errors with a series of compelling case studies, offering the reader valuable insights into how and why medical errors happen, and how to pre-empt them.

What will it take to put the patient in patient safety? We need to supplement evidence-based guidelines with an actively involved patient. We need to promote the notion, as patient-safety expert Patrice Spath, BA, RHIT, and her colleagues do: "Nothing about me without me," whereby every patient is concerned about the quality and safety of his or her own care and is willing to ask the difficult questions.

As Spath writes in her book, *Partnering with Patients to Reduce Medical Errors*, consumers do have strong opinions about staying safe. They want clinicians to treat them with compassion and honesty, and they want their opinions listened to and respected. "No patient should be afraid to ask a question, and no practitioner should appear offended by a patient who is willing to speak up," writes Spath. [21]

Spath and her colleagues recommend a variety of tools to teach patients how to speak up. At St. Joseph's Hospital in Tampa, Florida, for example, patients are given an information guide that includes "10 Tips to Help Us Keep You Safe." The guide asks patients to make sure every caregiver checks the patient's name band and washes their own hands before providing care and to ask what each of their medicines, tests and treatments are for. [22]

The healthcare industry itself is promoting the message that consumers be vigilant and actively questioning patients, notes Spath. In 2002, the Joint Commission on Accreditation of Healthcare Organizations (now called The Joint Commission) teamed up with the Centers for Medicare & Medicaid Services to launch the national Speak Up campaign urging patients to become more informed participants in their healthcare. The National Patient Safety Foundation partnered with the American Medical Association and the American Hospital Association to create brochures and fact sheets on topics such as how patients can help prevent hospital-acquired infections.

Truly committed organizations do more than hand out brochures, though, and Spath describes how hospitals like the University of Wisconsin Hospitals and Clinics in Madison use a variety of strategies to encourage patients to become actively involved in their care. Every patient admitted to the hospital is now interviewed by a pharmacist to compare previous medications with new ones that may be prescribed during the hospital visit. The hospital's patient-relations department exists for patients and their family to contact with questions and concerns. The hospital has even formed patient and family advisory groups to *educate the hospital* about patient-care issues and how it can improve patient safety.[23]

The patient is often the only consistent participant across a confusing and sometimes treacherous healthcare delivery system, writes Spath, and healthcare providers should teach patients how to help themselves during the journey. The patient's persistent and informed vigilance is a critical aspect of patient safety, and it's time to create more opportunities for consumer involvement.

There is another scenario in which more detailed dialogue between patients and physicians is sorely needed: when a patient is faced with several choices of treatment options that vary in intensity, risks and benefits. Patients have traditionally relied on their physician's opinion and treatment recommendations. That approach needs to be replaced with a superior alternative: the shared decision-making model, which defines new roles for both patient and physician when considering treatment options.

Consider the many medical conditions for which surgery is an elective (as opposed to absolutely necessary) option, among other treatment options, each of which may be effective. Medicare spends 40 percent of its surgery budget on elective surgeries for ten such conditions, including chest pain due to angina, hip and knee arthritis, silent gallstones (painless ones that may disappear on their own), prostate conditions and breast cancer, notes Shannon Brownlee in her book, *Overtreated*.

As we've seen in a previous section, the rate at which patients with the same clinical characteristics receive surgeries for these conditions varies greatly, depending on geographic location and individual physician. That means patients whose physician tends to treat chest pain due to angina aggressively will be more likely to get cardiac-bypass surgery than a patient whose physician typically recommends conservative treatments first. Evidence-based guidance is sorely needed to tackle this massively wasteful and potentially harmful variation in surgical practice.

But there's a type of evidence that is often missing from this decision-making. In "preference sensitive" situations like these, in which research says different treatment options are all viable, the "evidence" that is needed is informed patient preference, obtained through a meaningful dialogue between patient and physician that examines the risks and benefits of various treatment options in detail. Only through such a dialogue can both parties choose which treatment would be the most appropriate and most highly valued by the patient, while also permitting the physician to provide his or her medical expertise.

Because patients often have unrealistic expectations of treatment benefits and harms, and physicians are often poor judges of patients' values, there is massive overuse of treatment options that informed patients probably would not choose if they knew better. According to the Foundation for Informed Medical Decision Making, a not-for-profit organization advocating active participation of fully informed patients, when patients are not well informed and active in their medical decision-making, they wind up getting invasive and expensive procedures that often do not help them. The foundation's website (www.informedmedicaldecisions.org) lists plenty of examples, like unnecessary tests and treatments for back pain, early-stage prostate cancer and stable heart disease.

A better-informed patient is in a much stronger position to discuss his or her views of the evidence backing each option as well as their personal health and lifestyle priorities.

A growing number of decision-making aids have been created by a variety of entities to facilitate better information exchanges between patients and physicians, and promote productive discussion about costs and benefits of various treatment options. Sources of these aids include the Foundation for Informed Medical Decision Making and its commercial partner, Health Dialog; Healthwise; the Mayo Clinic; Dartmouth's Hitchcock Medical Center; and others.

Tools include videotapes, audiotapes with workbooks, booklets, CD-ROMs, websites or personalized health coaching in office-based kiosks. All of them offer evidence-based information about treatment options, an unbiased explanation of the advantages and disadvantages of each option and case studies of patients explaining their decisions to help other patients clarify their preferences and values about treatment.

Patients who are offered these aids become much more knowledgeable about the trade-offs of their choices and are in a much stronger position to choose treatments that reflect their priorities. A man faced with the choice between watchful waiting of his early-stage prostate cancer or radiation treatment or prostate surgery that may leave him impotent may be more wary of the risks after a detailed dialogue about them and may choose not to undergo the more aggressive treatment.

These shared decision aids affect what patients actually choose. Annette O'Connor, John Wennberg, and colleagues found, for example, that patients facing major elective surgery who had a shared decision-making encounter choose the more invasive surgical options 25 percent *less* frequently than if they had no shared decision-making encounter — with *no adverse effects* on patient satisfaction or health outcomes.[24] That is a startling finding.

In summary, three crucial activities are needed to improve physicians' decision-making and tackle the problems of uncertainty, variation and complexity in healthcare delivery: apply best practice guidelines to standardize medical practice when there is solid evidence of what works well; develop "homegrown" best practices by performing local experiments in care improvement at the bedside; and involve patients as much more active decision-makers of their care. We need to do all three things simultaneously.

Readers probably can appreciate how difficult all of this would be in the hurly-burly practice of physicians. There are formidable obstacles. Basically, if physicians are paid to do piecework, they have to stay on the assembly line and get the piecework done. Self-evaluation and adherence to guidelines take time and energy away from the core activity of seeing as many patients as possible to get paid as much as possible.

But a lot of harm is done in medical gray zones because many physicians are rushing to see more patients. These physicians don't get paid to take detailed patient histories; they don't self-evaluate; and they don't follow practice guidelines. The three fixes for clinical uncertainty that we have examined in this section won't work well unless other key forces are also in place, which we will consider in upcoming sections: deploying better evidence about what works best; holding physicians and hospitals accountable for delivering the best and safest care; changing physician and hospital payment incentives to leverage real improvement and efficiency; and practicing genuinely patient-centered care.

Reflection

Maybe someday the whole notion of evidence-based practice will disappear because of technology, like clinical decision aids and the greater promulgation and dissemination of clinical protocols. One day, we might just be teaching and implementing based on the evidence, without a second thought about how we got to that point.

With technology we can't even imagine today, maybe this issue will become a moot point in the future. Evidence-based practice will just occur because we'll have all of these tools; we'll have the evidence when we go to the keyboard; and that evidence will be widely disseminated. We both hope we live to see this during our professional lives.

Let's also hope for greater patient engagement as another way to put pressure on moving doctors toward a better evidentiary basis for their practices. If we, the doctors don't do it, patients are going to push us into it anyway. Patients are going to bring with them a lot of new information that might help doctors improve their evidence-based practice patterns. By asking us the difficult questions, patients are advancing the field as well. As difficult as it is for doctors when their patients bring them their ten-page downloads from the Internet, that type of patient involvement really is moving the ball down the field.

– S.K. and D.B.N.

Notes

1. David L. Sackett, Sharon E. Straus, et al. *Evidence-based Medicine: How to Practice and Teach* EBM, 2nd ed. (Philadelphia: Churchill Livingstone, 2000).

2. Centre for Evidence Based Medicine, University of Oxford. Comments by Dr. David L. Sackett on the occasion of receiving the Gairdner-Wightman Award, March 31, 2009. Available online at: www.cebm.net/index.aspx?o=4393.

3. Christopher Guadagnino, PhD, "Step-by-Step Medicine: Oft-Debated Consensus Practice Guidelines, Essential to Healthcare Reform, Gain Traction," *The Hospitalist* January, 2010. Available online at: http://www.the-hospitalist.org/details/article/518453/StepbyStep_Medicine.html.

4. David L. Sackett, W.M. Rosenberg, et al. "Evidence-Based Medicine: What It Is and What It Isn't: It's about Integrating Individual Clinical Expertise and the Best External Evidence." *British Medical Journal.* 1996; 312(7023):71-72.

5. James Reinertsen. "Zen and the Art of Physician Autonomy Maintenance." *Annals of Internal Medicine.* June 17, 2003; 138(12):992-995.

6. F.G. Kushner, et.al. "2009 Focused Updates: ACC/AHA Guidelines for the Management of Patients with ST-Elevation Myocardial Infarction (Updating the 2004 Guideline and 2007 Focused Update)" and "ACC/AHA/SCAI Guidelines on Percutaneous Coronary Intervention (Updating the 2005 Guideline and 2007 Focused Update)," *Circulation.* 2009; 120:2271-2306.

7. Peter Pronovost, et al. "An Intervention to Decrease Catheter-Related Bloodstream Infections in the ICU." *New England Journal of Medicine.* 2006; 355:2725-2732.

8. David Leonhardt. "Making Health Care Better," *New York Times*, November 8, 2009.

9. As detailed on the IHI's website: http://www.ihi.org/IHI/Programs/Campaign/.

10. As quoted by Charles Kenney in his book *The Best Practice: How the New Quality Movement is Transforming Medicine* (Philadelphia: Public Affairs, 2008).

11. James Reinertsen. "Zen and the Art of Physician Autonomy Maintenance." *Annals of Internal Medicine.* June 17, 2003; 138(12):992-995.

12. Christopher Guadagnino, PhD, "Pa.'s Hospital-Acquired Infection Battle," *Physician's News Digest*, February, 2006. Available online at: http://www.physiciansnews.com/cover/206.html. Additional details from Naida Grunden, *The Pittsburgh Way to Efficient Healthcare: Improving Patient Care Using Toyota Based Method.* (New York: Healthcare Performance Press, 2008).

13. Grunden, *The Pittsburgh Way to Efficient Healthcare.*

14. Ibid.

15. Christopher Guadagnino, PhD, "Hospitals Collaborate to Reduce Diagnostic Errors," *Physician's News Digest*, August, 2006. Available online at: http://www.physiciansnews.com/spotlight/806.html.

16. Pittsburgh Regional Healthcare Initiative. "The Story of Pittsburgh's Cardiac Registry and What It Promises for SWPA's Heart Patients," *PRHI Executive Summary*, February, 2004.

17. Ibid.

18. Jerome Groopman, MD. *How Doctors Think* (New York: Houghton Mifflin, 2007).

19. Ibid.

20. Sanjaya Kumar, MD. *Fatal Care: Survive in the U.S. Health System* (Minneapolis: IGI Press, 2008).

21. Patrice L. Spath, Editor. *Partnering with Patients to Reduce Medical Errors* (Chicago: Health Forum Inc., 2004).

22. Ibid.

23. Ibid.

24. Annette M. O'Connor, John E. Wennberg, et al. "Toward the 'Tipping Point': Decision Aids and Informed Patient Choice Access to High-Quality Patient Decision Aids Is Accelerating, But Not at the Point of Clinical Care." *Health Affairs.* May-June, 2007; 26(3):716-725.

MYTH BUSTER 2:

Comparative Effectiveness Research

"Developing the next new device or medication with potential blockbuster status is the current primary driver of the research enterprise. However, clinicians are faced daily with patients with common ailments for which there is no evidence to guide selection of one therapy or test over another."

– Patrick Conway and Carolyn Clancy,
health experts with the
U.S. Department of Health and Human Services.

[Patrick H. Conway and Carolyn Clancy. "Transformation of Healthcare at the Front Line," *Journal of the American Medical Association.* 301(2009): 763-765.]

When it comes to information for medical decision-making, more is not always better. We need the right kind of information. Thousands of peer-reviewed clinical research articles get published each year and unquestionably lead to lifesaving and life-sustaining advances in medical care. The Food and Drug Administration continually reviews this research to issue approval decisions about new drugs, new medical treatments, new medical devices and new surgical procedures.

The number of available therapeutic options for any given illness multiplies at a dizzying rate. For example, about two dozen approved combinations of antibiotic treatment are available for community-acquired pneumonia, varying in cost and effectiveness. There are more than 100 recognized treatments and strategies for autism.[1] They can't all be best. Which one works best for which patients? Which has the riskiest side effects? Which is most cost-effective? It's hard to know.

Paradoxically, giving more treatment options to physicians and patients does not mean they will make better choices among these options. Indeed, more options may lead to more clinical uncertainty and variation in physician practice patterns. More options may mean patients get more unwarranted tests and treatments, potentially exposing them to harm from invasive procedures, complications and error.

Consider the rapid growth in diagnostic testing technologies that have recently joined the old-fashioned x-ray, including computer-aided tomography (CT) scans, positron-emission tomography (PET) and various forms of nuclear imaging. Richard Popiel, MD, the vice president and chief medical officer of Horizon Blue Cross Blue Shield of New Jersey, shared a shocking statistic with us. As a result of multiple radiologic tests, one-third of Medicare beneficiaries in any given year receive radiation that exceeds the Chernobyl evacuation threshold by 50 percent. We are dousing our elderly with more radiation than ever before. Are all of those tests really necessary? We don't know.

Physicians often don't know which treatment is best for a patient because there are few places to look for an answer. Most clinical research is not designed to answer the question, "Which treatment option is best?" Consider a patient who is diagnosed with localized prostate cancer. He and his physician have a number of treatment choices, all FDA approved.

The physician can recommend a prostatectomy, the surgical removal of all or part of the prostate gland. That surgery can entail an open procedure, in which the surgeon performs the operation visually through an incision. It can be performed laparoscopically, using fiber-optic cameras and miniaturized scalpels inserted via catheters through small incisions. It can be performed with the aid of robotic and computer technologies, with miniaturized instruments and high-definition 3-D cameras. A surgeon can use lasers to vaporize cancerous tissue or cryosurgery to destroy it by exposing it to freezing temperatures.

The physician can recommend nonsurgical techniques, such as high-intensity, focused ultrasound (HIFU), which uses sound waves to heat and destroy cancerous tissue of the prostate. Or hormonal therapy, which uses medications to shrink prostate-cancer cells by depriving them of hormones they require to grow and spread.

The physician can recommend radiation therapy. One such option, proton therapy, uses a beam of protons to irradiate the diseased tissue. Another technique called intensity-modulated radiation therapy (IMRT) adjusts a radiation beam to paint the exact shape of the tumor. Brachytherapy inserts tiny pellets that emit low-energy x-rays directly into the tumor.

The physician can recommend active surveillance, or watchful waiting, in which the patient is regularly monitored without invasive treatment, particularly when a slow-growing prostate cancer is suspected or when the physician and patient believe that the risks of other treatment options outweigh the possible benefits.

Physicians know that each of these approaches works to some extent, but they don't know which approach works best for which type of patient. There is currently little guidance for informed decision-making, because research has not compared treatment approaches to each other in any systematic way. What do physicians do? They fall back on anecdotal evidence, conjecture, personal experience and personal judgment. Some prefer a conservative treatment approach for their patients, because that's how they were trained. Others tend to treat aggressively; that's how they were trained. The price of limited evidence can be high. Thousands of men have suffered complications and impotence from aggressive prostate-cancer treatment that was likely unnecessary.

We need comparative effectiveness research (CER) to fill the knowledge vacuum, research that is specifically designed to determine what works best for whom, with the greatest cost-to-benefit ratio. Comparative effectiveness research tests drugs, treatments, devices and procedures against each other to determine which ones work best, which are only marginally effective and which produce more risks for the same outcome. We need a lot more of these kinds of studies to give us good, solid science to help physicians and patients make clinical decisions that accurately reflect benefits, risks and yes, costs.

If we learn that different care options turn out to be similarly effective for a certain kind of patient, shouldn't we want to know if a certain treatment is far costlier than alternatives, yet no more effective? Because of a comparative effectiveness study conducted by National Institutes of Health researchers, for example, we now know thiazide diuretics, which cost pennies a day, are more effective than much more expensive drugs at reducing cardiac risk in older patients.[2]

As physicians learn more about the comparative effectiveness of the drugs, treatments and procedures they have been using, there will be less uncertainty about which to prescribe. There will be less unwarranted clinical variation and less waste and potential harm to patients.

This is a challenging agenda, but we have recently turned the corner on making it happen on the scale that's needed. Uncle Sam has put his confidence in CER with a $1.1 billion down payment on it, as part of the stimulus bill passed in early 2009. A few months later, the federal Institute of Medicine mapped out a clear agenda of priority areas for CER.

Let's take a closer look at why most clinical research doesn't help physicians and patients choose among competing treatment options; how CER is designed to fill that information gap and has worked in other countries; and how CER is now poised to grow rapidly here in the United States.

Traditional Research Doesn't Help Much

Most published clinical research does not help physicians choose which treatments to prescribe for their patients because it is primarily designed to demonstrate that a treatment option "works," but not how well it works in comparison to alternatives.

As the Institute of Medicine puts it in a recent report on CER,[3] traditional research studies are designed to demonstrate the degree to which a drug or treatment produces favorable results under carefully controlled conditions. Subjects and settings of these so-called "efficacy studies," however, are often very different from real-life clinical settings.

Effectiveness research instead measures "the benefits and harms of an intervention in ordinary settings and broader populations, and therefore can often be more relevant to policy evaluation and the healthcare decisions of providers and patients."[4]

For example, clinical trials often require subjects to be as similar to each other as possible to minimize the number of variables that could confound the results of the study. A drug may work well for a middle-aged diabetic man, for example, but less well for an elderly diabetic woman with heart disease and asthma. Researchers often use a homogeneous mix of patients (similar age, sex, race, ethnicity and severity of illness) and exclude from the study subgroups of patients who don't fit those inclusion criteria. By studying only an idealized subset of patients, though, research results are less able to be generalized to the kinds of patients that physicians actually encounter in their daily practice.

"Developing the next new device or medication with potential blockbuster status is the current primary driver of the research enterprise. However, clinicians are faced daily with patients with common ailments for which there is no evidence to guide selection of one therapy or test over another."[5] That's how U.S. Department of Health and Human Services health experts Patrick Conway and Carolyn Clancy sum up the status quo of clinical research. Drugs, treatments and procedures are tested primarily to gain approval by regulators. Research trials are designed to prove that a clinical intervention works, not to guide physicians on when and how to select them for patients, Conway and Clancy note.

Harold Sox, MD, a noted internist, member of the Institute of Medicine and nationally renowned expert on medical decision-making, recently co-wrote an article in the *Annals of Internal Medicine* stating that clinical research trials too often set out to answer the wrong question, "Does this work?" when physicians want to know "Is this better than that?"[6] To find out whether an intervention works, studies have rigorous methodological design requirements that actually cloud their usefulness to practicing physicians.

Bryan Luce, past president of the International Society for

Pharmacoeconomics and Outcomes Research, and colleagues sum up the dilemma nicely: "Without major changes in how we conceive, design, conduct and analyze RCTs [randomized clinical trials], the nation risks spending large sums of money inefficiently to answer the wrong questions — or the right questions too late."[7]

The typical standard for success of a typical clinical study is even more discouraging. Clinical trials generally compare a treatment to a placebo (for example, a sugar pill or an agent with no "active ingredient"). The clinical intervention being studied is given to one sample of patients, while an inert agent is given to another sample of patients so that both groups believe that they might be getting the active treatment. Outcomes are compared. If patients who received the real intervention have better outcomes than those who didn't receive it, and the intervention does not have significantly harmful side effects, the treatment is deemed to be efficacious and regulators approve it.

The new intervention literally has to work better than *nothing* for the medical community to embrace it! In the twenty-first century, our best science seeks to demonstrate that what the medical care physicians provide is better than nothing.

Only in rare exceptions do clinical trials of new drugs compare them head to head with alternative medications, for example, when the drug manufacturer wants to market the approved drug as superior to a competing drug (which is risky, from a marketplace competition standpoint, if the drug fails to demonstrate superiority), or when a placebo trial would be unethical, such as a study of AIDS drugs. Once the FDA approves a drug, few manufacturers initiate further studies that examine its long-term safety, its effectiveness in patients not included in the approval clinical trials or effectiveness relative to its alternatives.

The end result is that physicians still have very little guidance in picking which particular treatment is likely to work best for a patient.

Comparative Effectiveness Research Can Fill the Gap

Surely, physicians want to offer the best treatments to their patients. The trouble comes from assuming that the newest treatments are best. Marketplace competition drives much of the information physicians receive. Drug company representatives meet with physicians regularly to tout the benefits of the latest (and probably most costly) drug. They give physicians office samples to offer to their patients. Drug and medical device companies advertise new products heavily to physicians. The problem is aggravated further when patients expect to receive the latest cutting-edge therapies, spurred by the many billions of dollars that drug companies spend on advertising directly to consumers and by an arms race among health systems advertising the latest technologies.

But which treatments are best? Does new mean better? The staggering truth is that, for the most part, physicians often don't know. They need more research that answers these questions. Better-informed decisions means the right treatments would be given to the right patients. That means fewer complications and shorter (or prevented) hospitalizations. It may also mean that the newest and costliest drugs, treatments and procedures are not chosen when they offer little or no benefit over existing and less-expensive alternatives. Comparative effectiveness research offers the promise of improved quality and safety, as well as lower cost.

Studies that compare treatments can be eye opening. Are invasive procedures more effective than drugs? Not always. A recent study published in the New England Journal of Medicine concluded that patients with stable angina (chest pain that typically occurs with activity or stress) who had balloon angioplasty to compress the plaque deposits in their heart arteries fared slightly better than those treated with medication, but that benefit disappeared by 36 months.[8] When is knee surgery better than exercise? A recent study in the same journal found that physical and drug therapy was just as effective as knee surgery for osteoarthritis of the knee.[9]

Some public and private organizations currently conduct CER. Among them are the Agency for Healthcare Research and Quality (AHRQ), the Cochrane Collaboration, ECRI Institute and the Blue Cross and Blue Shield Association's Technology Evaluation Center. But the efforts of these organizations are fragmented, and less than 0.1 percent of the money spent on health research goes toward CER studies, according to Gail Wilensky, a former head of Medicare and a senior fellow at Project Hope, an international health advocacy organization.[10] We need more CER to "help us learn how to spend smarter and treat better," Wilensky says.

A more systematic CER agenda requires several choices. Comparative effectiveness studies may compare similar treatments, such as competing drugs; similar approaches to the same basic treatment, such as different levels of follow-up care after surgery; or very different approaches, such as surgery and drug therapy. All are needed.

A trickier question is how to deal with the issue of cost. Comparative effectiveness studies could restrict their focus to medical benefits, or they could also examine benefits and costs of competing medical treatments.[11] Cost analysis of treatment options is relatively straightforward when a less expensive treatment yields comparable or superior health gains. But how can researchers determine whether the additional medical benefits of a more expensive treatment are worth their added costs? The calculations can be complicated and controversial. How much is an extra year of life worth?

Researchers answer that question with a metric known as quality-adjusted life year (QALY), which combines quantity and quality of life into one unit. A year of life in perfect health is scored as 1.0 and death is scored as zero. A drug or treatment that results in extra years of life in less than full health would be scored between 0 and 1, for example, if the patient would lose a foot, suffer blindness or have to use a wheelchair. Comparative effectiveness studies that examine cost would report an intervention's cost per QALY gained.

Great Britain's National Institute for Health and Clinical Excellence (NICE), which was established in 1999 as an advisory body to the country's National Health Service (NHS), uses QALY calculations to decide what drugs, treatments and medical technologies it will pay for with its fixed national healthcare budget.[12] NICE uses committees of health professionals to review research and consider QALY equations to recommend whether the cost of particular therapies are worth the benefit.

To date, NICE has published appraisals of more than 100 specific technologies and has issued guidance on the use of more than 250 medical procedures and more than 60 sets of treatment guidelines. Over the past five or six years, NICE claims to have identified nearly

$1 billion in potential cost savings throughout the country's health-care delivery system. [13]

NICE estimates, for example, the net annual cost savings of full implementation of its hypertensive care guideline at more than $340 million. If all hypertensive patients were treated with the cheapest drug in each class in line with the guideline, NICE estimates an additional saving of $80 million compared with current prescribing. [14]

Not all of NICE's recommendations seek cheaper or fewer treatments. As an example, for metastatic spinal-cord compression (when a bone in a vertebrae presses on the spinal cord), NICE says implementing its prevention and treatment recommendations would *increase* surgery and cost an estimated $22 million more per year. But that is more than offset by a reduction in care costs by allowing patients to remain mobile, resulting in an estimated $27 million in net annual savings.[15]

NICE's recommendations for patient care protocols are translated into detailed behaviors that providers can implement. For example, its recommendations for primary-care physicians managing adults with hypertension include the following: "Drug therapy reduces the risk of cardiovascular disease (CVD) and death. Offer drug therapy to: patients with persistent high blood pressure of 160/100 mmHg or more or patients at raised cardiovascular risk (10-year risk of CVD of 20 percent or more, or existing CVD or target organ damage) with persistent blood pressure of more than 140/90 mmHg. In hypertensive patients aged 55 or older or black patients of any age, the first choice for initial therapy should be either a calcium-channel blocker or a thiazide-type diuretic."[16]

Does NICE guidance reduce unexplained clinical variation and improve quality? Some case studies suggest that it can, according to an appraisal of NICE by The Commonwealth Fund, a not-for-profit health-policy think tank.[17]

For example, the use of specific cancer drugs recommended by NICE increased by 50 percent from 2003 to 2005 across the country, while variation in their use also dropped significantly. After NICE recommended that multidisciplinary teams be used to manage lung cancer and colon cancer patients, more than 95 percent of providers implemented the advice.[18]

The lesson learned from Britain's experience is that CER offers a solid basis for treatment decisions and can trim waste from the system when multiple options are available. Combining effectiveness appraisals with cost-effectiveness appraisals, and putting providers on the hook for adopting the guidance, seems to work. There is no question that we need a similar body in the United States.

Cost-Effectiveness Study Remains an Uphill Battle

But opponents in the United States recoil from the "How much is a year of life worth?" question when it comes to CER influencing health-care decisions. They believe that cost comparisons would taint comparisons of clinical effectiveness and might ultimately be used to restrict access to valuable treatments. To them, the very concept of QALY is a chilling anathema.

Gail Wilensky, the former head of Medicare, has long supported CER, but she also advocates keeping cost-effectiveness analysis out of the equation for practical reasons. She believes that political sensitivities count and that CER studies must be perceived by all stakeholders as objective and unbiased. If the information is not credible, it will be useless.[19]

Because cost-effectiveness information in medical decision-making is more controversial than clinical effectiveness data, those cost-effectiveness decisions should instead be left to health plans, not to a national CER entity, Wilensky believes. "Because clinical effectiveness is the most basic and costly step in learning how to spend smarter, it should proceed first and in as politically protected a manner as possible," she writes.[20]

The Congressional Budget Office acknowledges that the practice of placing a dollar value on an additional year of life is controversial, that many people may be appalled by the notion and that a common sentiment among the American public is that no expense should be spared to extend a patient's life. These are serious cultural obstacles.

Nevertheless, in his 2007 Congressional testimony, Peter Orszag argued the dire need for comparative cost analysis as an essential feature of CER. The explosive growth rate of healthcare costs is the most important determinant of the country's long-term financial health, Orszag said, pointing out that the cost of treating similar patients in different regions of the country varies wildly, that higher spending does not translate into higher life expectancy or better health outcomes and that hard evidence is often unavailable about which treatments work best for which patients or whether the added benefits of more effective but more expensive services are sufficient to warrant their added costs.[21]

Orszag also acknowledged that building a solid base of CER information, whether or not it includes cost-effectiveness data, will take many years. Since a goal of comparative effectiveness analyses is to make physicians and patients aware of ineffective and wasteful treatment options so that they instead choose superior ones, we are going to need a sizeable body of research findings for a substantial number of medical conditions before we start sorting out what works better than what and for whom.

There's another major hurdle to injecting cost-effectiveness data into the mix: Medicare is currently forbidden from taking cost into account when making medical coverage decisions, so it would need new legal authority to adjust payments to physicians and hospitals based on whether they use care proven to be cost-effective. Medicare will generally cover any treatment or procedure that has medical benefits, regardless of its cost or its effectiveness relative to alternative therapies.

Wilensky's suggestion to finesse the cost-analysis piece remains an option. Private insurers have more latitude with what to do with the new CER information and could voluntarily adjust payments to physicians and hospitals to encourage the use of more effective care. They could simply provide the information to patients and physicians in the hope that it would positively modify their treatment choices.

They could choose not to cover drugs, devices or procedures that CER finds to be less effective or less cost-effective. Or, health plans could require enrollees to pay out-of-pocket for some or all of the extra cost of more expensive treatments that CER shows to be less effective or less cost-effective. However, private health plans might be reluctant to pursue the more aggressive approaches for fear of consumer backlash, as happened in the 1990s when marketplace pressures forced HMOs to back off from their aggressive cost-control policies.

Orszag's point is that plenty still needs to be done before CER translates into better quality and less waste in healthcare delivery. Getting the American CER research agenda off the ground is just the first step. We've started to do that through entities like the AHRQ, the primary federal agency supporting CER. But its CER budget to date has been too small ($30 million in 2008) to produce the volume of research needed.

New Momentum at Last

There is now fresh stimulus to jump-start CER in the United States in the form of new money and new direction. Congress recently recognized the importance of CER by allocating $1.1 billion over two years to support it as part of the American Recovery and Reinvestment Act of 2009 (popularly known as the stimulus bill). Those monies are just now reaching the research community.

Government officials dubbed the allocation a "down payment" on a national program of CER, and the U.S. Department of Health and Human Services in March 2009 created a fifteen-member Federal Coordinating Council for Comparative Effectiveness Research to coordinate research and advise the President and Congress how to make the best use of the allocation.

Political sensitivities won out, though, as cost-effectiveness was removed from the equation, at least for now. Skeptical lawmakers, lobbyists for drug and medical-device makers and some patient groups convinced Congress to word the bill to forbid the CER coordinating council from mandating healthcare coverage or payment decisions based on the research. The information we glean from the federally funded CER would be disseminated to physicians, patients, insurers and others, but none will be required to use it. Wilensky seems to have been right about the political climate surrounding CER.

What should the new money be spent on? We now have fresh direction to help answer that question, in addition to the new $1.1 billion down payment on CER. At the request of Congress, the Institute of Medicine issued a report in June, 2009, *Initial National Priorities for*

Comparative Effectiveness Research, that established a roadmap for the nation's CER agenda.[22] Comparative effectiveness studies, the report states, should focus on disorders that are the most common, that cause the greatest amount of illness and death and that are treated with most variation by physicians.

A solid agenda for CER is urgent, according to the report, because so many clinical-care decisions facing patients and physicians lack any solid foundation of knowledge about what works, how well, for what groups of patients and in what specific circumstances. Similar patients receive widely varying treatment in different settings, and they cannot all be receiving the best care.

Drawing upon definitions from several government agencies, the report offered a unified "official" definition of CER to set the agenda: "the generation and synthesis of evidence that compares the benefits and harms of alternative methods to prevent, diagnose, treat and monitor a clinical condition or to improve the delivery of care. The purpose of CER is to assist consumers, clinicians, purchasers and policy-makers to make informed decisions that will improve health care at both the individual and population levels."[23] The savvy reader will note that cost and efficiency are not part of the definition.

The IOM's Committee on Comparative Effectiveness Research Prioritization elicited a wide array of input from professional organizations and the public on what America's CER agenda should include and then deliberated over a list of 1,268 nominated research topics before whittling it down to 100 priority study topics. The list of priority topics is available on the report's website: www.iom.edu/cerpriorities.

Some topics are what most people might expect: what works in the doctor's office and what doesn't, how often should a patient with hypertension be seen — things that are the stuff of unexplained clinical variation. But of the 100 top topics, only eleven are concerned with particular drugs or biotechnology products. Many of the topics are "low-tech," which is testament to how much we don't know about seemingly fundamental care decisions.

Half of the IOM's recommended research topics, for example, focus on comparing different means of delivering healthcare (for example, how or where services are provided) rather than comparing specific treatments. The hope is that hospitals and health systems might better organize their facilities and personnel to deliver care in the manner that CER reveals to be superior.

Since heart disease is the leading cause of death in the United States, it seems appropriate that it was the second-ranked topic category (after how or where to deliver care) among the IOM's top 100 priority topics for CER, garnering eight recommendations — such as comparing the effectiveness of aggressive medical management and angioplasty in treating stable coronary disease, comparing different treatment strategies for type 2 diabetes and comparing innovative treatments for congestive heart failure.

Cancer, the second leading cause of death in the United States, is the focus of six recommended primary CER topics, including screening technologies for colorectal and breast cancers, and the use of imaging technologies for diagnosing and monitoring all cancers (the use of which has exploded over the past several years, prompting insurers to crack down on what they believe is overutilization).

The diversity of those topics speaks volumes about just how much physicians and patients don't know when they choose treatments for their ailments. One might have expected more CER priority topics to reflect the newest and least familiar technologies that have not had time to be proven. Instead, most of the priority CER topics seek to compare how or where services are provided, or treatments and therapies that physicians have been using for many years.

Future of CER

At least for now, cost effectiveness is off the CER table. Uncle Sam says Medicare can't stop paying physicians for prescribing Treatment A if CER proves that Treatment B works better and costs far less. If researchers discover that a prevailing procedure for congestive heart failure actually doesn't work as well as other treatments and costs five times more, physicians can continue performing it and get paid to perform it. Physicians can use information gleaned from CER research, or they can choose to ignore it.

We will have to wait for second-generation comparative effectiveness research proposals with teeth that explicitly examine cost-effectiveness and tie payment policies to credible findings. Before that can happen, the political climate must first permit a rational discussion about the value of CER quality and cost research, without demagogic labels such as "death panels" looking to "kill granny" by withholding expensive treatments. Politics has been called "the art of the possible" for a reason.

The IOM report states that the country needs a federal CER organizational infrastructure with the authority to set future CER priorities, support databases and registries, fund researcher training, conduct research and bring research findings into everyday clinical practice. Objectivity and transparency, it notes, will be central to the public's trust and confidence in the integrity of the CER program. Consumers, patients and caregivers have a key role to play in informing and framing CER to keep the research relevant and applicable to real-world settings. That active engagement also makes them more likely to trust the research findings and insist that their own care take account of the results, the report adds.

We believe that cost effectiveness research with teeth, or connecting payment to the adoption of CER guidelines, must become an integral part of those priorities. Policy-makers must persuade the public about an essential truth: comparative effectiveness research is not about rationing or cost control, per se. Comparative effectiveness research saves lives by injecting quality and safety — in the form of solid information about what works best and what works less well — into medical decision-making. It can go a long way in preventing complications and patient deaths from exposure to unnecessary drugs, tests and procedures.

It is folly to continue to pay physicians for performing tests and treatments that are shown to be ineffective. It is insidious that they get paid even more for performing even more, irrespective of effectiveness. Patients are being exposed to more procedures and risks than evidence says are justified. But the status quo is changing. Perhaps it is not changing as quickly as we would like, but we have finally come to a national consensus: CER is urgently needed to create a more rational basis for medical decision-making that is rooted in scientific evidence.

Reflection

Inevitably, the results of comparative effectiveness research will be tied to reimbursement. It's unpredictable how quickly this is going to occur, but our sense is that it will happen faster than we currently imagine. It has to, because most Western nations are already there, but we've been in national denial that this is, in fact, the case in our country.

There's a call for direct linkage by researchers writing in the October 2010 Health Affairs, who argue why Medicare should make coverage decisions based on CER as a way to achieve cost control without limiting access to medical services.

We think CER is going to be an irresistible force that will pummel everything in its path. It is a very powerful force for cost reduction, as evidenced by nations with centralized payment systems. And no, that's not just rationing. It's rational use of resources that is safer and less expensive.   *– S.K. and D.B.N.*

Notes

1. Commonwealth Fund. "What Works in Health Care? What Doesn't?" *Purchasing High Performance,* June 18, 2009.

2. Furburg et al. "Major Outcomes in High-Risk Hypertensive Patients Trial," *Journal of the American Medical Association,* 2002; 288:2981-2997.

3. Institute of Medicine. *Initial National Priorities for Comparative Effectiveness Research.* (Washington, DC: The National Academies Press, 2009).

4. Ibid.

5. Patrick Conway and Carolyn Clancy. "Transformation of Health Care at the Front Line," *Journal of the American Medical Association,* 2009; 301:763-765.

6. Harold Sox and S. Greenfield. "Comparative Effectiveness Research: A Report from the Institute of Medicine." *Annals of Internal Medicine,* 2009; 151:203-205.

7. B.R. Luce, PhD; J.M. Kramer, et al. "Rethinking Randomized Clinical Trials for Comparative Effectiveness Research: The Need for Transformational Change," *Annals of Internal Medicine,* 2009; 151:206-209.

8. E.D. Peterson and J.S. Rumsfeld. "Finding the Courage to Reconsider Medical Therapy for Stable Angina," *New England Journal of Medicine,* 2008; 359:751-753.

9. Alexandra Kirkley, MD; Trevor B. Birmingham, PhD, et al. "A Randomized Trial of Arthroscopic Surgery for Osteoarthritis of the Knee, *New England Journal of Medicine,* 2008; 359: 1097-1107.

10. Gail Wilensky was quoted in Geri Aston, "Pushing past the placebo: Legislating for a new kind of clinical trials," *American Medical News,* Dec. 1, 2008.

11. Congressional Budget Office. *Research on the Comparative Effectiveness of Medical Treatments: Issues and Options for an Expanded Federal Role,* December, 2007.

12. According to NICE's website (www.nice.org.uk).

13. Ibid.

14. National Institute for Health and Clinical Excellence. *Quick Reference Guide. Hypertension: Management of Hypertension in Adults in Primary Care.* June, 2006. Available online at: http://www.nice.org.uk/nicemedia/live/10986/30113/30113.pdf.

15. National Institute for Health and Clinical Excellence. "Metastatic Spinal Cord Compression: Diagnosis and Management of Adults at Risk of and with Metastatic Spinal Cord Compression," Available online at: http://guidance.nice.org.uk/CG75. A complete listing of NICE's published clinical guideline sets are available at: http://www.nice.org.uk/guidance/index.jsp?action=ByType&type=2&status=3&p=off.

16. National Institute for Health and Clinical Excellence. "Hypertension (CG34): Management of Hypertension in Adults in Primary Care." Available online at: http://egap.evidence.nhs.uk/CG34/guidance/unnumbered_section_4.

17. Chalkidou. Commonwealth Fund Issue Brief.

18. Ibid.

19. Gail R. Wilensky. "Cost-Effectiveness Information: Yes, It's Important, but Keep It Separate, Please!" *Annals of Internal Medicine* June 17, 2008; 148:967-968.

20. Ibid.

21. CBO Testimony: Statement of Peter R. Orszag, Director, "Health Care and the Budget, Issues and Challenges for Reform," before the Committee on the Budget United States Senate," June 21, 2007. Available online at: http://www.cbo.gov/ftpdocs/82xx/doc8255/06-21-HealthCareReform.pdf.

22. Institute of Medicine. *Initial National Priorities for Comparative Effectiveness Research* (Washington, DC: The National Academies Press, 2009).

23. Ibid.

MYTH BUSTER 3:

Accountability

"The central problem with our broken healthcare system is that costs are too high and they're rising too fast. Why? For too long, we've been seduced by the myth that because of the system's supposed complexity, average consumers could never make it work for them. Why not try what works? Here and there, in pilots and pockets, it's been proven beyond the shadow of a doubt that, if powered up with the right kind of data, healthcare consumers are more than capable of distinguishing between wasteful products and efficient ones, and between good quality and bad. Consumers don't need to adjust to a so-called healthcare system that everyone knows is terrible. Instead, healthcare needs to harness broadly the transformative power of consumerism. Only then will costs get under control."

– Mike McCallister,
chairman of the board and CEO, Humana Inc.

[Firsthand quote, received 10-15-10]

Doctors and hospitals should be held accountable for the quality, safety and efficiency of the care they deliver. But how to do that is a complicated question. We have a 20-year history of public healthcare report cards, good and bad. We've discovered unexpected answers to fundamental questions like what report cards should report, who reads them and why.

Accountability is multifaceted and is driven by several engines: report cards that people actually use; improvement mandates with teeth; and apology mechanisms for when things go wrong. We'll take a look at each in this section.

The stakes are high. Figuring out how to weed out sub-par care would save a lot of human and financial costs. Figuring out what patients need when they leave a hospital so that they're not hospitalized again in a few weeks, for example, could yield tremendous savings.

The Wall Street Journal writer Tom Burton notes, for example, that a public report card released by the Pennsylvania Cost Containment Council (PHC4) identified nearly 58,000 patient readmissions to the hospital in 2008, representing 19.1 percent of Pennsylvania patients who were discharged from the hospital after being treated for things like pneumonia, respiratory failure, stroke and hip fracture, and then hospitalized again within 30 days. The cost of those readmissions was a staggering $2.5 billion in hospital charges.[1]

Discovering which are the top-rated hospitals and using them cut the Hershey Company's healthcare expenses by 50 percent over several years as Hershey offered workers medical coverage based on the PHC4's reported outcomes, Burton notes. And, the Philadelphia police union's benefits-management company says it uses the reports to steer officers to the best hospitals, trimming its costs by about 17 percent compared to other plans.

Accountability Is Not Yet Consumer Driven

Hospital and doctor report cards can and do stimulate healthcare improvement, but sometimes in unexpected ways. Give consumers good information about where to go for the highest-quality services, and they will seek out the high-performers. Expose poor performers, and consumers will avoid them. The prospect of losing business will goad providers into improving their performance.

That has been the guiding rationale behind provider report cards made available to the public. But it doesn't work that way yet. Report cards are becoming more useful to consumers, offering data that is more relevant to them. Consumers will eventually embrace and act upon that data more vigilantly. Meanwhile, accountability for health-care providers still works without the consumer engine.

Do patients themselves select doctors and hospitals based on report-card outcomes? No, despite two decades of report-card efforts. About one-quarter of consumers surveyed in a 2002 Harris poll said they were aware of hospital report cards, but only three percent considered changing their care based on those ratings, and only one percent actually made a change, writes Robert Wachter, MD, in his book, *Internal Bleeding: The Truth behind America's Terrifying Epidemic of Medical Mistakes*.[2]

Consider the report-card pioneers, New York and Pennsylvania, which have been publicly reporting patient death rates after coronary-artery bypass graft (CABG) surgery for every hospital and surgeon in their states since the early 1990s. The reports compare the actual death rates with rates that would be expected when taking into account the severity of the patient's illness and coexisting conditions (risk- and severity-adjusted morbidity and mortality rates).

And yet, surveys of patients in Pennsylvania who underwent CABG surgery reveal that only a small minority was aware of the CABG report card before having the operation, and even fewer based their decision about where to have surgery on the rating of their hospital or surgeon, writes Harvard researcher Arnold Epstein, MD, MA.[3]

Thankfully, most people are healthy most of the time. Nobody goes around thinking, "I had better study the PHC4's myocardial-infarction report in anticipation of my heart attack next year." So, a big chunk of provider report-card data is not actionable until patients need care in the hospital.

Is it even worth patients' time to select hospitals and doctors based on outcomes? Given rampant practice variation and inconsistent safety outcomes, it is absolutely worth their time. The *Dartmouth Atlas* is proof positive that patients should be up in arms. The fact that they're not speaks volumes. The only people who are up in arms about the Dartmouth findings are national employers, in their case, because of the cost. They look at ZIP codes and demand to know why they are paying five times as much for the same procedure in one neighborhood as employers are in another, and for outcomes that are worse.

Employers care quite a bit about whether they are getting maximum value for their healthcare dollar. After all, they are paying for it under the traditional model of employer-sponsored health insurance. Groups that represent larger employers — like The Leapfrog Group — are actually doing something about it: reporting and comparing hospital quality-performance data so companies know what they're buying when they make healthcare purchasing decisions. The Leapfrog Group is an effective watchdog of the healthcare-purchaser community and it is getting real results.

While employers would very much like their employees to choose hospitals that deliver the highest value care (i.e., the best outcomes at the lowest cost), patients instead tend to base their choice of hospitals on, in this order: opinions of family members, opinions of friends and advice of their primary care doctor (who, of course, exists in a data-free environment with them). However, with the exception of the Leapfrog Group findings, which report on the 25% of American hospitals so far willing to report, very little useful information is available to consumers to compare and contrast hospitals on a national basis on the factors that matter most to family decision makers. This is true despite the plethora of public reporting entities available on the internet and elsewhere. Too often data is presented to show most of the providers performing at the average range, which does not inform consumer decision making. Leapfrog is the only neutral entity collecting and publicly reporting on hospitals nationally.

Few would question the importance of good data to drive the accountability of our healthcare system. The point was made nicely in a personal interview by the authors with Glenn Mitchell, MD, Chief Medical Officer and Vice-President, Clinical Safety, Sisters of Mercy Health System: "Improved data reporting and event reporting gives us a good shot at being able to get regulators, payers, our consumer base, health plans and hospital administrations to a table where we can finally fulfill a promise of arriving at a taxonomy that makes sense and is small enough to be useful, but is implemented across the country." The trick is figuring out how to get the right data out there in a way that encourages the right people to use it.

Accountability Is Hospital Driven

So back to the central question: who reads healthcare report cards, and why? The answer is counter-intuitive. In the twenty-first century, hospital organizations, not consumers, read these report cards most assiduously. Ironically, the people to whom report cards are directed are not the top users. Why? The argument could be made that hospitals have the most to lose or gain. Because marketplace competition is so important, it is common to see two-story-tall banners or billboards proclaiming Hospital X's high orthopedics ranking on *U.S. News & World Report*'s "Best Hospitals" list.

From the consumer perspective, report cards are too complicated. They are confusing, and their data about severity-adjusted morbidity and mortality makes no sense to consumers. Take the nation's largest hospital report card, Medicare's *Hospital Quality Compare*. There's very little consumer traction on that website, in part because it's not particularly user friendly, listing seven process-of-care measures related to heart-attack care, four related to heart-failure care, six related to pneumonia care, eight related to surgical care and three related to asthma care for children.

Outcome measures on the Medicare Hospital Compare website (www.hospitalcompare.hhs.gov) include "30-day, risk-standardized mortality rates and rates of readmission," with explanations like this: "The three readmission models estimate hospital-specific, risk-standardized, all-cause 30-day readmission rates for patients discharged alive to a non-acute care setting with a principal diagnosis of heart attack, heart failure and pneumonia. The statistical model for computing the 30-day risk-standardized readmission rates is a 'hierarchical regression model.'"

Even for savvy users, the ratings lack discriminatory power. When every hospital is found to be in the average range of performance, what is the value? So, the classic 20-year-old report card on severity-adjusted morbidity and mortality has no traction with consumers.

We also know that most doctors don't read report cards. Surveyed cardiologists and heart surgeons in New York and Pennsylvania say they don't believe the CABG report cards are an important indicator of a surgeon's or a hospital's quality of care, notes Epstein. Cardiologists say they rarely discuss report-card data with patients and don't typically use them in making referral decisions, he adds. Doctors are linked into their own referral network based on "you scratch my back, and I'll scratch yours." They're not paid to drive business based on outcomes, and report cards don't have the leverage to change that.

Hospitals read report cards and act on their information. They use report-card data to examine and improve their care processes. Low performers, like hospitals with higher-than-expected mortality rates or patient readmission rates, try to ferret out explanations for their scores. Maybe, for example, vigilantly readmitting surgery patients to the hospital actually winds up reducing mortality. Maybe medications that prevent certain kinds of complications are not being given, or maybe some other nonfatal element during the course of treatment is not being handled as well as it should be.

Hospitals use their performance information for marketing and other purposes. Many Pennsylvania hospitals, for example, said they used PHC4 CABG report information when recruiting staff thoracic surgeons and residents to affirm their quality status.

So, report cards do lead to quality improvement, because hospitals care about, study and act on their data. Mortality rates for CABG surgery in Pennsylvania have dropped by half, mirroring the years of PHC4's public reports of CABG mortality at Pennsylvania hospitals and outstripping improvements in states without public reporting.

When the national spotlight began to shine on healthcare safety and medical errors, report cards followed suit. Prior to 2006, few consumers had ever heard of a hospital-acquired infection (HAI). These are infections a patient catches while in the hospital, from, for example, catheters kept in too long, being on a ventilator or inadequate antibiotics during surgery. Hospitals themselves had no idea what the benchmark number was for HAIs.

Pennsylvania pioneered a national effort to mandate HAI reporting and in 2005 became the first in the nation to show hospital-specific data. While hospitals had included infection control as part of their quality-improvement programs for years, release of the state's first

HAI report by the PHC4 called into question whether those efforts were adequate by tallying HAI frequency, decrying the cost of these infections and heightening public awareness of their existence.

The HAI report card revealed that hospital processes play a much larger role in HAI risk than previously believed, exposing, as the PHC4 put it, the "myth of inevitability" surrounding the issue.[4] With its reminder that HAIs hurt or kill patients who came to a hospital to get well, the report card added moral urgency to the call for hospitals to reduce or eliminate HAIs.

No longer could HAIs simply be dismissed as inherent risks in healthcare or expected outcomes from the care of seriously ill patients, especially those in high-technology settings such as the operating room, the intensive care unit or the renal-dialysis center. There is no doubt that sick patients with complex conditions are at greater risk of hospital-acquired infections, but HAI research reveals that patients with less complex conditions also get these infections, and that care-related factors play a significant role. Perhaps the PHC4 report's largest practical impact has been in boosting providers' attentiveness to their patients. As soon as doctors and nurses are aware that something, in real time, is harming or killing their patients, they can become galvanized.

Infection numbers fell by 7.8 percent during the year after the first HAI report, as Pennsylvania hospitals responded by taking steps designed to lower infections, writes *The Wall Street Journal* reporter Tom Burton. Big savings followed. PHC4 report-card data showed that the average payment in 2006 for a hospitalization where a patient acquired an infection was $53,915, versus $8,311 with no infection. Pennsylvania hospitals could lower expenses by nearly $1 billion simply by eradicating preventable infections.

Insurers Are Learning that Consumers Don't Read Report Cards

Do health insurers use hospital report cards? Managed-care plans have their own accrediting body, the National Committee for Quality Assurance (NCQA), and demand accountability from hospitals in their contracting network, which is where they spend most of their funds.

Managed-care companies have done very little, on average, over the past decade to drive business to hospitals with high marks on public report cards. How come?

Failure can be blamed on the network system. When every Joint Commission-accredited hospital is in a health plan's network, then there is effectively no network. Philadelphia is a great example. Does Independence Blue Cross drive pancreatic surgery to Thomas Jefferson University Hospital, which has demonstrated better outcome on that surgery? The short answer is no. That would disrupt the marketplace. It is difficult to imagine that any major national managed-care plans drive business based on outcome at the hospital level.

The picture is slightly different for doctor report cards. Some health insurers actually generate their own to offer to their consumer members. However, the limitations of these report cards are readily apparent.

Under Cigna HealthCare's quality and cost-efficiency profiles, for example, a doctor can earn up to three stars in quality designation either for earning the NCQA Physician Recognition Award for adopting quality measures in diabetes care, cardiac and stroke care, spine care and care coordination-information system implementation or for being in the top third of his or her peer group in adhering to evidence-based measures, according to Jim Nastri, Cigna's vice president of product development and product management for consumer-driven products.[5]

But relatively few consumers use the doctor ratings. Cigna tracks the monthly hit rates of its online physician profiles, which Nastri says are still fairly low, and reports that perhaps one to two percent of the insurer's roughly 10 million members view the profiles.

Putting Consumers Back into the Accountability Equation

Consumers generally don't care about provider report cards. Why? The research is very interesting. Part of the reason is that the quality problem is "invisible" to most consumers. That's because patients fundamentally believe that doctors and hospitals are all trying to do a good job, according to Judith Hibbard, DrPH, professor of health policy at the University of Oregon. Patients generally don't believe that quality differs enough across providers to matter much.

Using report cards is also hard work. Presenting numerical data — such as the percentage of heart-attack patients given a beta blocker, as Medicare's *Hospital Quality Compare* does — makes it hard for consumers to figure out the meaning of, say, a five percent difference between hospitals. Instead, consumer researchers have found that it's best to present report-card data as grades or ratings, maybe supplemented with color-coded icons — like green for superior, yellow for average, and red for poor — to allow consumers to process the information and correctly interpret its meaning.

Consumers need a different kind of report card: one that portrays risk, not benefit. If a patient goes to a particular hospital, he or she wants to know the hospital-acquired infection and error rates, not the severity-adjusted morbidity and mortality for open-heart surgery. Pennsylvania's HAI report card is an example of what consumers care about.

Why do error rates resonate with patients? They've read decades worth of *The New York Times* and *USA Today* reports of medication errors and deaths in hospitals. Consumers are concerned. They know we still have to put an eraser on a pencil. An error is something they can get their arms around. Hibbard suggests that by emphasizing possible risk on report cards, consumers will be more likely to pay attention to the information. Give people a message about risk, rather than about gain and they will be more likely to think that choosing one particular provider over another makes a difference in the quality of care they receive.

In 2001, Hibbard and her colleagues examined the impact of a hospital report card called QualityCounts, which compared the performance of 24 hospitals in south central Wisconsin on complications and deaths.[6] The report used a green plus-sign in a circle to denote fewer mistakes, complications and deaths than expected; a white circle to denote average number of mistakes, complications and deaths; and a blue minus-sign to denote more mistakes, complications and deaths than expected. Hospitals were rated on their hip and knee surgery, cardiac care and maternity care.

Quality in hospitals' maternity and cardiac-care performance varied significantly, spurring consumer interest. Many performance reports fall flat with consumers because they fail to show much performance variation, Hibbard notes. That makes perfect intuitive sense. Consumers remembered the QualityCounts content for at least two years after release of the report. Report cards can work.

What does this imply for community-hospital mission statements? They should drop the mission statement that they're going to improve the health of the community. They should tell the community that they're going to be the safest hospital in that ZIP code, and then prove it. Or, that they're going to be the hospital with the lowest mortality rate for a heart attack. Or, that they're going to be the hospital that coordinates patients' care effectively after they're discharged.

Accountability Needs Mandates with Penalties

Consider an example of care coordination. The need for accountability and improvement is enormous. Hospitals are accredited by the Joint Commission, a private-sector, not-for-profit organization, and most states require that accreditation as a condition of hospital licensure. It wasn't until the Joint Commission mandated medication reconciliation two years ago that hospitals spent any time paying attention to the most important part of the hospital discharge process: here are the medications you took in the hospital; here's what you took before coming to the hospital; and here's what you have to take when you go home.

Here's the problem: patients who just come out of the hospital are often too infirm, elderly or disabled to actively participate in a successful discussion about a new medication regimen. The new regimen could omit essential medications that the patient has been taking for some time or may unintentionally duplicate a patient's existing medications. We know that medication errors such as omissions, duplications, dosing errors or drug interactions often cause great harm or even death.

Were errors made in a patient's new medication regimen while he or she was shuttled to and fro in the hospital? Does the patient know how to act on the new regimen? Was his or her community doctor informed about it? Prior to the Joint Commission mandate, it was a free-for-all.

The Joint Commission, since 2006, has required hospitals to document the medicines that each patient takes and to communicate that information to other providers involved in the patient's care.[7] What's the lesson here? Hospitals needed a mandate before they would improve this dangerous and important care process. But even a mandate hasn't yet worked.

In early 2009, the Joint Commission noted that many hospitals were struggling to develop and implement effective and efficient medication-reconciliation processes. So the commission said it would suspend the use of medication reconciliation in its accreditation scoring while its surveyors consult with hospitals, doctors, pharmacists, nurses and others to evaluate their processes and discuss further improvement opportunities. A tweaked mandate is expected by January 2011.[8]

The time has come to stop averting our eyes from preventable errors committed by individual doctors and other providers. Mandates with penalties for noncompliance are justified. How much longer should we wait until we hold individuals accountable for behaviors that have been proven to be harmful and deadly, such as failure of doctors and nurses to wash their hands? That's the question posed by patient-safety experts Robert Wachter, MD and Peter Pronovost, MD, PhD, who recently co-wrote an article in the *New England Journal of Medicine* about balancing a position of "no blame" with personal accountability in patient safety.[9]

The "no blame" position gained prominence with the watershed Institute of Medicine's 1999 report *To Err is Human*, which launched the modern patient-safety movement and has spawned improvement initiatives across the country. The report's main theme is still true, write Wachter and Pronovost. Most errors are innocent slips by well-meaning practitioners. Individual blame is counterproductive. System defects and error-prone situations should be corrected to minimize the harm of errors. For example, illegible handwriting needn't cause harm because computerized, drug order systems can catch medication errors before they reach patients. The rate of surgical complications and bloodstream infections from catheters can be slashed by implementing simple process checklists.

But sometimes doctors who know about safe practices still ignore them, posing real risk to patients. In those cases, we need mandates with penalties for noncompliance, Wachter and Pronovost argue. As an example, they point to hand hygiene, simply washing one's hands before touching a patient, a proven preventer of hospital-acquired infections. A decade ago, rates of hand hygiene in most American hospitals were often below 20 percent. Today, despite a decade of informational campaigns, hand-gel dispensers placed in or near every patient's room and even financial incentives, most hospitals continue to have hand-hygiene rates that range only from 30 percent to 70 percent. That's no longer a systems problem, and doctors should be held accountable.

Other examples show that process improvements have failed to eradicate preventable errors. Programs in which surgeons write their initials on a patient's limb in advance of surgery — or take a time out in the operating room to go through a preoperative safety check — are proven ways to prevent wrong-side surgeries like operating on the wrong knee or amputating a diabetic's healthy foot, egregious errors that still occur about 4,000 times a year in the United States.

Many or most of the estimated 100,000 annual deaths from HAIs in the United States could be prevented by strict adherence to infection-control practices, including hand hygiene, note Wachter and Pronovost. "As long as transgressions carry no risk of penalty," they write, "some providers will ignore the rules," because they don't believe they're risking a patient's safety or don't believe the safety practice is effective or feel they are too busy to bother.

Here's their suggested prescription for doctors who habitually and willfully ignore proven safety practices despite education, counseling and systems improvements for important safety problems like poor hand hygiene. Chronic failure to clean hands? A one-week suspension from clinical practice, accompanied by completion of a two-hour online educational module on infection prevention. Failure to perform a "time-out" safety check before surgery or failure to mark a patient's surgical site to prevent wrong-site surgery? Mandatory corrective education and loss of operating-room privileges for two weeks. Persistent failure to adhere to the practice improvement after the initial penalty? Permanent loss of clinical privileges at that hospital for a doctor; firing for nurses and other employed hospital staff. Other options include stress management and other behavioral interventions for chronic offenders.

Accountability Also Means Saying You're Sorry

What should doctors and hospitals do when a patient is harmed by a medical mistake? Historically, they've kept quiet and tried to cover up the mistake for fear of being sued for medical malpractice. But the moral thing to do is to disclose errors to patients, apologize, offer to investigate what happened and be engaged in fixing the mistake. That kind of accountability honors the harmed patient and all future patients by potentially preventing a similar mistake from happening again. Counter-intuitively, it may also lower medical liability (malpractice) costs for doctors and hospitals.

Patients respond more favorably to doctors who apologize and accept responsibility for medical errors than to those who do not apologize or give ambiguous responses, according to Albert Wu, MD, MPH, associate professor of health policy and management at the Johns Hopkins Bloomberg School of Public Health.[10] Wu has spent years researching the effects of medical-error disclosure and apology. What he's learned is that patients who are harmed by medical errors generally want to learn what happened, know someone accepts responsibility and hear what steps are being taken to prevent future similar incidents. They also want an apology.

Patients describe the experience of previously friendly and forthcoming physicians and nurses suddenly clamming up after a bad outcome for a patient, and they find this very chilling and distressing, says Wu. The most common reason for lawsuits appears to be patients' desire to get some kind of information about a bad outcome when that information is not forthcoming through official channels.

Doctors can try to sweep medical mistakes under the rug and hope no one notices. If the mistake is discovered, though, patients will likely be angry; lawsuits will be filed seeking punitive damages; and coverage in the press is likely to mention the word "cover-up" rather prominently, says Wu. Most of us would think that apology is tantamount to an admission of guilt, but patients do not seem to see it that way. Wu doesn't think there has ever been a case at Johns Hopkins where the fact that the doctor apologized wound up figuring into a lawsuit, and if it did, it was only to the positive: patients who observed that the doctor was honest, sincere and seemed to understand that they had suffered, actually thought better of the doctor as a result.

Wu says he believes that apologies are part of treating the patient with the respect and compassion that he or she deserves. Patients have the right to learn about mistakes made in their care, and doctors at the hospital are obligated to disclose these events to patients and families. These disclosures, paradoxically, can actually improve the doctor-patient relationship.

How, then, should doctors and hospital officials tell patients and their families about incidents that harm them? Most physicians have never been trained in what to say. It's not likely to be taught in medical school. Seeing the need for a toolkit to help doctors prepare for these discussions, Wu produced an educational video in 2004. The video *Removing Insult from Injury: Disclosing Adverse Events* features short vignettes of doctors talking with patients to illustrate the best methods for disclosing medical errors. The vignettes describe real cases where patients were harmed and in which a doctor is disclosing to a patient what happened. One involves an overlooked mammogram and another a chemotherapy overdose, while a third shows a physician who is slow to answer pages about a hospitalized patient whose condition deteriorates as a result.

Wu says that doctors should initially tell the patient everything they know about what happened, no more and no less. The conversation might go something like this: "It looks like something bad has happened. We are not sure exactly what has occurred. We are looking into it, and we will let you know as soon as we find something out." While that kind of news is upsetting to get, the patient would feel like he or she was being appropriately informed and might be better able to cope with any resulting medical problems.

That initial discussion should take place as soon as the doctor learns that an adverse event occurred and can say something intelligent about it. The more that discussion occurs in real time, says Wu, the more it really becomes part of the normal discourse between doctor and patient, simply informing the patient about his or her condition, and the less it seems like something that ought to merit a malpractice suit. The longer a doctor delays and withholds information, the more he or she is uncomfortable, Wu believes, and it becomes more evident to the patient that something is amiss, not just with his condition but with how he's being handled.

Successful formal apology systems have been put into place. A coalition of doctors, lawyers, insurers and patient advocates called The Sorry Works! Coalition was formed in 2005 and is dedicated to promoting full disclosure, apologies and compensation for medical errors.[11] If poor care causes a bad outcome or adverse event, the coalition says, the doctors and hospital (along with their medical malpractice insurer) should apologize to the patient or family, or both; admit fault; provide an explanation of what happened and how the hospital will ensure that the error is not repeated; and offer fair compensation. Attorneys representing the providers and plaintiffs usually negotiate the compensation, and the case is usually closed in a few months.

Does a program like Sorry Works! actually work? The coalition says it does and cites successful disclosure protocols upon which it is based, developed at the Veterans Affairs Hospital in Lexington, Kentucky, and replicated in other organizations such as the University of Michigan Health System.

The Lexington VA experience suggests that proactive investigation, full disclosure and even offering to settle early for a reasonable restitution amount when it seems appropriate are likely to produce good outcomes for patients. The Lexington VA saw its malpractice settlement and litigation costs sink over a seven-year period using the protocols, with an average payout of $16,000 per settlement, compared to the national VA average of $98,000 per settlement.[12]

Using a similar full-disclosure model, the University of Michigan Health System cut its number of pending lawsuits in half and reduced litigation costs per case from $65,000 to $35,000, resulting in annual savings of approximately $2 million in defense litigation bills.[13] Similar disclosure programs have worked well at places like Stanford University Medical Center; the National Naval Center in Bethesda, Maryland; Children's Hospitals and Clinics of Minnesota; and several Kaiser Permanente hospitals.

Accountability in healthcare is a multifaceted concept. A variety of well-designed mechanisms are available to hold doctors and hospitals accountable for the quality, safety and efficiency of the care they deliver. Transparency initiatives like hospital report cards should focus on risk data and be consumer friendly in design. They should be supplemented with mandates and penalties for doctors who willfully ignore proven and accessible safety enhancements in clinical care. And when something does go wrong, saying, "Sorry," works.

Reflection

As this book was being written, the government was actively bolstering the level of transparency and accountability on its Hospital Compare website by bringing together quality measures from various sources — such as CMS, AHRQ and CDC — in a way that the public can really understand. Uncle Sam is into the act now, bringing together these disparate data streams. Key information is finally all there in a searchable, easy-to-understand, well-presented format.

What must happen next, we believe, is to connect this new accountability to the payment process. Under healthcare reform, we believe this will happen. — *S.K. and D.B.N.*

Notes

1. Thomas M. Burton. "Hospitals Find Way to Make Care Cheaper-Make It Better," *Wall Street Journal*, November 8, 2009.

2. Robert M. Wachter and Kaveh Shojania, *Internal Bleeding: The Truth Behind America's Terrifying Epidemic of Medical Mistakes* (New York: Rugged Land, 2004).

3. Arnold M. Epstein. "Rolling Down the Runway: The Challenges Ahead for Quality Report Cards," *Journal of the American Medical Association*, 1998; 279(21):1691-1696.

4. Christopher Guadagnino, PhD. "Appraising PHC4's Infection Report," *Physician's News Digest*, January, 2007. Available online at: http://www.physiciansnews.com/cover/107pa.html.

5. Christopher Guadagnino, PhD. "Physician Report Card Validity," *Physician's News Digest*, April, 2008. Available online at: http://www.physiciansnews.com/cover/408.html.

6. Judith H. Hibbard, Jean Stockard, and Martin Tusler. "Hospital Performance Reports: Impact on Quality, Market Share, and Reputation." *Health Affairs*, 2005; 24(4): 1150-1160.

7. Joint Commission Sentinel Event Alert, Issue 25, January 25, 2006. *Medication Reconciliation*. Available online at: http://www.jointcommission.org/sentinelevents/sentineleventalert/sea_35.htm.

8. The Joint Commission. "Medication Reconciliation National Patient Safety Goal to Be Reviewed, Refined," March 5, 2010. Available online at: http://www.jointcommission.org/PatientSafety/NationalPatientSafetyGoals/npsg8_review.htm.

9. Robert M. Wachter and Peter J. Pronovost. "Balancing 'No Blame' with Accountability in Patient Safety," *New England Journal of Medicine*, 2009: 361(14):1401-1406.

10. Christopher Guadagnino, PhD. "Effects of Medical Error Disclosure and Apology," *Physician's News Digest*, February, 2005. Available online at: http://www.physiciansnews.com/spotlight/205.html.

11. As described on the organization's website: www.sorryworks.net.

12. Doug Wojcieszak, John Banja, MD, Carole Houk, JD. "The Sorry Works! Coalition: Making the Case for Full Disclosure," *The Joint Commission Journal on Quality and Patient Safety*, 2006; 32(6):344-350.

13. Ibid.

MYTH BUSTER 4:

Next Generation Pay-for-Performance

"Pay-for-performance models offer small drips of money on top of an existing payment system that doesn't give us the quality we want. It is not sustainable as a business model and is transitional, at best."

"We were astonished, however, to see in the data (such as that associated with diabetes) how much improvement there might be in payment to physicians in particular, especially those in primary care, when science-based care is adequately compensated... These dollars would permit primary-care physicians to support the kinds of infra-structure, communications and interactions they need to help patients be compliant and engaged in their care and avoid the very complications the Prometheus Payment model seeks to prevent. The current system does not accommodate these efforts at all; but if what we have designed were widely adopted, the savings to the system in terms of all dollars spent would be enormous."

– Alice G. Gosfield, JD,
first Chairman of the Board of Prometheus Payment Inc.

[Alice G. Gosfield, JD, first chairman of the board of Prometheus Payment Inc. Quoted by Christopher Guadagnino, PhD, in "Bundled Payment Reform," *Physician's News Digest*, January, 2009.]

[Alice G. Gosfield, JD, "Making Prometheus Payment Rates Real: Ya' Gotta Start Somewhere," Prometheus Payment Inc., June, 2008.]

The health maintenance organizations (HMOs) got it partially right in the 1990s. The capitation model, which pays primary-care physicians a fixed amount each month for whatever type or quantity of services they give a patient, was designed to prevent overuse of tests and healthcare services while encouraging physicians to keep their patients healthy. But capitation was interpreted in the marketplace as "deny service." Once physicians got hold of the deny-service argument, they poisoned the well by telling patients, "My hands are tied. I can't give you an MRI because the mean managed care company won't let me." A massive backlash against HMOs followed.

Choice and more choice: that's our mantra when it comes to medical care. We hate HMOs because they restrict our choice of physicians and sometimes of care. HMOs slowed medical cost spikes a bit in the 1990s, but marketplace demand for less restrictive health plans have pushed HMOs to the back of the bus, where they account for less than a quarter of nationwide health-plan enrollment, while the HMOs themselves have loosened their cost-squeezing grip.

Here we are in the 2010s, with a healthcare system that is still trying to figure out ways to spur efficiency, effectiveness and safety. Our reimbursement system is still largely based on fee-for-service, paying more for greater volume and intensity of care. That continues to corrupt physicians' medical decision-making: when faced with clinical uncertainty, the natural thing to do is order more tests and services in the hope that they are appropriate and effective.

That's an easy equation to remember, and no provider forgets it. But erring on the side of more care remains an expensive and potentially dangerous problem. Can't physicians simply follow what evidence says is the best treatment approach for a given patient? Reminding physicians when they aren't following the available science does not work; physicians have plenty of reasons why they insist on doing things their way despite the evidence.

As third-party payors, health insurers that take our money and write the checks for physicians and hospitals are fully aware of this challenge. They know firsthand that unexplained clinical variation drives tremendous waste and overutilization of medical resources. It costs them a bundle. Like a mountain with no summit in sight, medical-care costs continue to rise each year, forcing insurers to continually raise premiums and explain to their customers each year why their coverage is going to cost 10, 20 or 30 percent more than last year. Medicare faces that same cost mountain, further eroding the national budget.

Will Paying More Produce Better Quality?

What are payors doing about it? They're trying plenty, but their efforts are not enough. Unexplained clinical variation remains rampant, and ineffective care is costing billions of dollars. Payors are trying to sweeten physicians' and hospitals' paychecks to inject a bit more quality, safety and efficiency into their care. They have embraced a form of bribery known as "pay-for-performance" (P4P) to try to get physicians and hospitals to do the right thing.

Here's how it works: "Dear physician, if you prove to us that you follow these proven clinical processes for good care or achieve this level of successful outcomes for your patients, we'll reward you with a little extra money." Sometimes payors supplement the carrots with sticks, like withholding some money if providers commit avoidable errors.

Who can argue with such an approach? Payors ante up to prove to their customers that they care about quality; physicians and hospitals make a little more money; and patients get better care. The P4P concept is rapidly evolving, and new initiatives are cropping up around the country. We'll take a look at some of them in this section.

But we believe it's not enough, that P4P is a bandage on a gushing wound. Physicians' practice patterns are notoriously difficult to change. Most P4P incentives tend to be too weak. Research demonstrates that at least 20 percent of a physician's annual income needs to be on the table to motivate him or her to change practice patterns. Most P4P programs don't come close.

The chief driver of wasteful and harmful clinical variation still remains: a piecework reimbursement system that rewards more care and more intense care. P4P programs are grafted onto that dysfunctional payment system.

Another glaring problem is fragmented care, and it continues to pose a huge challenge. It's partly the price we pay for the deeply embedded culture of autonomy in physician training. It's partly the hierarchical pecking order in clinical practice among surgeons, specialists, primary-care physicians, nurses, physician assistants, pharmacists, physical therapists and others. Does it make sense to think that paying each of these caregivers separately, even with P4P bonuses, will reduce miscommunication, waste and error stemming from poor coordination among them?

P4P tinkers on the edges of these problems. We believe that P4P is a transitional model to a more fully integrated payment approach. If we're serious about encouraging physicians and hospitals to curtail unexplained practice variation, to practice evidence-based medicine when guidelines exist, to closely examine and improve their practice patterns and to behave as an interdependent clinical team, we're going to need to bundle their payments somehow.

That means tying together payment for physicians, hospitals and other caregivers so that they are jointly motivated to get patients' care right, catch errors, work cooperatively and track whether what they did worked. Some sort of bundled payment approach essentially gives a fixed amount of money to all providers involved in a patient's care and tells them to divvy it up.

It goes something like this: "Here's what the evidence says effective heart-attack care will cost. Here's a basket of money; you all share it the way you see fit. It covers everything that science says a patient needs to recover, including surgery, anesthesia, drugs, medical devices, nurse and physician assistant services, hospital facility costs and follow-up care for 60 days after your patient is discharged from the hospital. We've factored in your patient's age and how sick he was before his heart attack.

"We've thrown in a chunk of extra money, on top of what the evidence says is required to do all of these things, because we realize that not all patients respond alike in real life, despite similarities on paper. If you work cooperatively and do your best as a care team, your patient may get better sooner and you can all come out ahead and make a profit. Remember, it's now in your best financial interest to coordinate your activities with one another and to do all you can to prevent your patient from having to come back to the hospital with avoidable complications."

P4P incentive programs are proof that our healthcare payment system is becoming more sophisticated, but they must ultimately be folded into some form of bundled payment structure to fully transform the quality and efficiency of our healthcare. That transformation has also begun, as we'll see.

Sticks and Carrots for Hospitals

Every so often you read about a medical error that defies credulity. A surgeon amputates a patient's healthy leg instead of the one he's supposed to. A patient suffers massive infection from a sponge accidentally left in her abdomen after surgery. The federal government has finally learned that paying for the consequences of medical errors makes no sense and is doing something about it.

In late 2008, the Centers for Medicare & Medicaid Services (CMS) stopped paying hospitals for treating certain medical complications that should have been prevented. Now that hospitals must pay for the consequences of these preventable errors, they're on the hot seat to repair broken care processes that cause them. CMS's "will not pay" list includes things like objects inadvertently left in after surgery, severe pressure ulcers (bed sores), surgical site infections, urinary-tract infections caused by catheters and pneumonia caused by ventilators. The list continues to expand. The perverse thing is that hospitals, until now, had been paid all along to treat patients for these preventable mistakes.

Medicaid programs (which pay for healthcare services to the poor) and commercial insurance companies in several states have seen the light and are also beginning to penalize hospitals for poor quality care. Time will tell how much of a dent this "no more reward for poor performance" policy will make in preventable hospitalized-patient complications.

CMS is wielding more sticks to prod hospital quality improvement. It withholds a hospital's full Medicare payment unless hospitals report quality performance data on more than seventy standardized measures, including various medical conditions (heart attack, health failure, chronic lung disease, pneumonia, adult diabetes and chest pain), surgical procedures, patient readmission rates and several other quality and safety indicators. We'll have to wait and see what CMS does with this information. It is making some of it available to consumers. Some form of P4P program can't be far down the road.

CMS wants to add a heavier stick, one that is causing quite a buzz within the hospital community: withholding Medicare reimbursement for preventable readmissions. That means, if a hospital discharges a patient after heart surgery, but a couple of weeks later he or she has to go back into the hospital because of an infection that could have been prevented, the hospital eats the cost of the follow-up care. The trick is determining what's preventable and what's not. That battle is being waged right now among stakeholders. There's a lot at stake, and those extra reimbursements mean a lot of money on the line for hospitals.

CMS is also in the carrot business. It continues to pilot a P4P incentive program with 230 hospitals that it began back in 2003. The hospitals (who all volunteered for the program) must adhere to proven quality measures when they care for patients with heart attack, heart failure, pneumonia, coronary-artery bypass graft and hip and knee replacements. Medicare pays high-performing hospitals bonus payments of up to two percent and penalizes poor performers with one percent lower payments.[1]

Unless participation in such a program becomes mandatory, good hospitals may self-select into it while poorer performers, the real targets for change, would be reluctant to participate. CMS said it would take that possibility into account as it evaluates the program, and it has proposed that Congress extend the program nationally. We'll have to wait and see what kind of traction it has.

Some private insurers are also adopting the hospital P4P concept. They're paying bonuses to hospitals that do things like lower mortality (patient death) and readmission rates, minimize hospital-acquired infections, reduce surgical complications, use proven quality checklists for treating ICU patients, have physicians use computerized (and less error-prone) drug ordering systems and meet certain nurse-to-patient staffing ratios. Give heart-attack patients aspirin when they enter the ER, and give them a blood pressure-reducing beta blocker when they leave the hospital. These are practices that are proven to save lives. Prove that you do it, and earn more money.

But because these hospital P4P programs are voluntary, insurers have to be "easy graders" to encourage hospitals to participate.

Below-average performers still get some reimbursement increase, while superior performers get a little more, and most hospitals have a very good chance of scoring in the middle of the range. We still need to encourage skittish hospitals to come to the carrots, it seems.

Carrots for Physicians

Physicians are getting into the P4P game too, as private insurers like Blue Cross Blue Shield, Aetna, UnitedHealth and others have begun rewarding them for adhering to nationally vetted best-practice guidelines that promote efficient and superior care.

The longest-standing type, actually going back more than a decade, offers bonuses to primary-care physicians who are paid a flat monthly rate, called capitation, to provide all healthcare services to HMO patients. Because that capitation payment is blind to outcomes or quality, insurers have supplemented it with bonuses for following guidelines such as the Health Care Effectiveness Data and Information Set (HEDIS) measures, developed by the National Committee for Quality Assurance (NCQA). Meet a measure's target performance level, like asthma medication use or high blood pressure control, and earn a bonus.

CMS's P4P first experiment for physicians, launched in 2005, involved ten large practices (each with at least 200 physicians) and combined traditional fee-for-service Medicare payments with a bonus pool accumulated from any savings that physicians could squeeze by better managing their patients' healthcare needs. Practices were rewarded for meeting clinical performance standards for treating diabetes, congestive heart failure, coronary artery disease, hypertension and cancer screening.

Physician improvement was modest. Physicians' quality scores increased between one percent and 11 percent over the project's three years, depending on the measure.[2] CMS has launched the experiment again and is currently testing it on small and solo physician practices in California, Arkansas, Massachusetts and Utah.

The next challenge is to expand these programs nationally. As a prelude to a nationwide Medicare P4P physician program, in 2007 CMS launched the Physician Quality Reporting Initiative (PQRI), a "pay-for-reporting" program. It pays financial bonuses (currently two percent of their annual Medicare reimbursement) to physicians and other healthcare providers who report from a list of about 180 quality measures on their Medicare patients. The measures include things like diabetes mellitus, chronic kidney disease, preventive care, coronary-artery bypass graft, rheumatoid arthritis, back pain, hepatitis C, heart failure and community-acquired pneumonia.[3]

The quality metrics cover a gamut of medical conditions. For example, what percentage of a physician's patients aged 18 through 75 years with diabetes mellitus had their most recent hemoglobin A1c (blood sugar level) greater than 9.0 percent (indicating poor control)? What percentage of patients aged 50 years and older and treated for a hip or spine fracture had documented communication from their physician that a fracture occurred and that the patient was or should be tested or treated for osteoporosis? What percentage of patients aged 50 years and older with a diagnosis of osteoporosis was pre-scribed drug therapy within 12 months? What percentage of female patients aged 65 years and older was assessed for the presence or absence of urinary incontinence within 12 months?

In 2008, CMS says, the average bonus payment to individual physicians and other healthcare professionals was just over $1,000. That was for reporting their performance on the measures. CMS may soon convert the PQRI to a P4P program.[4]

CMS has also launched a program offering a two percent incentive payment (of the practice's total Medicare reimbursement for the year) to physician practices that prescribe drugs with a computer instead of writing them by hand on paper pads. Electronic prescribing systems are proven to reduce prescribing errors by alerting physicians about a patient's medication history and possible adverse events such as improper dosing, drug-to-drug interactions and allergy concerns. A physician who successfully reports under both this and the PQRI initiatives could receive up to a four percent pay boost from Medicare in a year.[5]

Still No Proof

We have begun to address quality and safety gaps in our healthcare delivery system with programs like these, and that is a tremendously important accomplishment. It puts a national spotlight on healthcare quality and patient safety. It stimulates physicians and hospitals to think about their practices. It may even promote some meaningful change.

But it's hard to know whether P4P programs are capable of driving the magnitude of improvement that we desperately need. Will P4P curtail waste, decrease the unwarranted use of medical services and improve efficiencies in care delivery? Frankly, not many performance measures address overuse.

Are P4P incentives sufficiently powerful to motivate physicians to deliver appropriate care? That's also hard to know. Research findings on this question are mixed, showing either modest influence or no additional influence over physicians not getting P4P bonuses; a recent Rand Corporation analysis bears this out.[6] Because the same P4P measures are often also part of other quality-improvement programs, like accreditation requirements and public reporting initiatives, it's tough to disentangle the net effects of P4P incentives.

How much of a bonus do you have to pay a physician to make significant changes in his or her practice patterns? A lot more than P4P currently offers, it would seem. P4P experiments thus far tend to use relatively small annual financial incentives (approximately $1,500 to $5,000 per physician). Health services research suggests the magic number needs to approach 20 percent of a physician's annual income, or $30,000 for a primary-care physician who earns $150K a year.

P4P could also produce unintended consequences. Appropriate care guidelines can paradoxically spur physicians to deliver inappropriate care, like prescribing aspirin to all hypertensive patients, in order to earn the bonus (some patients don't take well to aspirin). Physicians may neglect other important aspects of care by fixating on the incentivized measures to improve their overall quality scores.

P4P incentives may create perverse incentives for physicians to "game the system" — perhaps by sending the sickest congestive-heart failure patients to other physicians or by reporting only four diagnoses when a patient actually has five — to achieve the best P4P profile. We don't know if these things happen, but P4P skeptics have raised these issues as concerns.

"Next Generation" P4P: Bundled Payment

Then there is the serious problem of our pernicious payment system, which P4P incentives don't wipe away. Physicians continue to get paid for volume and intensity of care. They don't get paid to coordinate their activities with other caregivers inside and outside the hospital.

Hospitals do have some incentive to get patients out of the hospital quickly. Since the early 1980s, Medicare and some private insurers have used a payment scheme known as diagnosis-related groups, or DRGs, which had been hoped to squeeze more efficiency out of hospitals. The approach is essentially a patient classification scheme of about 500 kinds of hospital cases, with payments that reflect the average cost of treating patients with particular diagnoses — a head injury, a heart condition, pneumonia — in an efficient hospital. The hospital makes money by getting patients well quickly and loses money on patients that end up costing more to treat than the average amount for their condition.

Although the DRG system did slow the rate of Medicare's cost growth somewhat in its early years, the system tends to overpay for certain procedures, particularly expensive surgeries such as cardiac bypass. How did hospitals respond? Rationally: they invested heavily in these services with high margins that could bring in 30, 40 or 50 percent more money than the hospital's cost of providing them. Cardiac catheterization labs sprang up like daisies. A heart-attack patient comes to the emergency room and evidence-based guidelines say drug treatment alone is called for. Or, the hospital can earn a 40 percent profit by performing an angioplasty. The incentive is problematic.

Meanwhile, physicians get paid separately, on an a la carte basis, for the services they provide to patients in the hospital. The invasive cardiologist will get paid for performing the angioplasty. Heart surgery is big business.

Then there's the coordination problem. When a patient is hospitalized, say, for a hip replacement or heart operation, they will be handed off several times from physician to physician across multiple care settings — emergency room, operating room, intensive care unit, hospital ward, rehabilitation unit — for their "episode" of care. They will be seen by various physicians, nurses, therapists, pharmacists, hospital discharge planners and other people important to their recovery.

Handoffs between these caregivers are dangerous moments in healthcare, when serious "voltage drops" in information occur. The patient's next physician has no details about that CT scan he or she recently received, so another one is ordered. The patient is sent up to the seventh floor of the hospital, while his records somehow didn't make it there and have to be hunted down.

Hospitals are trying to get better at patient handoffs through their own internal quality-improvement programs. But think of the sheer number of patients involved: thousands a day in the larger hospitals. The problem remains huge and there's still no potent financial incentive to accelerate improvement. There has to be a better way to spur better coordination among all of a patient's caregivers.

Enter bundled payment, an incentive structure designed to align the incentives of all involved. Bundled payment in some form, we believe, represents the state of the art in leveraging the highest quality care with the least wasteful duplication and variation in medical services. It's being tested by CMS, private insurers, large health systems and physician groups.

The core mechanism is simple: a single paycheck to be shared among various healthcare professionals in multiple settings for treating a specific condition over a specific period of time.

How much should that combined check be? That's an important and complex question. We're going to ask physicians, nurses, therapists, pharmacists and others to accept this amount as payment in full, and divvy it up as they see fit, for all of the healthcare services they'll provide to a patient with a specific illness, like a heart attack, for a specific time period, an "episode" of care. That episode might be defined, for example, as occurring from the time a heart-attack patient enters the hospital to 30 days after he or she is discharged from the hospital.

So, what's the right amount of money to win buy-in of participants and encourage them to improve quality and trim waste? We have to study a mountain of medical claims and patient records to figure out the historic cost of that heart-attack care. We have to scour the medical literature for the best guidelines and consult with clinical experts to reach consensus on which ones to use. We have to figure out what kind of healthcare services the evidence says a patient needs for heart-attack treatment and set an equitable flat fee to cover those services. That fee needs to be adjusted upward for sicker patients (like those who have a lot of other illnesses) and downward for patients with fewer co-morbidities.

The single bundled payment covers the entire array of healthcare services by multiple providers, including the hospital facility, physicians, laboratories, imaging centers, pharmacies and even follow-up office visits. Everyone has a vested financial interest in quality and efficiency, getting care right the first time, because they won't be paid extra for procedures that don't work. They will all lose money from errors, patient complications and patients coming back to the hospital because something went wrong.

Patients can be tracked after their hospital stay to determine whether the (now collaborative) care actually prevented short- and longer-term complications and duplication of services. The model employs evidence-based guidelines, allowing for incentive payments for significant quality improvements and savings for less wasteful and more efficient care. Advocates of this payment model call it "next-generation P4P." It's here now.

CMS actually tested global payment in the early to mid-1990s for heart-bypass surgery with some success. Medicare spent about 10 percent less on heart-bypass operations at seven participating hospitals than was expected without bundled payment, while quality of care remained high. But that was the 1990s, and some providers objected to a government program designating some providers as higher quality than others and paying them differently. As a result, follow-up experiments with bundled payment were delayed.

CMS has taken up the charge again with a bundled payment pilot program launched last year in Texas, Oklahoma, New Mexico and Colorado: the Acute Care Episode (ACE) demonstration. A lump sum (global) payment will be shared among physicians and hospitals for orthopedic procedures (like hip and knee replacement surgery), cardiovascular procedures (like cardiac bypass) and inpatient surgical procedures (like coronary-artery bypass graft surgery, cardiac-valve replacement surgery, cardiac-pacemaker implantation and replacement, cardiac-defibrillator implantation and coronary-artery angioplasty).[7]

ACE demonstration sites have the option to pay a bit more from the lump payment to individual clinicians, teams of clinicians or other hospital staff who demonstrate measurable improvement in clinical quality and efficiency. CMS expects to pay less for the conditions treated under bundled payment and says it will share a portion of any savings with Medicare patients themselves, up to about $1,000. That's a carrot to encourage patients to participate (and yes, it's subject to federal, state and other income taxes).

To see what kinds of innovations care teams come up with, CMS will be watching closely for things like ensuring that antibiotics are provided before surgery and discontinued at the proper interval, 30-day readmission and mortality rates and other measures.

That's the federal government side, but will bundled payment work in the private sector as well? It already is. The Robert Wood Johnson Foundation has granted $6.4 million to pilot a bundled-payment model developed by the not-for-profit corporation Prometheus Payment Inc. The model is focusing not only on surgical procedures, but on care of chronic illness as well. Prometheus's initial list of medical conditions is impressive: hip and knee replacement, coronary-artery bypass graft (CABG) surgery, cardiac catheterization, bariatric surgery, hernias, congestive heart failure, chronic obstructive pulmonary disorder, asthma, coronary-artery disease and hypertension.[8]

Prometheus combines clinical practice guidelines with an evidence-based budget for what it historically takes to deliver optimal services for a particular condition. It adjusts the payment for how sick the patient is and covers all of the caregivers who treat that patient for that condition (for example, heart surgery).

A hospital and caregiver team decides among themselves who will provide what services within an episode of care. Providers decide how to configure themselves. Physician groups may join with hospitals, therapy providers, imaging facilities or any other entity with whom they think collaboration would be worthwhile to achieve better results for patients and better payment for themselves. They approach a private health plan and strike a deal to provide those services under an evidence-informed case rate contract. Those providers can also have traditional reimbursement arrangements with the insurer for some patients, so the model needn't replace the old system overnight.

The contract sets aside a bonus pool to reward providers who adhere to practice guidelines, achieve target performance levels on clinical process and outcome measures and produce high levels of patient satisfaction. It's like having P4P built in.

If they reduce the number of avoidable complications in a patient's care, the participating providers can earn sizable monetary savings. We currently pay dearly for potentially avoidable complications. According to Prometheus, upwards of 30 percent of all the fee-for-service payments for heart attacks and 60 percent of payments for diabetes care is spent on these complications.[9] Think about those numbers for a moment. They are staggering. The contracted evidence-informed case rate builds in some money to allow for complications, roughly half of the amount historically associated with treating a given type of illness. If providers can collaborate to avoid those complications, they stand to pocket a lot of money, certainly a lot more than the small payment incentives under most current P4P models.[10]

The centerpiece of the model is that it creates an explicit incentive for clinical collaboration among independent providers and practitioners. Here's how it works. A physician who adheres to best-practice guidelines and achieves good outcomes will achieve a high performance score. Seventy percent of that score is based on what he or she did, while the remaining 30 percent of the score is tied to what other providers treating that patient did. Effective collaboration is rewarded. The model has built in a feedback loop, issuing performance reports so providers can modify their behavior for better results.

Under the existing payment system, physicians have actually been penalized for innovative improvements that made care more efficient. For example, when orthopedic surgeons created minimally invasive knee and shoulder surgery using cameras and scalpels inserted through small incisions via catheter tubes, a five-day hospital stay became a two-day stay, and the only thanks that surgeons got from the traditional reimbursement system was a reduction in payment. Under bundled payment, any quality and efficiency improvements that save money, get poured back into the pot to be directly distributed among the hospital, surgeons, anesthesiologists, pathologists, radiologists, medical consultants, post-acute care providers and home care and rehab professionals.

Bundled Payment Seems to Work

The bundled payment model is actually working. Let's look at two examples, both from integrated health systems, in which the same company owns the insurance company, the hospital and the physicians (by employing them).

Geisinger Health System has been in the news a lot recently. When President Obama pushed Washington to focus on healthcare reform in 2008, he used Geisinger as an example in his speeches, calling it a model for high-quality care at lower than average costs.

Not-for-profit Geisinger serves approximately 2.6 million people living in 43 counties of northeastern and central Pennsylvania. It's testing a bundled payment model for specialty care. Ronald Paulus, MD, is the system's chief technology and innovation officer.

Geisinger used to charge for elective coronary-artery bypass graft (CABG) surgery the way most hospitals do: separate bills for the hospitalization, for surgeon and other physician fees and for follow-up care, including care for complications.

Beginning in February, 2006, Geisinger began charging for elective CABG surgery very differently: a single, bundled case rate covers every service the patient needs, starting from his or her visit to the physician that triggered the decision to have surgery through 90 days following the surgery, Paulus explains.[11] The bundled rate also covers all related complications, hospital readmissions and follow-up care during that time interval.

There's also an agreement jointly signed by the patient and clinician before surgery that outlines the patient's commitment to communicate with healthcare team members, to involve his or her family in care, to adhere to medications and other important care steps and to follow appropriate follow-up and preventive care. Geisinger calls the program "ProvenCare." The press has dubbed it surgery with a warranty.

Geisinger has since extended ProvenCare to eight interventions: CABG surgery, hip replacement, cataract surgery, bariatric surgery (stomach reduction), percutaneous angioplasty (using catheters to unblock vessels), spine surgery for low back pain, erythropoietin management (hormone that controls red blood cell production) and perinatal care (pregnancy).

Chronic disease care is on the horizon, as Geisinger hopes to develop ProvenCare programs for the most common ones, like diabetes, coronary-artery disease, congestive heart failure and kidney disease.

The model works this way. Clinical workgroups (the initiative was largely led by physicians) select evidence-based guidelines and craft workflow processes with specific "who is accountable for what" points in the process. For elective CABG surgery, Geisinger clinicians use 40 process steps from the American Heart Association and the American College of Cardiology guidelines for cardiac surgery. These steps are used for every patient to eliminate unwarranted practice variation, as well as to ensure that the surgery is, in fact, the most appropriate intervention for a particular patient.

Physicians reached full compliance with the guidelines within a few months. That's an important accomplishment. Paulus says translating scientific evidence into process steps gets patients all the things that they need and none of the things that they don't need during a care encounter.[12] ProvenCare employs a multidisciplinary team-based approach in which physicians, nurses, pharmacists and other care team members carefully coordinate their care. It hard-wires practice guidelines into the care process with an electronic health record infrastructure so clinicians don't rely on individual heroism or goodwill or memory to see that these right things get done.

Geisinger tracks performance metrics and gives providers timely feedback to stimulate learning and improvement. This is the right recipe for effective healthcare delivery, and similar models are being implemented by health systems around the country, like Minnesota's Mayo Clinic, Salt Lake City's Intermountain Healthcare and California's Kaiser Permanente.

The model appears to be working, as physicians have improved patients' outcomes for elective CABG surgery. Here are results from the program's first 18 months: A 21 percent decrease in patients with any complications (from 38 percent to 30 percent). A 44 percent decrease in hospital readmissions within 30 days (from 6.9 percent to 3.8 percent). A 10 percent increase in patients discharged to their homes. A half-day reduction in length of hospital stay.[13] Pretty impressive.

If bundled payment can succeed in integrated health systems like Geisinger, can they work with private insurers and independent provider groups who don't all work for the same boss? Experiments are under way in other parts of the country, including Massachusetts, to prove that it can.

Since January, 2009, several hospitals and provider groups have signed on with Blue Cross Blue Shield of Massachusetts for a bundled payment arrangement using what the insurer calls an "alternative quality contract" (AQC). As of late November, 2009, Blue Cross reported that 20 percent of its provider network is now in the AQC, covering more than a quarter of the insurer's Massachusetts-based HMO members.

One of those provider groups is Atrius Health, an alliance of five community-based medical groups representing more than 800 physicians and more than 1,250 other health professionals in over 30 sites in eastern Massachusetts. In July, 2009, Atrius signed a five-year AQC covering more than 106,000 patients. The AQC combines two forms of payment: a global fixed payment per patient (adjusted for age, sex, health status and inflation) and substantial performance incentives tied to the latest nationally accepted measures of quality, effectiveness and patient experience of care.[14]

The contract's global payment covers all services the patient receives, including primary, specialty and hospital care, as well as ancillary, behavioral health and pharmacy services. That means when a physician spends more time with a patient and helps him or her avoid an unnecessary hospitalization, the patient receives better care, and the physician and hospital can receive performance incentives up to 10 percent above the global payment amount.

The contract is designed to pay for quality and appropriateness of care rather than volume, complexity and intensity of care. The financial incentives are designed to eliminate waste and overuse of resources, while a robust set of performance measures creates accountability for quality, safety and outcomes — like keeping patients' cholesterol levels low, or reducing the rate of blood clots and pneumonia after surgery.

Those performance measures are key features in the bundled payment model and safeguard against inappropriate under-treatment (for example, saving money by withholding appropriate services — the old charge against HMOs). The performance measures hold providers accountable for both the delivery of appropriate services and the good health outcomes of their patients. The physicians and hospitals signed on to the AQC are jointly accountable for the total quality and costs associated with each patient covered by the contract, counteracting any incentives to withhold necessary care.

Atrius physicians discuss clinical variation and ways to improve quality in the physician office and hospital settings. They close the feedback loop and refine the way they provide care. They reinvest the money they save through increased efficiency and reduced waste into further improvements — things like e-mail exchanges with patients (e-visits), group visits for patients who share a common chronic illness and follow-up home visits for patients after hospitalizations. In between office visits, physicians' staff contact patients to promote better nutrition, physical activity and compliance with taking their medicines. These preventive health interventions may not sound like rocket science, but they are absolutely huge opportunities to prevent illness.[15]

Think for a moment about the implications of this last piece. A tremendous chunk of our healthcare is currently devoted to treating maladies like diabetes, obesity and heart disease that we inflict upon ourselves through our lifestyle choices. Under our current healthcare payment system, effective preventive health intervention means that physicians and hospitals lose money because it takes time and energy; it is not reimbursed; and patients will start to need fewer tests, treatments, drugs and surgeries. That's truly a toxic incentive system. But alternatives like bundled payment are starting to change that.

Here is the direction in which we are headed. Physicians and hospitals will be rewarded for encouraging us to stay healthy and for teaching us how to stay healthy. We have to do our part, of course, but we will now have an influential coach and partner cheering us on, our physician, who will be paid to offer that help.

A fair and effective healthcare payment system is evolving that can give us the best and safest results from the most appropriate treatments, based on the best medical evidence, by the right kind of provider at the right time. That is a revolution in quality and safety improvement. It will drive a tremendous amount of waste out of our system. And it is already underway.

Reflection

Some of these early bundled payment models are working. Although getting bundled payment off the ground may be more difficult than we thought, aligning income with these models will make it happen at a quicker pace.

The Prometheus bundled payment approach may turn out to be a bellwether experiment that shows it can be done. Leading integrated-delivery systems, like Spectrum Health System in Grand Rapids, Michigan, are becoming beta sites for Prometheus. Early experience with Prometheus predicts that we can learn to coordinate healthcare services and align the incentives of various providers, especially if the payment system is aligned.

Healthcare reform will add a lot of fuel to this rocket. We've been tinkering around the edges up until now. Effective pay-for-performance, under healthcare reform, is really going to happen faster and with more income at stake than ever before.

– S.K. and D.B.N.

Notes

1. Christopher Guadagnino, PhD. "Payors Expand Quality Incentives," *Physician's News Digest*, November, 2003. Available online at: http://www.physiciansnews.com/cover/1103.html.

2. Center for Medicare & Medicaid Services. *Medicare Physician Group Practice Demonstration Fact Sheet*, August, 2009. Available online at: https://www.cms.gov/DemoProjectsEvalRpts/downloads/PGP_Fact_Sheet.pdf.

3. Christopher Guadagnino, PhD. "Physician Pay-for-Reporting Launched," *Physician's News Digest*, July, 2007. Available online at: http://www.physiciansnews.com/cover/707.html.

4. Centers for Medicare & Medicaid Services. "Overview: Physician Quality Reporting Initiative (PQRI)." Available online at: https://www.cms.gov/pqri/.

5. Centers for Medicare & Medicaid Services. "Overview: Electronic Prescribing (eRx) Incentive Program." Available online at: https://www.cms.gov/ERXIncentive/.

6. Rand Corporation. "Analysis of Physician Pay for Performance," *RAND COMPARE*. Available online at: http://www.randcompare.org/analysis-of-options/analysis-of-physician-pay-for-performance.

7. Centers for Medicare & Medicaid Services. "Details for Medicare Acute Care Episode (ACE) Demonstration." Available online at: http://www.cms.gov/demoprojectsevalrpts/md/itemdetail.asp?filterType=none&filterByDID=99&sortByDID=3&sortOrder=descending&itemID=CMS1204388&intNumPerPage=10.

8. Christopher Guadagnino, PhD. "Bundled Payment Reform," *Physician's News Digest*, January, 2009. Available online at: http://www.physiciansnews.com/wp-content/uploads/2009/01/pm_jan_lores.pdf.

9. Alice G. Gosfield, JD. "Making Prometheus Payment Rates Real: Ya' Gotta Start Somewhere," *Prometheus Payment Inc.-Robert Wood Johnson Foundation*, June, 2008. Available online at: http://www.gosfield.com/PDF/MakingItReal-Final.pdf.

10. Ibid.

11. Christopher Guadagnino, PhD, "Value-Based Clinical Innovation Projects," *Physician's News Digest*, October, 2007. Available online at: http://www.physiciansnews.com/spotlight/1008pa.html.

12. Ibid.

13. Geisinger, "ProvenCare by the Numbers." Available online at: http://www.geisinger.org/provencare/numbers.html.

14. Atrius Health. "Atrius Health and Blue Cross Blue Shield Sign Alternative Quality Contract," press release, July 20, 2009. Available online at: http://www.atriushealth.org/news/AlternativeQualityContract.asp.

15. Ibid.

MYTH BUSTER 5:

Training Team Captains for Patient-Centric Care

"Physicians must be dedicated to continuous improvement in the quality of care. This commitment entails not only maintaining clinical competence but also working collaboratively with other professionals to reduce medical error, increase patient safety, minimize overuse of healthcare resources and optimize the outcomes of care."

> – Joint Charter by the American Board of Internal Medicine (ABIM),
> the American College of Physicians — American Society of
> Internal Medicine and the European Federation of Internal Medicine.

"The clinical transaction — what happens between the physician and the patient — is the common thread in all of medicine. It is where art and science combine in the subtleties of a deeply personal, human interaction that has significance for patient satisfaction, competent healing and cost effective care."

> – Blue Ridge Academic Health Group.

[ABIM Foundation, American Board of Internal Medicine, ACP-ASIM Foundation, American College of Physicians-American Society of Internal Medicine, European Federation of Internal Medicine. "Medical Professionalism in the New Millennium: A Physician Charter," *Annals of Internal Medicine,* 2002; 136(3):243-246.]

[The Blue Ridge Academic Health Group. *Reforming Medical Education: Urgent Priority for Academic Health Centers in the New Century* (Atlanta: Robert W. Woodruff Health Sciences Center, 2003).]

Decades of evidence shows us that high-quality healthcare can and must cost less. The only way to reduce cost is by reducing waste. It must be true that if physicians order the right drug or treatment for the right patient, for the right indication and at the right dose, they will achieve a good outcome at a lower cost. The patient will leave the hospital sooner, will be happier and will tell ten potential patients about the positive experience they had at that institution.

Physicians need the proper skill set to achieve these goals. Unfortunately, despite their best intentions, physicians remain burdened with tremendously wasteful, unexplained clinical variation in their day-to-day practice. Most clinicians don't even recognize that a minority of their decisions at the bedside are based on solid Grade-A, randomized, controlled trial evidence. We know that autonomous physician decision-making, without solid evidence backing those decisions, leads to waste and a propensity for medical error. We also know that when evidence does exist, some physicians adhere to it and some don't. Our healthcare system gets a patient's care right about half of the time.

As we've seen thus far in this book, we need to do several things in tandem to address these problems: improve physician decision-making processes, deploy some kind of comparative effectiveness research, tie it to physician payment and combine pay-for-performance with bundling. We must also provide the right kind of training for physicians.

Physicians need a different skill set than they have today. We need a sea change in how we train tomorrow's physicians to help them build essential competencies that are now lacking. The model of physician as autonomous expert working in isolation from other caregivers is ineffective, wasteful and potentially dangerous. The culture of physician as autonomous expert must be unlearned.

The problem begins in medical school. We're using a 50-year-old medical education model to build the physician of the twenty-first century. A medical-school graduate who walks across that stage in May, 2010, will be in practice in May, 2040, possibly May, 2050. What will the world be like in May, 2040, and what will the physician of the future need to know?

A watershed report released by the Institute of Medicine ten years ago, "Crossing the Quality Chasm: A New Health System for the 21st Century," provides crucial direction. In that report, the IOM proposed a national healthcare-improvement agenda with six fundamental things that healthcare should be: safe, effective, patient-centered, timely, efficient and equitable.[1] Those six aims form a vision of what competencies tomorrow's physician must possess. But the report left us without a roadmap of how to achieve those aims.

What skill set, then, will tomorrow's physicians need to possess? They must put a premium on quality and safety. They must do a much better job of paying attention to their patient's preferences. They must focus on preventive care, rather than wait for patients to come to their offices in crisis. They must learn to coordinate care efficiently with other caregivers. Tomorrow's physicians will be quality-focused, patient-centered, team-oriented promoters of prevention and wellness.

Our physician-training system has begun to make some progress on those aims. As we noted in Part 1, Myth 5, the Accreditation Council for Graduate Medical Education's ACGME Outcome Project has begun requiring all accredited residency programs to incorporate six general competencies into their curricula: medical knowledge, patient care, professionalism, interpersonal and communication skills, systems-based practice, and practice-based learning and improvement.

Yes, this new competency-based training approach is encountering obstacles, like any disruptive innovation will. Curricula are already crowded; there are shortages of trained faculty; and many teachers and students are skeptical of the new training. But this new vision of medical professionalism is establishing a beachhead. Various teaching modalities, such as the use of simulated patients, are facilitating these goals. Innovative pilot projects, like the patient-centered medical home, are underway to reward physicians for practicing these competencies. A transformation of medical training and practice has already begun.

Learning to Practice Quality and Safety Improvement

Teaching a new set of skills to physicians faces onerous challenges, as we saw in Part 1, Myth 5. Our current medical training culture doesn't convince physicians to accept the lifelong need to monitor and improve their care delivery. Physicians learn by example that they are part of a hierarchical pecking order that prizes autonomy over collaboration and teaches that fallibility is shameful. Physicians are acculturated to believe that being held accountable for the quality and safety of their care is an affront to their personal autonomy, because in many ways it is.

That culture is gradually changing. The culture of personal autonomy is slowly being replaced by a new culture of accountability, which an expanding body of science proves will result in better, safer and more efficient patient care. Quality improvement is becoming a professional expectation for physicians.

In 2002, the American Board of Internal Medicine (ABIM), American College of Physicians — American Society of Internal Medicine and the European Federation of Internal Medicine released a Charter on Medical Professionalism,[2] a sort of professional creed that stated:

"Physicians must be dedicated to continuous improvement in the quality of care. This commitment entails not only maintaining clinical competence but also working collaboratively with other professionals to reduce medical error, increase patient safety, minimize overuse of healthcare resources and optimize the outcomes of care. Physicians must actively participate in the development of better measures of quality of care and the application of quality measures to assess routinely the performance of all individuals, institutions and systems responsible for healthcare delivery."

This expectation is resonating throughout our healthcare delivery system. We hear it from patients, from employers, from health insurers and from politicians. We also hear it from professional organizations like the American Medical Association and the Accreditation Council for Graduate Medical Education (ACGME), an accrediting agency that now requires residency programs to add things like interpersonal and communication skills, effective teamwork and personal practice improvement to their curricula. Residency programs are beginning to equip young physicians with the skills they will need to compete in today's (and tomorrow's) healthcare system, such as how to use information technology to track wellness data across their patient population and how to respond to adverse outcomes from medical errors.

Quality-improvement curriculum can be integrated throughout

medical school and residency training. Various training modalities are being used, including exercise-based discussions, video sessions followed by debriefing, simulations, case-based discussions and lectures. All are designed to train physicians for the current environment where medical errors, system shortcomings and report cards have become the norm.

Several residency training programs across the United States have begun to implement new curriculum spurred by ACGME's new quality-improvement requirements, and measure its impact. Preliminary results are encouraging. They show that quality improvement needn't be an anathema to young physicians, that it can be taught successfully and that it improves patient care.

The University of South Florida, for example, designed a residency-training program for surgical residents that combines lectures, role-playing and mentoring to reduce medical errors.[3] The training bore fruit. During the 18-month course of the study involving thirty-three residents, there were significant reductions in complications (from 26 to 18 per month, on average) and reductions in total numbers of errors (from 18.5 to 13.2 per month on average). Those differences reflected effective training.

Curiously, the researchers noted that residents may have reduced their surgical complication and error rates simply by virtue of being sensitized to the problem of surgical errors, which may have helped them consider causes and prevention strategies independent of the training. Whether it was because of the training itself or the increased vigilance it prompted, quality and safety of care improved. Error training in surgery works.

Preventable medication errors often occur when a patient is transferred from one care setting to another, such as being transferred from a hospital ward to the OR for surgery or being discharged from a hospital to a home or nursing setting. Patients admitted to a hospital commonly receive new medications or have changes made to their existing medications. A new medication regimen that is prescribed when a patient is discharged from the hospital may inadvertently omit needed medications that patients have been receiving for some time or may unintentionally duplicate existing medications. A process known as medication reconciliation tries to avoid such inconsistencies across transitions in care by reviewing the patient's complete medication regimen at the time of admission, transfer, and discharge and comparing it with the regimen being considered for the new setting of care.

Atlantic Health, a two-hospital health system in north central New Jersey, tested the effectiveness of using multidisciplinary teams (quality improvement, nursing, pharmacy and physician faculty) to teach medication reconciliation in their residency programs.[4]

The program was so successful that it led several Atlantic Health residency programs to change their medication-reconciliation protocols, such as putting a medication-reconciliation form in every patient chart before the resident sees a patient, making sure the chart information was accurate and up-to-date and making sure that family members got the information. Residents weren't allowed to perform a medical procedure unless they had a complete medication-reconciliation form for their patient.

As further testament to the effectiveness of the training, Atlantic Care has implemented changes throughout its entire health system, like providing wallet cards with medication lists for patients, families and staff; making pre-appointment telephone calls to patients reminding them to bring their current list of medications; and posting confidential Web pages to allow patients to track their medications online.[5] Needless to say, Atlantic Health now incorporates medication-reconciliation resident education into its new resident-orientation programs.

Teaching quality and safety improvement is possible. We expect that medical schools and residency programs will continue to expand their commitment to curricular reform and embrace more sophisticated methods of teaching quality and safety. Medical education is retooling slowly but appropriately. We view all of this as a fitting redefinition of medical professionalism.

Let's take a close look at three more essential competencies of tomorrow's physicians: delivering care that is patient-centered, promoting wellness in patient populations and practicing in a team-based manner.

Learning to Practice Patient-Centered Care

So much of healthcare delivery is currently designed for the convenience of providers instead of patients. Physician practices are organized by specialty type, often requiring patients to make multiple appointments for the same health problem. Physician's schedules are set according to their needs, while patients are kept waiting.

But patient-centered care means a lot more than convenient care. It means restoring a meaningful physician-patient relationship. One group of academic medicine experts known as the Blue Ridge Academic Health Group summed up nicely the importance of restoring the patient-physician relationship. Here's how they put it: "The clinical transaction — what happens between the physician and the patient — is the common thread in all of medicine. It is where art and science combine in the subtleties of a deeply personal, human interaction that has significance for patient satisfaction, competent healing and cost-effective care." [6]

The paternalistic model of physicians telling their patients, "Here's what's wrong with you. Take this pill," is yielding to one that encourages active involvement of patients in their care management. Empathetic listening and communication skills must become part of physician training.

The Institute of Medicine in its 2004 report, *Improving Medical Education: Enhancing the Behavioral and Social Science Content of Medical School Curricula*, noted that half of all causes of morbidity and mortality in the United States are linked to behavioral and social factors, and lamented that the medical profession has yet to successfully incorporate knowledge of psychological and social variables into standard medical practice.

"To make measurable improvements in the health of Americans," the report said, "physicians must be equipped with the knowledge and skills from the behavioral and social sciences needed to recognize, understand and effectively respond to patients as individuals, not just to their symptoms." The report noted that "communication skills, which are emphasized in the behavioral and social sciences, will assist physicians in building therapeutic relationships with their patients and increase the likelihood that patients will follow their advice."

Physicians are trained to focus on "what is the matter" with the human body and mind, as part of their bio-clinical education. But, "what matters" to the owner of the body and the mind may not be congruent with "what is the matter," for a number of reasons, says Dartmouth Medical School researcher and professor John Wasson, MD.[7]

For example, an overweight, prediabetic may never lose weight until he or she deals with the issues that are driving the overeating, including emotional issues. Only about 40 percent of diabetics who are overweight have confidence in managing their weight problem; 60 percent don't, says Wasson. Unless physicians are prepared to help their patients overcome their lack of confidence in losing weight, their patients aren't going to be able to improve.[8]

Being patient-centered therefore requires physicians to understand both "what is the matter" with the patient (for example, being diabetic and overweight) as well as "what matters" to the patient. Once physician and patient are on the same page, the physician can know how to give their patient the best information and support they need to better manage what matters to them and what is the matter with them.

"Merely telling someone they have a high body mass index, or prescribing insulin for hyperglycemia, will not result in as good an outcome in terms of diabetic control and weight reduction as providing the information and treatment in a context in which the patient can become confident in managing both the blood sugar and weight," says Wasson. Confidence is the key. Only about 25 percent of adult Americans strongly agree that they have received patient-centered collaborative care defined in this way, says Wasson.[9] We still have a long way to go.

Consider other examples, like the physician unaware that a patient has significant pain while encouraging the patient to be more active because he happens to have coronary artery disease. A large managed-care company in New York State asked Wasson and his colleagues to consult with them because a number of women were doing badly in their asthma management and the company didn't understand why. Wasson found that a third of the women were in domestic-abuse situations and were not quite as focused on their inhaler use as patients without such an obstacle.[10]

Wasson believes that the ultimate way physicians can find out what to do with patients is to find out how confident they are with self-management strategies and stratify their patients accordingly, regardless of disease. For example, when a patient says they are very confident (about 30 to 50 percent of typical patients rate themselves a nine or 10 on a 10-point scale) they usually do not need a lot of extra support.

Physicians can use assessment tools, such as C.A.R.E. Vital Signs, or www.HowsYourHealth.org, to help patients who lack confidence.[11] These tools ask patients to rate their pain and confidence levels so that physicians can follow up with them on the issues that matter most to them.

Newly minted physicians are beginning to emerge from their education with much stronger training in interpersonal communication skills than their mentors did, thanks to new and evolving curriculum and training opportunities. In Jefferson Medical College's "Medical Practice for the 21st Century" course, for example, first-year students role-play and critique each other's history-taking interviews, which include sensitive scenarios such as taking a sexual history and dealing with domestic violence abuse. When they enter residency training, new physicians are evaluated in clinical settings with real patients as to how well they interview, examine and counsel their patients, says Lindsey Lane, MD, former associate professor of pediatrics and director of undergraduate medical education at Jefferson Medical College.[12]

Medical schools also use "simulated patients," trained actors who role-play difficult scenarios, while students get coached on how to handle them, says Laurel Milberg, PhD, associate director of education for the University of Pittsburgh Institute for Physician-Patient Communication.[13] When the "patient" cries or expresses anger, for example, students are encouraged to resist the urge to recoil from the emotion or to try to talk the patient out of expressing it, and instead to "lean into" the emotion by saying something like, "It seems as though you are serious about how you feel," says Milberg.

Learning to Promote Wellness Systematically

Quality improvement and patient-centeredness are two crucial physician competencies that must come into the mainstream of medical education and training. A third key skill set physicians must learn is the ability to coordinate care efficiently and promote wellness proactively in their patient populations.

Effective wellness promotion requires physicians to move past the one-patient-at-a-time mindset, and to adopt a population health framework. We envision a rapid growth in the "mass customization" of clinical information to promote wellness in patient populations, and we believe physicians must become skilled in its techniques.

Mass customization is an industrial term. Recall Henry Ford's famous quote: "You can have any color you want, as long as it's black." Mass customization essentially means: Here's the Toyota Corolla; here are the ten colors you can choose and the three engines and the five accessory-package choices. They'll build you the basic Corolla and customize it to your needs.

Extend that analogy to clinical care. We envision the flow of information between physicians and patients in a broad scheme of mass customization of clinical information. For example, suppose that you're a general internist of the future, and in your medical practice are twenty-five teenagers who are brittle diabetics and who are in and out of the hospital because they refuse to take their insulin — which is a common problem with teenagers.

Mass customization means that you're going to have a special channel of communication just for that group, password protected, so they could log-on anytime to learn and listen and interact with you and your teammates in a different way from what we could possibly do today with a one-size-fits-all brochure or CD. You might engineer an e-mail push, on a daily basis, to warn your teenage diabetics about getting ketoacidosis if they don't take their insulin.

What kind of physician would you need to implement mass-customization techniques like that? You'd need somebody with teamwork training and leadership skills who is able to understand new fields and has data-analysis capabilities, really good communication skills, and some scientific and clinical understanding of diabetes. That's a totally different way of looking at physician education than we currently do. Promoting coordinated, preventive care among a population of patients runs counter to the way that most physician practices are currently organized. They're pretty much designed to treat each patient individually and not think across groups of patients.

A major campaign being tested around the country is designed to overcome these obstacles and reposition the doctor-patient relationship with the physician as the central care coordinator. It's called the patient-centered medical home. Medicare recently announced that it will climb aboard and support existing medical home partnerships between commercial health plans and physician groups.

The patient-centered medical home seeks to counteract the challenges facing the healthcare system today. There is a worsening shortage of physicians entering primary care. There are inequities and inefficiencies in the healthcare delivery and reimbursement system. There is lack of coordination of care among physicians that wastes money and endangers patients. Truly patient-centered care requires a fundamental shift in the relationship between patients and their primary-care physicians, who must help their patients navigate a fragmented healthcare system by forging a much higher level of personalized care coordination and access. This involves taking the time to learn patients' health-related needs beyond an acute-care episode, making the practice's resources more readily available to them, identifying key medical and community resources to meet their needs and following up closely to ensure those needs are met.

Fundamental to this medical-home model is a population-based approach to care management, ideally facilitated by an electronic-medical-record infrastructure, to identify those patients with chronic care and other special needs and to facilitate more proactive care management than is typically seen in the current system, like reminding diabetic patients to monitor their blood glucose level — before they have an emergency that requires a trip to the emergency room. These are among the competencies tomorrow's physicians are going to need.

Even a very basic medical-home model can achieve cost savings and quality enhancement. Look, for example, at North Carolina's Primary Care Case Management Medicaid program, in which every patient is matched with and given 24/7 access to a primary-care physician, along with locally based disease-management and nurse-educator support that is integrated with the physician practice. The state contributes about $20 million a year to reimburse physician practices for the extra care-coordination activities. In return, the program has led to improved outcomes for diabetics and asthmatics, and to a reduction in healthcare costs to the tune of $200 to $220 million per year.[14]

Physician practices around the country are testing this medical-home concept, and medical training is beginning to embrace its principles. For example, fourteen family-medicine residency programs around the country are involved in a six-year demonstration project called Preparing the Personal Physician for Practice Residency, which will study various ways to incorporate the concepts into residency education.

Patients with multiple chronic diseases probably need to get more care, not less, and if they got more care up front, they will probably need fewer hospital admissions and high-cost services that really strain the system, says Ronald Paulus, MD, Geisinger Health System's chief technology and innovation officer.[15] Geisinger Health System has an active medical-project for its primary-care physician practices, dubbed Personal Health Navigator. Yes, the number of patient office visits goes up, and pharmacy costs go up under the model, but that is more than compensated for by a decrease in hospital, nursing home, and other related costs, says Paulus. In preliminary data during the first year, Geisinger saw a 20 percent reduction in hospital admissions and readmissions, and a seven percent reduction in total medical spending.

Learning Team-Based Practice

We've looked at three core competencies that tomorrow's physician will need: quality improvement, patient-centeredness, and the ability to promote wellness proactively in their patient populations. The physician of tomorrow is also going to need to be skilled in teamwork through interdisciplinary education and training with nursing, pharmacy and other health professionals. We see the physician of 2040 as central to a command post and getting data feeds from team members who are experts in their own areas: the patient educator, the home-health aide, the community epidemiologist who notices an uptick in swine flu over the past four days, the nurse and the pharmacist. An expanding array of teamwork simulation exercises provide this kind of training.

We want to train a generation of "Sully" Sullenbergers, so that when they have to land that plane on the Hudson, they'll be able to do it. It was not a miracle on the Hudson: he was trained and had practiced for a disaster. High-risk industries like aviation and nuclear power have proven that leadership skills and teamwork can be taught and then employed in high-stakes situations. We're gradually beginning to apply those lessons to medical training.

The simulation labs that we have now include all kinds of rooms with recording equipment, and we're improving the patient-centeredness of care slowly by teaching young physicians how to be better interviewers, how to elicit information and how to deliver bad news. We're doing a much better job than a generation ago.

How did physicians one generation ago learn technical skills, like putting in a central line and doing a spinal tap? On the poor and the disenfranchised in teaching hospitals, largely without the patients' knowledge or permission. We're doing better on teaching the technical skills. For example, faculty will watch young physicians put a central catheter line in a robot and will correct their technique. What we really need to be doing next is to videotape trainees delivering a lifesaving emergency procedure code and give them tools and techniques to improve their leadership skills while doing it. They need to be taught teamwork in a simulated environment.

In aviation, most fatal accidents — up to 70 percent, in one study — can be attributed to communication errors. A training approach known as crew resource management (CRM) is proven to decrease those errors, writes David Lindquist, MD, assistant professor of Emergency Medicine at Rhode Island Hospital, Warren Alpert School of Medicine at Brown University.[16]

Used primarily in the airline industry for improving safety, CRM teaches interpersonal teamwork skills like maintaining situational awareness so that flight crews can anticipate and pre-empt safety breaches, or respond to them without panic if they occur. CRM training has since been adapted to different industries and organizations, including healthcare.

CRM teamwork principles can reduce medical errors by one-third, according to Lindquist. The chief obstacle, he notes, is encouraging physicians to overcome their deeply ingrained but incorrect belief that they, as the most senior members of the healthcare team, are solely responsible for preventing errors. Every member of the care team is responsible, and physicians must be trained to seek out input about the care process from other care team members. Nurses and other care team members must similarly be trained to speak up and express their concerns about possibly unsafe situations.[17]

Various entities have developed teamwork communication training modules for clinical settings. One example is TeamSTEPPS (Team Strategies and Tools to Enhance Performance and Patient Safety), which was released in 2006 and is available for download via the Agency for Healthcare Research and Quality's website.[18]

Consider an example of TeamSTEPPS in action, as described on AHRQ's website. The University of North Carolina (UNC) Health Care System has trained more than 600 staff and faculty in nine different areas within the organization in its surgical, pediatric and neonatal intensive care units; its bone marrow transplant unit; and its respiratory therapy, labor and delivery, and radiology departments. Training consisted of a one-hour TeamSTEPPS online module, readings and a one-hour interactive classroom session with role-playing.

Physicians reported that the training prevented errors. During a pediatric rapid-response team event on a unit that has a mixed population of adults and children, for example, a physician requested a specific drug and dose. The nurse verbally checked back with what she thought she heard the physician say before handing over the drug. The physician responded, "Whoa! This is a baby; that's too much." This kind of intervention is low-tech, but the human error it prevented could have been lifesaving.

The training also removes potentially deadly hierarchical inhibitions to speak up to avert patient harm. A UNC Health Care nurse remarked that only after the training did she feel comfortable calling a "team huddle" before ECMO cannulation, a procedure that requires isolation in a scrupulously sterile environment to avoid risk to the patient. The procedure entails a temporary artificial support of heart-and-lung function for patients who have reversible heart failure from pulmonary, cardiac or other disease. Blood is drained from the patient to an external pump that pushes the blood through a membrane gas exchanger for oxygenation and CO_2 removal and returns the blood to the patient's circulation.

Contamination could mean serious or deadly infection. The UNC care team now performs a time-out and puts a sign on the door that says, "Sterile procedure in progress." Before TeamSTEPPS, nurses regarded that precaution as the physician's responsibility and were reluctant to question the process.

Putting quality and safety improvement at the forefront of physicians' practice, learning to deliver more sensitive and responsive patient-centered care, learning to promote wellness proactively and learning teamwork skills in patient-care settings are all competencies that have become expected of physicians.

Until these skills become more widely taught and practiced, physicians will continue to build waste into the way they practice medicine. Instead of promoting prevention and wellness among their patients (which they're generally not paid to do), physicians will continue to treat patients reactively and episodically: one patient with one problem, one at a time. They will continue to order every test and treatment to tackle each problem, and make decisions largely in isolation from other physicians and caregivers.

New training opportunities are expanding to build these new core competencies. As we gradually discard dangerous cultural obstacles in medical training and intensify our demand for this new competency training, we will ensure a supply of physicians who are well prepared for the next 40 years of practice and beyond.

Reflection

Some very powerful residency-training developments emerged as this book was being written.

The ACGME, through its residency review committees (RRCs), is the body that approves medical-residency programs around the country. The ACGME is contemplating a mandate, by 2012, that residency-program directors release house officer-specific error reports. That means that two or three years from now, the RRCs would be empowered to demand answers to questions like, "What are you doing to train your residents to reduce medical error?" RRCs will also be required to look at outcome-of-care information on a per-residency-program basis and to rank residency programs publicly.

Now that would be super-powerful. The ACGME is poking its nose under the kimono and is going to demand these kinds of changes. This is a critical frontier for changing the medical-training model for the future. Instead of arguing over the 80-hour work week for medical residents, we're going to have better information about something much more important: how individual residency programs stack up with respect to quality and patient safety.   – S.K. and D.B.N.

Notes

1. Institute of Medicine, *Crossing the Quality Chasm: A New Health System for the 21st Century* (Washington, DC: National Academy Press, 2001).

2. ABIM Foundation, American Board of Internal Medicine, ACP-ASIM Foundation, American College of Physicians-American Society of Internal Medicine, European Federation of Internal Medicine. "Medical Professionalism in the New Millennium: A Physician Charter," *Annals of Internal Medicine,* 2002; 136(3):243-246.

3. Michael T. Brannick, Peter J. Fabri, et al. "Evaluation of an Error-Reduction Training Program for Surgical Residents." *Academic Medicine,* 2009; 84(12):1809-1814.

4. Donna M. Daniel, Donald E. Casey Jr. et al. "Taking a Unified Approach to Teaching and Implementing Quality Improvements across Multiple Residency Programs: The Atlantic Health Experience," *Academic Medicine,* 2009; 84(12):1788-1795.

5. Ibid.

6. The Blue Ridge Academic Health Group. *Reforming Medical Education: Urgent Priority for Academic Health Centers in the New Century.* (Atlanta: Robert W. Woodruff Health Sciences Center, 2003).

7. Christopher Guadagnino, PhD. "Practicing Patient-Centered Collaborative Care," *Physician's News Digest,* November, 2006. Available online at: http://www.physiciansnews.com/spotlight/1106.html.

8. Ibid.

9. Ibid.

10. Ibid.

11. John Wasson and Steve Bartels. "CARE Vital Signs Supports Patient-Centered, Collaborative Care," *Journal of Ambulatory Care Management,* Jan.-Mar., 2009; 32(1):56-71.

12. Christopher Guadagnino, PhD. "Physician-Patient Communication," *Physician's News Digest,* July, 2006. Available online at: http://www.physiciansnews.com/cover/706.html.

13. Ibid.

14. Mercer Cost Effectiveness Analysis — AFDC only for Inpatient, Outpatient, ED, Physician Services, Pharmacy, Administrative Costs, Other). From presentation by Al Dobson, Patient-Centered Primary Care Roundtable, March 12, 2007.

15. Christopher Guadagnino, PhD. "Value-Based Clinical Innovation Projects," *Physician's News Digest,* October, 2007. Available online at: http://www.physiciansnews.com/spotlight/1008pa.html.

16. David G. Lindquist, MD. "Improving Patient Safety Using Crew Resource Management Principles Taught via Medical Simulation," *Prescriptions for Excellence in Health Care Newsletter Supplement:* 2009; 1(7) Article 5. Available at: http://jdc.jefferson.edu/pehc/vol1/iss7/5.

17. M. Leonard, S. Graham, and D. Bonacum. The Human Factor: The Critical Importance of Effective Teamwork and Communication in Providing Safe Care. *Quality and Safety in Healthcare,* 2001; 10(suppl 1):i85-i90.

18. Agency for Healthcare Research and Quality. TeamSTEPPS: National Implementation. Available online at: http://teamstepps.ahrq.gov/index.htm.

MYTH BUSTER 6:

The Transformative Power of Convenient Care

"Retail clinics provide less costly treatment than physician offices or urgent care centers for three common illnesses [otitis media, pharyngitis and urinary tract infection] with no apparent adverse effect on quality of care or delivery of preventive care."

– *Conclusion of a 2009 peer-reviewed study published in the* Annals of Internal Medicine.

[Ateev Mehrotra, MD, Hangsheng Liu, PhD, et al. "Comparing Costs and Quality of Care at Retail Clinics with That of Other Medical Settings for Three Common Illnesses," *Annals of Internal Medicine*. September 1, 2009; 151(5):321-328.]

The concept of retail medicine, non-physicians providing healthcare treatments outside of a physician's office, may seem radical. Some physicians object to it. We believe that putting nurse practitioners in a convenient location like a chain drugstore is a concept to be embraced. Why? The main reason is that the current system is such a mess: not customer friendly, not efficient, not based on guidelines and not based on scientific evidence. Imagine any kind of primary, non-emergency care at any time, with a money-back guarantee, a follow-up phone call, an electronic medical record — all of those variables baked into the business plan. Who would think that healthcare transformation could occur while shopping?

Retail medicine, as well as other innovative forms of convenient care, are promising venues for safe, effective and cost-effective healthcare that address many of the issues we've examined so far in this book.

The New Model Encounters Obstacles

Let's consider some of the barriers and facilitators to the convenient-care model. Facilitators first: a public unhappy with the rigmarole of doctor appointments, many not even having a primary-care doctor, difficulty accessing care and high cost. But in this case, those barriers to good healthcare were the critics for a retail-medicine company such as Take Care Health Systems, which started about six years ago and now offers primary-care services in local Walgreens pharmacies throughout the country.

Still, barriers to Take Care were many. One was the question of whether insurance companies would pay for a visit to a licensed nurse practitioner outside of a doctor's office. It turned out that the major insurers in the marketplace were readily convinced that this was a good idea. The reason why is twofold: solid science supports the fact that these nurse practitioners do a great job, and compelling economic evidence shows that if instead of facing a $300 initial fee to walk into a hospital emergency room, you just walk in the door of your neighborhood drugstore and have your problem resolved for $45, you save everybody a bucket load of money. Health plans were smart. They realized they could get the same bang for a much smaller buck. And most retail clinics accept insurance co-payments.

One somewhat unexpected barrier to the convenient-care concept was the loud and organized voice of pediatricians nationwide. You would think that, with their Snoopy ties, relaxed demeanor and friendly office staffs, pediatricians would embrace the idea of a nurse practitioner helping. But, of course, it's all about the pocketbook. So, pediatric groups nationwide organized against retail medicine from its inception and remain hostile. The reason? The perception that retail clinics are "cream-skimming." The quick and easy visit by Johnny, the second grader with a sore throat that turns out to be strep, is what keeps pediatric doctor offices in business.

So, instead of the pediatrician getting a reimbursable office visit out of it, off Johnny goes to Take Care for a rapid strep test. His parents get the results and get a prescription from the nurse practitioner. Johnny then walks over with mommy and daddy ten feet to the pharmacy to get his penicillin script filled, or the prescription can be sent electronically to any pharmacy that accepts electronic prescriptions. You can't get much better than that: no appointment, no waiting, $45 fee. Pretty amazing.

Other groups that opposed retail clinics were various state and county medical societies who, in many instances, were initially resistant but then became supportive once they realized that it was better to join them than to fight them.

Take a typical marketplace: Kansas City, where David Nash spoke at the Kansas City Medical Society in October, 2007. The doctors were dead set against any kind of retail clinic. While publicly the medical society was pillorying retail clinics, individual doctors were dropping their cards off at the clinic sites, smartly thinking that the nurse practitioner would use them as their referral backup source. Very appropriately, all the retail clinics restrict their care to a narrow group of symptoms and diagnoses, and don't stray beyond them. So, if somebody walked in with chest pain, the nurse practitioner would say, "Maybe we should call an ambulance, but if you need follow-up, here's Doctor Jones's card. Go see Doctor Jones."

Why the Model Succeeds

Take Care then led the creation in October, 2006 of a national organization called the Convenient Care Association of America (CCA), which shares best practices and common standards of operation among its members. There are a couple of dozen firms now in this business, which run some 1,200 clinics in 32 states, having served more than 3.5 million patients.

A worsening shortage of primary-care physicians and a growing interest in the idea of universal healthcare coverage means the demand for retail-based clinics will likely continue to grow, perhaps dramatically. Fewer and fewer medical students are attracted to primary care when they can make triple or quadruple the income as specialists. About a third of retail-clinic patients report that they do not have a regular source of primary care. These clinics serve a valuable public-health service by offering a critical entry point to the healthcare system.

Retail-based clinics are proving to be popular, and for good reasons. The CCA touts them as promoting "consumer-driven" priorities like price transparency, convenience and cost savings. Some 40 percent of patients reported in a CCA survey that they would have gone to a hospital emergency room or an urgent care center, or forgone treatment altogether, had there not been a convenient-care clinic available. Clinics prominently display their healthcare services and pricing, so patients know costs up-front. The clinics may further reduce overall system costs by providing more convenient preventive care, like flu shots, and potentially nipping in the bud symptoms that would be a lot costlier to treat if people deferred seeking care.

These clinics are generally open seven days a week, with extended weekday hours. No appointments are necessary, and visits generally take 15 to 20 minutes. Even for someone with a primary-care physician, these clinics give an alternative to waiting for an appointment or wondering if the symptoms even justify making one. If someone's condition is beyond the scope of the clinic's treatment services, or if the person needs ongoing care, he or she will be referred to local physicians. And, although the clinics only offer a limited range of treatments — for sore throats, common cold and flu symptoms, cough, sinus infection, allergies, immunizations, blood-pressure testing, health screenings and a few others — these account for an impressive quantity of care that people regularly need.

Who's using retail-based clinics, and what is the cost impact? We get a fascinating glimpse at some answers from a Rand Health study of 1.35 million patient visits to these clinics between 2000 and 2007. Patients between 18 and 44 years old accounted for nearly twice as many visits to retail clinics as to primary-care physicians. Very few retail-clinic patients (about two percent) were triaged to an emergency room or doctor's office, showing how savvy patients are about choosing the clinic appropriately for their treatment. A full 90 percent of retail-clinic visits were for preventive services or for ten simple acute illnesses, which account for 12 percent of all emergency-room visits, according to research cited in *Population Health Management* magazine.[1]

That means big cost savings to the system. Do the math. A visit to a typical retail clinic in Minneapolis cost $55 less than at a primary-care doctor's office, and $279 less than a visit to an emergency room. (Those figures, as cited in the article, come from an actual payor: Minneapolis-based HMO HealthPartners.) BlueCross/BlueShield of Minnesota saved more than $1.2 million in 2007 from its members going to retail clinics. BlueCross was so impressed that it eliminated co-pays altogether for clinic visits.

What about Quality?

The big remaining question everybody has about retail clinics concerns quality. Is the care they provide comparable in quality to what you'd get from a primary-care doctor? All evidence points to yes, and a look at the clinics' operating guidelines and infrastructure shows why.

The clinics' nurse practitioners are board certified and licensed to diagnose and treat health problems. They do so with the support of evidence-based clinical practice guidelines vetted by national medical societies such as the American Medical Association and the American Academy of Family Physicians. They perform physical exams, order and interpret laboratory tests and x-rays, and prescribe medications and treatments. They offer patient education about health risks and illness prevention. Some provide prenatal care, gynecological exams and pap smears.

The clinics use electronic medical records to display practice guidelines at the moment of care and to help coordinate care between the clinic and the patient's regular sources of primary care. The diagnosis, prescriptions and treatment are available at the touch of a button. The patient gets a copy of his or her health record at the end of the visit. At the patient's request, the clinics can fax the record to the primary-care provider, if the patient has one, or help find one if he or she does not.

Isolated medical care is not good care, and the retail-clinic industry knows that. It maintains that its model is not an attempt to take over traditional primary care, but to complement it. Collaboration with physician groups is a priority, and the CCA requires its member clinics (which comprise nearly all retail clinics out there) to establish relationships with local primary-care doctors, specialists and emergency-room providers. Clinics must also encourage patients to establish relationships with primary-care doctors.[2]

Retail clinics set up their physician referral base in various ways, depending on the marketplace. They either have a medical group that backs them, a medical society network or individual doctors. The model varies from town to town. But the clinics' practitioners do actively look to forge relationships with local doctors.

Physicians supervise the clinics' nurse practitioners. Based on experience from 42 states, the CCA says a single physician can provide effective collaborative support to a number of clinic practitioners by regularly reviewing patient charts from a remote location, without requiring an on-site presence. That provides quality assurance while minimizing costs. Clinics also collect and report quality and safety outcome data, and monitor patient satisfaction, which generally exceeds 90 percent.[3]

How well do retail clinics adhere to evidence-based practice guidelines? A heck of a lot better than do traditional medical centers, which follow clinical guidelines about half of the time. The adherence rate by convenient-care clinic practitioners? Over 99 percent.[4]

Take Care was eventually purchased by Walgreens, which was a wonderful idea. How often does the typical insulin-dependent diabetic visit her endocrinologist? The answer is twice a year, maybe three times. How often does the typical insulin-dependent diabetic visit her local chain pharmacy? Every three to four weeks. Where might these kinds of patients get their ongoing, coordinated chronic care? They may end up getting it from a convenient-care clinic in a retail space. Convenience and quality converge.

Other chains are in the business, like MinuteClinic in CVS drugstores and RediClinic in H-E-B supermarkets. The models look a lot alike, with a little bit of tweaking here and there. But the main elements are the same: improved access, no waiting, care covered by insurance in most places and an electronic medical record acting as a backbone that features tightly managed clinical guidelines. Jefferson Medical College helped to organize and vet a process whereby its faculty members review and approve Take Care's clinical practice guidelines. The CCA and the Jefferson School of Population Health have entered into an agreement to develop a certification process to ensure that CCA members follow core standards.

So back to this question: Is the care that retail clinics provide comparable in quality to what you'd get from a primary-care doctor? There's a criticism that is leveled at all non-physician, "mid-level" practitioners, as they are sometimes called: you're going to miss the colon cancer or miss the malignant melanoma. Sure, that definitely could happen, just like it happens in private practice. We're not aware of any evidence in peer-reviewed literature saying that nurse practitioners are anything but better than other primary-care doctors.

David Nash, MD, chaired the Take Care Scientific Advisory Board and helped to bring together a group of national ambulatory-care experts who vetted convenient-care clinic guidelines, processes and feedback tools. Firms like Take Care do regular quality-improvement review of their work and evaluate feedback from patients. What we see in these clinics is an infrastructure, a set of processes, that we knew would be helpful in providing patients with the best possible quality. Not only do they tackle the access problem and the cost problem; they also tackle the quality problem.

There is yet another barrier to rapid proliferation of the convenient-care clinic model: a patchwork quilt of state laws controlling the scope of practice that nurse practitioners have. Some states allow them to prescribe drugs, and some don't. Some of these state restrictions will have to be lifted to allow the model to operate effectively across the country.

What is the future of the convenient-care clinic model, in light of remaining reservations by some doctors? In some markets, Take Care and their ilk provide doctors with additional business via consultations. In other markets, Take Care is clearly skimming the less ill pediatric cases. So we understand why the pediatricians are upset. But the argument that quality will suffer is a smokescreen.

We think the model has great potential, especially in light of the primary-care doctor shortage. With the recent passage of health-insurance reform, we believe these centers will be potentially overrun because they will have millions of new customers who are empowered with health insurance and would otherwise have to wait a year for an appointment with a primary-care doctor (which they're clearly not going to do). These clinics seem to be able to tackle cost, quality, and access simultaneously and fairly effectively.

Potential Transformative Power

Walmart has taken a different approach to the convenient-care concept. At first, a private company ran the convenient centers inside the retail giant's big-box stores. Then Walmart decided to take over the centers. As the nation's largest employer with one of the most sophisticated retail distribution-channel computers in the world, Walmart has the infrastructure to deliver efficient care. Add the fact that one out of four Americans is in a Walmart every day, and you've got to believe that the company could have an impact on the health-care delivery business.

Walmart has used its incredible market power to create an extremely low-cost, generic prescription-drug pricing structure. More recently, the retailer announced that it will deliver the generics to patients' homes for free. That's formidable! When Walmart began offering health insurance to its employees, it created electronic health records and expanded its $4 generic drug plan from the 350 medications available to customers to more than 2,000 for employees.

Last year, Walmart added a "Life with Baby" health and wellness initiative for employees and their spouses, pairing them with a registered nurse throughout the pregnancy and the child's first year, offering counseling on smoking cessation and breastfeeding and providing other educational resources.

If Walmart ever decides to make preventive healthcare a big part of what the retailer is about and offer it to customers, Walmart could really change the face of healthcare. The sheer reach of preventive care that the stores could provide could change our national health statistics in a short time. Millions more people getting immunizations and health screenings could lower the risk of contagious disease and avert the spending of millions of dollars for no-longer-needed acute care. The impact would be especially significant in rural areas, where there is a scarcity of healthcare practitioners and other retail health clinics.

Two years ago, Jefferson Medical College invited as a guest speaker Walmart's first chief medical officer, John Agwunobi, MD, MPH, MBA, who is also an admiral in the U.S. Public Health Service Commissioned Corps and a former Assistant Secretary for Health for the U.S. Department of Health and Human Services. Agwunobi could change the face of healthcare just by reducing smoking in his own employee ranks: millions of Walmart workers smoke.

Walmart no longer has a contract with the private company that was delivering convenient care, so shoppers generally won't see a nurse practitioner inside a Walmart anymore. But we believe that will come back with a vengeance. We bet that eventually Walmart and the other big-box stores — Target among them — will do more preventive care in their stores than doctors do currently.

The other big player in retail-chain healthcare delivery is MinuteClinic in CVS drugstores, which is connected to Caremark's pharmacy benefit management (PBM) services. Five or six pharmacy benefit managers — Caremark among them — process, pay for and keep the information from more than 90 percent of all prescriptions written in the United States. More than 210 million Americans nationwide receive drug benefits administered by these third-party prescription drug administrators. Every prescription that's in the Caremark family of providers is tracked. From a data-mining perspective, that's of extraordinary importance.

Consider an example. Pharmacy benefit managers can tell you, at the ZIP code level, which particular prescription drug is being used, where and why. This connectivity will enable us to get to the next level, which is to identify who's using a particular drug, why they are using it and — the Holy Grail of quality feedback — what the outcome is. That would be the ultimate "clinical trial:" prescription-drug data on nearly the entire population showing what works and what does not.

We envision this kind of connectivity as shedding light on everyday medical practice outcomes. We have not yet harnessed the latent capacity that these data-tracking connections bring with them: they can ask patients to come back or to fill out a survey and report actual outcomes of a prescribed course of treatment. That is an immensely powerful tool to close the feedback loop for doctors and teach them what treatments are actually working and not working well.

Healthcare at Home

Another important venue of convenient care is the home diagnostic market. In Japan you can buy a toilet that does a barrage of amazing diagnostic tests (for example, whether you have blood in your urine or whether you need a colonoscopy). At-home diagnostic tests and monitoring devices could give a patient a valuable heads-up about a medical problem and enable him or her to seek medical intervention earlier, preventing further medical complications.

These tests and devices help patients prevent and manage chronic disease. For example, people can measure their cholesterol and triglyceride levels to help minimize the risk of cardiovascular disease. A home test kit allows people with diabetes to test for glucose and even small amounts of protein in their urine — an early sign of kidney dysfunction. The more someone is inclined to measure something, the more likely he or she is to do something about the results. Or, as the mantra goes, what gets measured gets improved.

Hundreds of at-home diagnostic kits have been approved by the Food and Drug Administration and allow people to analyze saliva, urine and blood for a wide array of health-status indicators including HIV, hepatitis, drug abuse, pregnancy and fertility, tuberculosis and other infectious diseases, West Nile virus, colorectal cancer, prostate cancer, allergies, anemia, urinary tract infection, diabetes, cholesterol level and blood-thinning medication level.

At-home devices linked to Web-based services can monitor conditions like sleep apnea (an airway obstruction usually caused by tissue in the back of the throat), which is known to aggravate other chronic conditions like diabetes, heart disease and depression. Many patients are reluctant to go to a specialized sleep clinic for a couple of nights to be diagnosed, so they live with their condition until it becomes worse.

Instead, there is now an at-home monitoring device that fits on a headband, with tubes going into the patient's nose, that records sleep patterns, snoring patterns, airflow, pulse rate, blood-oxygen level and other data. The data is sent via the Web to specialists who interpret it, make a diagnosis and suggest treatment. Similar Web-based personal devices may also monitor chronic conditions like heart disease and diabetes.

This at-home testing and monitoring is a growing area. Caveat emptor: all of these diagnostic tools are going to have to be built with great care and safety specifications, but the technology exists already for many such tests; what's left is fine-tuning. We think you'll see more home cholesterol monitoring, home blood-protein monitoring and other monitoring that we thought could only be done in the hospital.

A key corollary to the home diagnostic market is in the area of personalized medicine. Cracking the human genome has given us amazing insight into what is sometimes called predictive medicine. Here's how that would work. Let's pretend that you have hypertension (high blood pressure). You come to us, and your treatment is relatively straightforward. We have a huge compendium of products we could use. The challenge is that there are largely unpredictable and idiosyncratic reactions to almost every drug for this kind of problem. Translation: it's a hit or a miss.

We envision one day when you will be able to come into the office to have a few cells removed from inside your cheek and placed into an analyzer. The analyzer will give us your genetic readout and your particular predilection for worsening high blood pressure, or give us the prediction of which drug, based on the chemistry of that product and your genetic makeup, would work best for you. We're clearly not there yet, but we have some clinical examples in this area of predictive medicine, such as searching for a particular breast cancer gene or searching for a particular gene that tells us the way that your body will metabolize a particular drug differently than other people.

The Internet will speed up home diagnostics because it will allow a lot more information to be shared a lot faster than it could be over the telephone. A doctor will be able to monitor patients remotely with tele-monitoring for heart failure, apnea or anything where there's a sine wave coming out. That capability brings up all kinds of challenges. Is it appropriate for use in your house versus in the hospital? How ill do you have to become to warrant its use? What are the guidelines in practice for doing this? The home diagnostic market is wide open.

The growth of this market can also positively impact the patient-physician relationship, fostering meaningful dialogue and feedback that truly customizes optimal care. We'd like to think that you, the patient, should be the center of everything. It's likely that many patients are going to genuinely educate their providers about what works and what doesn't.

Other Convenience Venues

Other types of convenient-care venues exist, among them, medical tourism and concierge medicine. There are Joint Commission-accredited hospitals in other countries, and patients can have open-heart surgery, including all physician fees, for something like $7,000. Your insurance may or may not pay for it, but if you have to pay out of pocket for the operation anyway, there can be a huge advantage. Many patient procedures can be very expensive, and some overseas prices are less than half of what they are in the United States.

The reason doctors go into concierge medicine is that they get tired of the treadmill of piecework based on patient volume where the more patients they see, the more they get paid. That creates all kinds of bad pressures on doctors and patients. Doctors who go into concierge medicine say they can spend more time with patients and develop better longer relations with them. The doctor has a limited number of patients — the typical number is 2,000, tops.

The patient pays a retainer-type fee, maybe $2,000 a year, for a menu of healthcare services and same- or next-day office appointments. They can reach their doctor any time, and the doctor knows them. Intuitively, you would expect a doctor who knows you better to remember that you have an allergy, even without using a computerized medical record.

We're attracted to the idea, especially if there's a real contract with the patient. We'd like to see it say something like, "I promise to keep you healthy, and you promise to participate in your care. Together, if we get it right, providers of medical services should get a bonus. If we don't get it right, it should be free." While the concierge model is perhaps most attractive to higher-income patients, they are likely to be active patients and motivated patients are wonderful. If you're paying two grand out-of-pocket, you're going to be more attuned to your health and follow your prescribed treatments.

What does convenient healthcare mean? It sounds counterintuitive that it could be more customer friendly, patient-centered, efficient, guideline-based, and rigged for meaningful feedback and improvement. But that is precisely the promise that it holds. Convenience in this context means a lot more than "less hassle." It reflects the growing trend of patients becoming more active and involved in their healthcare choices. That includes getting evidence-based care in new venues that may simultaneously be effective and less expensive. Convenient healthcare may be a threat to the traditional status quo. That's a good thing.

Reflection

The nation is recognizing very quickly that the notion of a patient-centered medical home, while wonderful, can't become operational because of the current shortage of primary-care doctors. Hence, convenient care may be an interim strategy until such time that we can train a sufficient number of primary-care doctors. We're going to see more medical care in big-box stores all around the country. Patients get it. They like convenient care and they're going to demand better!

There's also a new movement called the "quantifiable selfers" — people who are measuring their REM sleep every night and Tweeting about it. They're measuring their glucose and they're bragging about how many laps they swam. We expect this new movement to coalesce with retail medicine and create a newly energized consumer of the future. *– S.K. and D.B.N.*

Notes

1. Tine Hansen-Turton, Caroline Ridgway, Sandra Festa Ryan, David B. Nash. "Convenient Care Clinics: The Future of Accessible Health Care-The Formation Years 2006-2008," *Population Health Management.* October, 2009; 12(5):231-240.

2. Ibid.

3. Ibid.

4. Ibid.

EPILOGUE

Here we are, over a decade since the publication of the landmark Institute of Medicine report, *To Err is Human*, and we have made little progress since then. An excess of medical errors and preventable patient harm is still posing a critical public-health crisis and represents a true epidemic. Healthcare quality is uneven. Unexplained clinical variation remains rampant. Healthcare costs continue to spiral out of control. There is no easy fix, but we are gradually moving in the right direction on a number of fronts.

Historic Legislation Misses the Mark

On March 23, 2010, President Barack Obama signed into law the Patient Protection and Affordable Care Act, marking a watershed event in the delivery of healthcare in our country. The law accomplished one really important thing: it recognized that universal access to healthcare is critically important. But it was the culmination of a tangled, partisan legislative battle and ended up being insurance reform rather than real healthcare reform.

The legislation ignores three out of four essential pillars of meaningful health reform. Those four pillars are: (1) create value in the system, (2) cover everyone, (3) coordinate care, and (4) promote prevention and wellness. The new law addresses only the second pillar. While it is laudable that we have extended insurance coverage to the uninsured, ignoring the other three pillars will create many unforeseen challenges.

Creating value in the system means we must recognize that, despite spending more for healthcare than any other society in the developed world, we do not achieve value for the money we spend. Our healthcare spending continues to rise, threatening the health of our national economy. And yet, we rank 39th on societal measures of well-being. Unless the financing system puts pressure on the delivery system to eliminate waste and inefficiency, it faces ruinous inflation.

We must implement a program that makes a bargain with our healthcare providers: "No outcome, no income." Namely, we should have more widespread pay-for-performance programs, bundled payment and related mechanisms that emphasize payment only to be received when care is based on solid evidence and achieves appropriate outcomes. The current legislation does continue to fund nearly a dozen federal demonstration projects, which are a small step toward achieving the value equation.

Another pillar, coordination of care, is also ignored in the new leg-islation. There are in excess of 16,000 Current Procedural Terminology (CPT) codes for medical billing, and not a single code for care coordi-nation. Ample published evidence recognizes that only through the coordination of care will we be able to reduce waste and thus decrease cost. A small percentage of chronically ill individuals con-sume a very disproportionate share of our healthcare resources. Through improved care coordination, we could go a long way toward improving outcomes, improving safety, decreasing waste and decreasing overall cost to the system. Care coordination should be a fundamental part of provider payment models.

The final pillar, promote prevention and wellness, also gets short shrift in the new legislation. It is true that the 2009 stimulus bill and related spending has sent modest resources to organizations like the Centers for Disease Control and Prevention and elsewhere, but there remains no nationally coordinated attack on prevention and wellness.

Our system is a disease-based system, not a wellness system. We know that lifestyle behavior — like alcohol use, smoking, diet, lack of use of seat belts, violence or drug abuse — drives almost half of healthcare costs. That's a humbling thought. For most Americans, more medical care is not the most promising route to better health.

What percent of American adults do all of the following: don't smoke, are close to the appropriate body weight, exercise for 20 minutes three times a week, eat fruits and vegetables regularly and wear a seat belt when driving? Answer: three percent. The American personality is still more like, "Let's take Lipitor on the way to McDonalds."

We haven't been able to connect prevention and wellness to the mainstream healthcare system because the system is disease-based. We need a nationally coordinated effort recognizing that for every dollar spent on prevention and wellness, we can achieve at least a two-to-one return on our investment. A society can make no greater invest-ment than an investment in prevention and wellness for its citizens.

By addressing only one of these four pillars of health reform, this new legislation is likely to cost more than anyone can possibly imagine.

If you look back at the historical record of 1962 to 1963, leading up to the creation of Medicare under Lyndon B. Johnson, the original estimates of total Medicare spending were off by a factor of 500 percent.

The new law does nothing to address overall utilization of resources: more tests, more drugs, more treatments, more surgeries. In fact, it crafts the potential for *way more* utilization on top of what we currently are doing. It merely releases pent-up demand for healthcare services by the previously uninsured. In the absence of creating value, coordinating care and promoting prevention and wellness, healthcare coverage for everyone cannot be sustained.

The experience in Massachusetts is a potential harbinger of what reform will mean on the national level. In 2006, that state passed a law that has expanded health-insurance coverage to 97 percent of the population through the shared responsibility of individuals and employers. But the reform has not halted rising healthcare costs in the state, which risk breaking the state's budget.

Massachusetts Attorney General Martha Coakley released a report on March 16, 2010, *Examination of Health Care Cost Trends and Cost Drivers*, which revealed enormous price variation in medical procedures at different hospitals across the state and declared that the state cannot afford to ignore unsustainable healthcare cost escalation. Hospitals and physicians costing twice as much as their peers deliver no better care or service.

There is no correlation between price and quality of healthcare in the state. Hospital prices are not related to the sickness of the patients, the complexity of procedures performed or actual hospital costs. Instead, large and prestigious hospitals dominate the market by using their financial leverage to win more reimbursement from insurance companies. In response, Massachusetts is contemplating bundled healthcare payment for the entire state and has a commission making further cost-control recommendations.

What's missing from meaningful healthcare reform at the national level is a deeper understanding of the true drivers of waste, error and uneven quality. In U.S. healthcare, we do more things to more people at a greater intensity than any other country in the world. That's a deeply culturally ingrained fact. Our rugged individualism compels us to stop at nothing. Do everything to tackle each problem. Get the job done. Give that prescription, that test, that treatment — especially if the patient has insurance. That impulse is fueled by a willing payment system, a limited evidentiary base and very little feedback for physicians to learn whether what they're doing is producing the intended outcome.

Building those four pillars of health reform is going to take a lot of political courage. It is easier to malign the insurance industry, the pharmaceutical industry and other "culprits" than it is to create fundamental changes in a broken system. While we applaud the President for his leadership in making this first step toward system reform, it is simply not enough. In the coming months and years, we will witness the release of pent-up demand for healthcare services, as millions of Americans enter an already broken system, which will potentially cripple it fatally for the future.

The Work Ahead

We know that unexplained clinical variation in practice in the United States remains one of medicine's greatest challenges. According to the work of Jack Wennberg and others who helped create the *Dartmouth Atlas of Healthcare*, geography is destiny. Healthcare is rationed every day in the United States by socioeconomic status, race and, of course, a patient's residence. The variation in healthcare that physicians deliver is simply too great to contend that they all are equally adept at providing the best and most efficient possible care for their patients. There is, regrettably, a bell-shaped curve of physicians' practices and the medical profession is tasked with reducing these unexplained variations. In short, physicians must abandon their slavish adherence to autonomy and place their patients at the center of their reasoning.

While most clinicians do not recognize that a minority of their decisions at the bedside are based on solid Grade-A evidence from randomized, controlled trials, the people who pay the bills for what clinicians do clearly are cognizant of this fact. The evidence is overwhelming that autonomous decision-making, without a solid evidentiary basis, leads to waste and a propensity for medical error. Furthermore, nearly a decade of published evidence points to the fact that there is uneven adherence to the evidence when it does exist, and that according to the best published sources, the U.S. healthcare system gets it right just about half of the time.

Is this failure the result of poor doctoring? No. This uneven adherence to the evidence is in part the reflection of widespread system failure. Surely our healthcare industry must get beyond the conversation focused on simple things such as hand washing and penmanship to tackle the more difficult systems issues that lead to failure, that lead to error. We must recognize that healthcare will never be error-free; what we must strive for is care that is harm-free.

That brings us full circle to the core challenge to meaningful reform of our healthcare delivery system, which remains largely unaddressed. We believe that better, safer and more efficient healthcare absolutely requires less unwarranted variation in the way physicians practice. Unexplained clinical variation drives tremendous waste. It ensures a great deal of underuse, overuse and misuse of medical services. It can lead to medical errors and complications that harm and kill patients. It stems from limited scientific certainty available to physicians about what works best for which patients and from failure to adopt proven guidelines. It is sustained by our healthcare payment system that largely encourages piecework, irrespective of effectiveness. It is deeply rooted in the way we train physicians to prize autonomy and hierarchy over team-based and patient-centered care.

Here's what we need. We must accelerate efforts to discover and disseminate better evidence about what tests, drugs and treatments work best and deliver the right tools to physicians so that they can use information effectively in their clinical decision-making. We need to help physicians close the feedback loop on their practice, study their outcomes and improve the safety and quality of their care. We must hold physicians and hospitals accountable for delivering the best and safest care. We must tie payment to evidence-based improvement and efficiency. We must train physicians as team captains for patient-centric care. We must also promote alternative, convenient models of healthcare that encourage patients to be vigilant about their health.

We're making slow, gradual progress on at least six fronts. First, tackling the problems of uncertainty, variation and complexity in healthcare delivery is extraordinarily difficult work. Physicians and hospitals in various parts of the country are stepping up; by applying guidelines to standardize medical practice when there is solid evidence of what works well; by developing new best practices from the ground up through local care-improvement innovations at the bedside; and by involving patients as active decision-makers of their care. We need to do all of these things simultaneously on a national level.

Second, comparative effectiveness research has newfound respect and a jump start by fresh federal funding. But we will have to wait for second-generation proposals with teeth that will give physicians the incentive to use proven treatments by tying payment to credible research. Pay for what works. Pay more for what works better. That shouldn't be controversial. We need the research to make it possible.

Third, we now have a variety of mechanisms to hold physicians and hospitals accountable for the quality, safety and efficiency of the care they deliver. Transparency initiatives, like hospital and physician report cards, seem to work best when they focus on risk and safety information and are consumer friendly in design. Metrics matter. All providers can't score the same, or transparency is meaningless (until that magical, mythical day when all providers are uniformly excellent in minimizing the harm of medical errors and avoidable complications). Report cards should be supplemented with mandates and penalties for physicians who willfully ignore proven safety enhancements in clinical care. And when something does go wrong, physicians and hospital personnel should be able to disclose and apologize to patients without fear of reprisals.

Fourth, our payment system must reward physicians for the time and energy they need to cultivate effective preventive health interventions, not penalize them as it currently does. A tremendous chunk of healthcare delivery is currently devoted to treating maladies like diabetes, obesity and heart disease that patients can manage through lifestyle choices. Alternatives like the patient-centered medical home, pay-for-performance and bundled payment can change that. Demonstration-project success stories should make policy-makers less leery of implementing these models on a wider scale. A fair and effective healthcare payment system should give us the best and safest results from the most appropriate treatments, based on the best medical evidence by the right kind of providers at the right time. Make no mistake:

payment reform may be controversial, but it is pivotal to success.

Fifth, a sea change is underway in how we train tomorrow's physicians to build the new skill set they will need for the coming decades. The model of the physician as an autonomous expert working in isolation from other caregivers is giving way to curriculum that no longer ignores quality and safety improvement. New physicians-in-training are getting more opportunities to practice delivering sensitive and responsive patient-centered care, to promote wellness more proactively and to orchestrate teamwork skills in patient-care settings. We expect demand for these competencies to intensify, and new competency training opportunities to multiply.

Sixth, a growing market for convenient healthcare is offering many alluring features: customer-friendly, patient-centered, efficient, evidence-based, less expensive and a system that is amenable to provider feedback and improvement. If convenient-care venues improve access and encourage patients to care more about their health, we're all for them.

High-quality healthcare must cost less. The only way to reduce cost is by reducing waste, which requires a better evidentiary basis to reduce clinicians' unexplained practice variation. Lower cost and higher quality are complementary. It must be true that if we use the right drug or treatment on the right patient for the right indication and in the right way, we will achieve a good outcome at a lower cost. The patient will leave the hospital sooner, will be happier and will stay healthier. A healthier population should be our ultimate goal, and a healthcare system that evolves along the path we've outlined should certainly welcome healthier patients. Absurdly, that's not yet the case.

About The Authors

Sanjaya Kumar, MD, MPH, MSc, is Founder, Chief Medical Officer and Chief Technical Officer of Quantros, Inc., a leader in web-based healthcare data management and decision support solutions to further patient safety and quality. Today, more than 2,200 healthcare facilities in the USA use Quantros applications to drive improvements in quality of care delivered, patient safety initiatives, and compliance programs.

Dr. Kumar spent his early years in West Africa and the extreme poverty eventually defined the course of his career. Overwhelmed by horrific, yet preventable adverse medical outcomes, he decided being a physician would be an effective way to improve the quality of healthcare and address patient safety concerns.

Drawing on his extensive background in medicine and technology, Dr. Kumar directed his medical training, direct patient care experiences and epidemiological and biostatistical data management and analysis skills towards developing clinical informatics solutions that would impact quality measurement and patient safety monitoring. In 1997, he founded Quantros, Inc. and introduced the predecessor of Quantros ACE™, an automated self-auditing and compliance management tool, to the healthcare industry. Solutions for patient quality, safety, risk management and surveillance soon followed.

Dr. Kumar serves on numerous quality improvement committees, task forces and working groups including the Association for Healthcare Risk Management (ASHRM) Data Safety Committee and the National Patient Safety Foundation Safety Product Vendor Selection Criteria Committee. He is a frequent speaker at national health care conferences and meetings and has hosted a number of conferences as well. Dr. Kumar has been widely published in peer reviewed medical journals and is the author of *Fatal Care: Survive in the U.S. Health System*.

Dr. Kumar earned his medical degree at the University of Benin and received extensive postgraduate medical training in the UK. In pursuit of defining healthcare delivery models and programs, Dr. Kumar received a Master of Science degree in Health Planning and Financing from the London School of Economics and Political Science. While furthering his career in the U.S., Dr. Kumar also earned a MPH in Epidemiology from the University of Massachusetts.

David Nash, MD, MBA, is the Founding Dean of the Jefferson School of Population Health on the campus of Thomas Jefferson University in Philadelphia, Pennsylvania. Dr. Nash is also the Dr. Raymond C. and Doris N. Grandon Professor of Health Policy. The Jefferson School of Population Health represents the first time a health-sciences university has placed four Masters Programs under one roof, namely: Masters in Public Health; Health Policy; Healthcare Quality and Safety; and Chronic Care Management. The goal of this innovative school is to produce a new type of healthcare leader for the future.

Dr. Nash is a Board Certified Internist and is internationally recognized for his work in outcomes management, medical staff development and quality-of-care improvement. In 1995, he was awarded the Latiolais Prize by the Academy of Managed Care Pharmacy for his leadership in disease management and pharmacoeconomics.

Repeatedly named by *Modern Healthcare* to the top 100 most powerful persons in healthcare, his national activities include membership on the Board of Directors of: the DMAA; The Care Continuum Alliance; Chair of an NQF Technical Advisory Panel; membership in the American College of Surgeons' Health Policy Institute; and the ACP Clinical Guidelines Project.

Dr. Nash was recently appointed to the Board of Directors of Humana, a Fortune 200 company headquartered in Louisville, KY. He also serves on the Board of Main Line Health — a four hospital system in suburban Philadelphia, PA. From 1998 to 2008, he served on the Board of Trustees of Catholic Healthcare Partners, Cincinnati, Ohio, where he chaired the Board Committee on Quality and Safety.

He is a consultant to organizations in both the public and private sectors including the Technical Advisory Group of the Pennsylvania Health Care Cost Containment Council. From 1984 to 1989, he was Deputy Editor, Annals of Internal Medicine, at the American College of Physicians. Currently, he is Editor-in-Chief of four major national journals: *P&T; Population Health Management; Biotechnology Healthcare;* and the *American Journal of Medical Quality.*

Dr. Nash received his BA in economics (Phi Beta Kappa) from Vassar College, Poughkeepsie, New York; his MD from the University of Rochester School of Medicine and Dentistry; and his MBA in Health Administration (with honors) from the Wharton School at the University of Pennsylvania.